JOHN HUGHES: A LIFE IN FILM

For my wife, Mira Advani Honeycutt.

JOHN HUGHES:
A LIFE IN FILM

Kirk Honeycutt

Race Point
PUBLISHING

Race Point Publishing
A division of Quarto Publishing Group USA Inc.
276 Fifth Avenue, Suite 205
New York, NY 10001

Please see page 207 for the photography credits

ISBN: 978-1-631060-22-9

Author: Kirk Honeycutt

Editorial Director: Jeannine Dillon

Managing Editor: Erin Canning

Senior Design Manager: Heidi North

Interior Design: Renato Stanisic

Cover Design: Mary Ann Smith

Library of Congress Cataloging-in-Publication data is available

Printed in China

2 4 6 8 10 9 7 5 3 1

www.racepointpub.com

CONTENTS

FOREWORD

BY CHRIS COLUMBUS

In 1988, I made a high profile picture that was devastated by most critics and opened to a $2.4 million weekend. It was the second film I had directed. In the months that followed, studios stopped sending me scripts. It appeared that my directorial career was over, or at least on hold for several years. I resigned myself to the fact that I would go back to my much more successful job as a screenwriter.

But there was one person who still believed in me as a director.

John Hughes.

He started sending me scripts to direct. The first one didn't work out (there's more about that in this book). The next screenplay he sent, a comedy about a child who is left alone in his house over the holidays, was something I sparked to immediately. It was called *Home Alone.*

My first interview with John was at his Lake Forest complex. I entered John's office and sat there. Alone, waiting. At some point, John's young, usually frightened assistant walked in, carrying a fresh pack of Carlton cigarettes, a disposable lighter, and a glass ashtray. These items were carefully placed on a table beside John's chair.

The assistant left the room and after a few minutes, John walked through the door. He opened the pack of cigarettes and lit up. This particular ritual happened before every single meeting I ever had with John Hughes. Nothing ever changed about it. Except the assistants.

Following my first interview with John, I got the *Home Alone* directing gig. I was ecstatic to be making this film, and even more thrilled to be working with one of the great comedic minds. But I soon learned that collaborating with John could be a bit of a double-edged sword. The guy was incredibly film savvy, bitingly funny, and perceptive. But he was also an eccentric, frustrating person.

John loved to work late, starting preproduction meetings at around 10:00 p.m. at his home in Lake Forest and continuing till four or five in the morning. At the time, I was prepping *Home Alone* with our crew from 7:00 a.m. until 8:00 p.m. every day. That meant seeing my wife and six–month-old baby every night for a quick dinner before driving to John's house for a marathon meeting session. The most maddening part of these meetings was the first three or four hours. During that time, John would tell us stories—tales about

his new farm, about working with Machiavellian studio executives, his days at Chicago's Leo Burnett advertising agency… Then there were nights when he would dig out an old VHS tape, a director's cut of one of his earlier movies, like *Planes, Trains and Automobiles*, and screen the entire film. Obviously, the film geek in me loved this. But we had real work to do. And when you're prepping a film and getting by on about two hours sleep, screening a three-and-a half-hour cut of *PTA* was not on the agenda. But it was on John's agenda. Thankfully, the night-owl meetings stopped once we started shooting *Home Alone*.

And after those first few grueling months of preproduction, John turned into a director's dream. He showed up on the first day of shooting *Home Alone* and only came back on one occasion, when John Candy shot his lengthy cameo. During the postproduction process, John always supported my vision of the film and rarely interfered creatively. But when he did, his advice was smart, precise, and always made the picture better.

When I left Chicago for San Francisco to direct *Mrs. Doubtfire*, John never really got over it. For some reason, he felt that we should spend the rest of our days in Chicago, making films together. But filmmaking is a moveable feast. If you only make movies in one particular location, you run the risk of limiting yourself artistically and visually. I wanted to make films all over the country, all over the world. But John didn't feel the same way. He assumed, as he said, that I was in "the Chris Columbus business" and he took it personally that I wanted to move on. But that wasn't the case. I would have worked with John again in a second. And even though we didn't keep in touch, I assumed, maybe naively, that we would make many more films together.

That wasn't meant to be. Hearing the news of John's death was truly shocking. I had lost a great collaborator and the world had lost a great filmmaker. When you look back at some of the critical reaction to John's work, there were a lot of reviewers who didn't take him seriously. But John was a true visionary. Today, many of his films are regarded as classics. And some of them, even the movies that are so firmly rooted in the world of the 1980s, feel as fresh today as the day they were released.

John's films have inspired a few generations and they will continue to do so for many, many more decades. His work has profoundly changed millions of lives. I know that he profoundly changed mine. Without John, I may not still be directing today. I owe everything that's happened in my cinematic life over the past twenty-five years to John Hughes.

I would give anything for one more meeting with John. I'd love to listen to all of those stories again. How cool would it be to rewatch the three-and-a-half-hour rough cut of *Planes, Trains and Automobiles* with John? I didn't realize how lucky I was. If only I could be sitting alone in a Lake Forest office, waiting for some terrified assistant to enter and place an ashtray, lighter, and Carlton cigarettes on the table.

INTRODUCTION

The job interview was not going well for Michelle Manning. A graduate of the University of Southern California's famed film school, she had worked as production supervisor in 1982 for Francis Ford Coppola on films shot back-to-back in Oklahoma, *The Outsiders* and *Rumble Fish*. Yet working for Coppola, certainly among the most famous movie directors in the world, did not prepare you for a studio job. His Zoetrope Studios wasn't a real studio. It was a one-man band of extravagant showmanship

within a hierarchy-busting organization of high-risk entrepreneurialism and experimentation with the latest movie technology. It was not where one learned the nuts-and-bolts basics of the film business.

Since her Zoetrope colleague, cinematographer Caleb Deschanel, had joked that every year working with Francis would take fifteen years off your life expectancy, Manning was looking to get out.

Ned Tanen, the gruff and outspoken former president of Universal Pictures, had recently left the studio to set up an independent production company, Channel Productions, on the lot to produce movies for Universal. Manning wanted a job with his new company.

Normally someone coming on board a studio-based film company as a development executive or producer would bring along a considerable list of contacts at the talent agencies, know the

Opposite: John Hughes leaning against a row of lockers on the set of *The Breakfast Club* in 1985. Above: Director Francis Ford Coppola presents his Zoetrope Studios to the press in Hollywood, California (1981).

1

top writers and directors, and have been tracking screenplays in development around Hollywood.

Knowing only the Zoetrope family and no agents to speak of, Manning was not impressing her potential new boss. When Tanen asked her if she knew of any screenplays Channel might be interested in, Manning suddenly remembered a conversation she had overheard.

She had recently accompanied Warner Bros. executives Mark Canton and Lucy Fisher on the

corporate jet to a preview of *The Outsiders* in Phoenix. The two were grumbling bitterly about a teen comedy circulated by one of the town's top agents, ICM head Jeff Berg. The executives very much wanted to buy the script, but Berg was adamant its young writer would also direct the film despite having never directed.

This news was music to Tanen's ears. At Universal he championed youth movies such as *American Graffiti* and, against considerable opposition, *Animal House*. He had overseen *Fast Times at Ridgemont High* by first-time director Amy Heckerling and first-time writer Cameron Crowe. Plus he had two teenage daughters. He loved that teenage space.

"Who's the writer?" asked Tanen.

"I think it's the guy who wrote *Mr. Mom* and the *Vacation* movie," she said.

"I've always been a champion of first-time directors," insisted Tanen. "Call Jeff Berg. Let's see the script."

Not entirely clear if she was in fact hired, Manning nevertheless phoned Berg. He messengered the screenplay to Manning that afternoon.

Since there was still no furniture in Channel's new office suite, Manning read the screenplay while sitting on the floor. Enthused about what she read, she gave the screenplay for *Sixteen Candles* to Tanen to read that night.

The next morning Tanen put in a call to Berg. The following day, the writer, whose name was John Hughes, boarded a plane in Chicago headed for Los Angeles.

John Hughes hit Hollywood like few writers in its history. His meteoric rise would establish

Left: The wild success of "youth" movies like *National Lampoon's Animal House* (1978) helped pave the way for the John Hughes films of the 1980s.

Above: Molly Ringwald, John Hughes, and Michael
Schoeffling on the set of *Pretty in Pink* (1984).

him in a position of dominance in comedy for well
over a decade. He would create a hit-making production company that, had he surrendered to his
entrepreneurial inclinations, could have expanded
into music, television, and other entertainment
platforms.

He did all this despite focusing initially on
a genre most American filmmakers shun—teen
comedies.

John Hughes gave the world Molly Ringwald,
Anthony Michael Hall, the Brat Pack, *Ferris Bueller*, Macaulay Culkin, "Don't You (Forget About

Me)," and helped make John Candy a household
name. More importantly, his voice resonated
with millions of teenagers who otherwise did not
relate to so-called youth movies, movies that John
Hughes would insist were really films for adults
who wanted to ogle teenage girls in showers.

He connected with an entire generation in a way
that hasn't been duplicated since. He broke down
the veneer of high-school stereotypes to discover
not what separates teens, but what unites them.

His films connected because they spoke to teens
as if they were adults. He saw no reason why the
thoughts and emotions of sixteen-year-olds were

any less valid than his at thirty-six. Meanwhile, this baby boomer treated the adult world as so pretentious and phony that it deserved to be conned.

This uncanny connection and understanding was not intellectual, but *felt*. John was the characters he created on paper.

What fueled this empire of the Teen King was a writer unique not just to Hollywood, but to the understood norms of any kind of writing. His preferred method of working was late at night and into the early hours of the morning, blasting the latest music out of the British rock and punk scene while drinking coffee and chain-smoking.

This M.O. produced completed screenplays in such a rapid-fire manner that it became the stuff of Hollywood legend. The number of days tends to fluctuate but he claims he wrote the first draft of *The Breakfast Club* in two days; *Planes, Trains and Automobiles* in three; *Mr. Mom* in four; *Vacation* in a week; and *Ferris Bueller's Day Off* in four days while at the same time rewriting *Pretty in Pink*.

The story goes that Howard (Howie) Deutch, set to direct *Pretty in Pink* from John's screenplay, came to his Brentwood house one evening to talk through a rewrite. John disappeared upstairs to write while Deutch fell asleep on the couch. At dawn, John came bounding down the stairs to wake up his director and hand him about forty-five pages and demand to know what he thought of them.

Deutch took a look. In his hands was the first draft for *Ferris Bueller*. The finished script was a "go" picture at Paramount the following week.

A young producer named Lauren Shuler summoned John for a story conference on *Mr. Mom*. "I gave him notes," she recalled. "He turned to my assistant with a typewriter and said, 'Ann, please get up.' He then sat at the typewriter and knocked out the pages. Just like that. He wrote the rest of the script in two hours."

The reality behind this myth of the nearly instant screenplay is that, while he believed in quick *first* drafts, he rewrote scripts constantly to accommodate casting, locations, and developments during rehearsals. "All through production I fix this and I fix that, constantly changing and making additions. So I work on a script for nine months," he insisted.

"John came from advertising and was able to distill an idea," noted Michael Chinich, who at one time ran his production company. "A guy takes a day off. Well, from that idea he would be able to create a whole world. The title of *Pretty in Pink* evolved from a song title. One Friday, Ned (Tanen) needed a picture for a Thanksgiving release. John told him about *Planes*. Ned said that's a great idea and by Monday he had a draft. Done."

As prolific as his screenwriting was—the website IMDb credits John with forty-six writing credits—many more screenplays were never finished, or if finished, never made. To this day, unfilmed John Hughes screenplays gather dust at several Hollywood studios. These do not include the number of scripts and treatments he never bothered to finish.

His longtime agent, Jack Rapke, explained: "He would go to the computer, which I called Command Central, and take a run [at a story idea] like Jack Kerouac. If he couldn't finish it, he felt that ultimately there was something wrong with the concept. This was his process: to sit down and jam it through."

One unfinished script John was willing to abandon, said Rapke, was bought by Bobby and Peter Farrelly. They turned it into *Dumb and Dumber*, the hit that launched the brothers' careers. As part of the sale, John insisted his name be removed from the credits.

Among his closest associates some felt his prolific output worked against his artistry. They encouraged him to edit his thoughts and not involve himself in so many projects, to focus on getting the worthy ones up and running correctly before creating the next wave. John never paid any attention. Perhaps he couldn't.

For John loved the writing process. Next to his family it was the most important thing in his life, as fundamental as breathing. He liked and was extremely good at producing, marketing, and, thanks to a terrific ear for popular music, creating soundtracks to his films. Directing he eventually wearied of, disliking the early morning hours, time away from family and the crisis-control atmosphere that permeates the job.

As a director, Hughes made only eight films over a seven-year period (1984 through 1991). He directed to protect his material. He rightly believed these screenplays could only be directed by him. He knew what he wanted and knew from experience that other directors would not carry through his vision.

His M.O. here was to shoot nearly a million feet of film per picture—vastly more than the industry norm—and to encourage improvisation.

Take a sequence in *Ferris Bueller's Day Off*, which many feel is his best picture. Playing hooky from school, Ferris (Matthew Broderick) and his best pal Cameron (Alan Ruck) fool the school's harried principal on the telephone to spring Ferris's girlfriend Sloane (Mia Sara) from school too.

"One unfinished script John was willing to abandon was bought by Bobby and Peter Farrelly. They turned it into *Dumb and Dumber*."

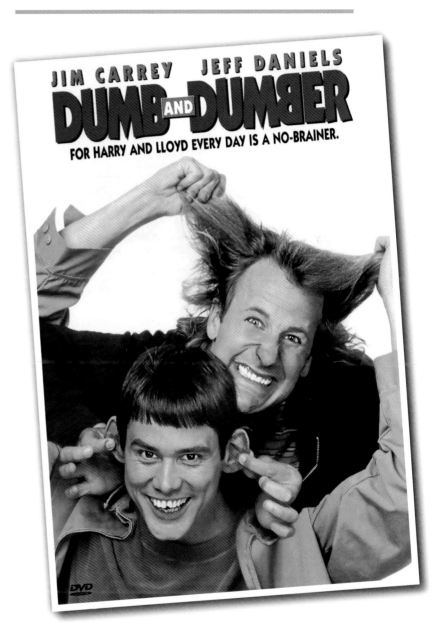

Above: *Dumb and Dumber* was an unfinished movie script written by John Hughes. He sold it to the Farrelly Brothers who turned it into the smash comedy hit in 1994.

"He was a very, very sensitive man. I don't think you can be the genius that he was without having those sensitivities." —Jack Rapke

Anticipating Principal Rooney's reaction to the old my-grandmother-has-died excuse, Ferris double-teams Rooney (Jeffrey Jones). First, Cameron, masquerading as Sloane's dad, calls Rooney's office. Absolutely certain this "dad" is Ferris, Rooney berates him with nasty insults, only for his secretary, Grace (Edie McClurg), to inform him that Ferris Bueller is on the other line.

The look on Rooney's face when he realizes the person he is talking to is NOT Ferris is explosively funny, but no more so than the chaos of juggling phones and obsequious pleadings Rooney and Grace must perform to mollify Sloane's father while handling Ferris's call.

Aware that his two performers had considerable experience in improvisation, John made two requests. He asked Broderick and Ruck, scheduled to have the day off, be on the set with live phone lines to deliver their dialogue so as to guide the actors on camera. Then he asked Jones and

Right: Principal Rooney (Jeffrey Jones) and his secretary, Grace (Edie McClurg), plotting to catch Ferris Bueller cutting school in the Hughes hit, *Ferris Bueller's Day Off* (1986).

Left: The Hughes family in Las Vegas, Nevada (1991). John and Nancy are in the center with their sons, John Hughes III (left) and James Hughes (right).

McClurg to improvise as the film crew adjusted to their actions on the fly.

"It was a real lift for everybody," recalled Jones. "It was a riot. The camera was mounted on a dolly and the crew had to move lights while we were shooting. It woke everybody up on set. It was a smart thing for John to do—everybody had to bring his game up. It was incredibly difficult and fun, and it shows in the final scene."

John never went to film school or spent time studying film and its history, although he certainly watched vintage films and admired Hitchcock, Wilder, Truffaut, Chaplin, Sturges, and many others. At the height of his power and fame, he made an unusual confession to *The Hollywood Reporter*: "I still haven't reconciled whether movies are an art form or not."

Here too, John went against the grain in Hollywood.

There is no sign that John ever considered himself part of the counter-culture, as so many baby-boomers did. Indeed, as a conservative Republican, he may have felt an outsider in liberal Hollywood, where he seldom socialized.

A significant anti-authoritarian streak runs through his films, though. Teachers, principals, and parents are rudely treated. In his personal life, this took the form of an anti-Hollywood attitude and personal grudges that lasted forever. Neither Molly Ringwald nor Anthony Michael Hall, for instance, had spoken to John in twenty years when he died.

A longtime Chicagoan, John lived in Los Angeles for less than half a decade, never gave up his Illinois home, and tried with some success to make Hollywood movies at arm's length from the town. He had no close friends in the industry. Indeed, he battled with its "suits" almost on a daily basis.

He hated it when studio executives gave him notes on his screenplays. He hated it when actors turned down roles in his films.

"He was fragile so a note could actually break the glass house," said Rapke. "He was a very, very sensitive man. I don't think you can be the genius that he was without having those sensitivities."

To those in his good graces, John was affable, witty, and warm. To those out of favor, he was remote—if he spoke to them at all. Unwilling or unable to confront anyone whose actions angered him, he instead froze such a person out, acting as if they were invisible.

Ascribing to him a "WASP interiorization," his one-time publicist Fredell Pogodin explained, "He lived in his head a lot, like a cartoon character with a thought bubble coming out. He was inherently a socially reticent human being and on some level more interested in young people than adults."

Which is a good thing if you're the Teen King. He had an ability to enter the heads of young people without judgment and to capture their reality: how fledgling emotions confuse kids, how words often get in the way, and how affairs of the heart will always trump sex.

As his clout in the industry grew, John became increasingly combative, if not irrational, in his approach to filmmaking, firing handpicked directors, always to the detriment of his own pictures, and later unnecessarily running up costs.

The legend of the instant screenplay was eventually replaced by tales of capricious personnel changes—of the right-hand man dismissed

because of a name John found scratched on his phone log, or directors fired within days of production for no reason that made sense.

That wounded sensibility Rapke noted transformed over time into a paranoid distrust of friendships outside of his family. When he withdrew from filmmaking and eventually any kind of public life, he cut himself off from old friends, former colleagues, and most certainly the press.

He raised the drawbridge on his twin castles, in the tony Lake Forest district outside Chicago and his Redwing Farm in western Illinois, to spend his retirement with family and produce writing no one else would see.

His family was so precious to him that, ultimately, he abandoned first directing and then filmmaking altogether to spend more time with them (the Hughes family, his sons, John III and James, and his widow Nancy, declined to be interviewed for the book, and consequently, a few others close to the family also turned down interview requests). By all indications Hughes was a dad unlike those depicted in his movies. He played a major role in his sons' lives and never lost connection to his offspring as his fictional dads did. Fatherhood was clearly his greatest achievement in his own eyes.

The Hollywood establishment and film critics might have responded differently had John focused on adult stories and themes. They appreciated how successful his films were, and certainly studio heads loved the money he made for them. Everyone wanted to be in the John Hughes business. But forget about Oscars, tributes, or critical accolades.

Martha Coolidge, who directed such films as *Valley Girl*, *Real Genius*, and *Rambling Rose*, noted that if you make teen films, "Most studio executives don't see your films. You can go to events where you're being honored and it's clear the major critics have not seen your films. It doesn't matter how much money they made.

"If you look at the great love stories in the world going back to antiquity, they're about teens or young adults. That's a dramatic time of life. What happens in the teenage years informs the rest of our lives."

Chicago's two most famous critics, Roger Ebert and Gene Siskel, gave John a fair hearing in print and on their celebrated TV show. But his films lacked the siren call most of the nation's critics respond to, which is to say adult themes, social issues, and artistic ambition. John made movies about teenagers. And later kids, dogs, and even a baby.

So, as a lifelong film critic and journalist, I'm glad for the opportunity to revisit the extraordinary storytelling career of John Hughes and to look at his films afresh.

While I never met John, I spoke with him occasionally on the telephone in my capacity then as a film reporter at *The Hollywood Reporter*. If memory serves, I first called him to follow up on a press release concerning a nationwide search for a young boy to play the title character in *Dennis the Menace*.

"No experienced required—or desired," he joked. "I find kids who have worked in commercials have picked up a lot of bad habits. I want a fresh kid, a five-year-old with an outgoing personality. I knew I'd have to look outside the business. Not a lot of five-year-olds have agents. My Dennis is out there somewhere riding his bike."

I talked to John maybe a dozen times over the course of the years. The saddest conversation was the day his great friend John Candy died. I believe that day to be a transformative one for John, the

Above: Comedian John Candy in 1981.

day he began to realize that, as Ferris Bueller says, "Life moves pretty fast—if you don't stop and look around, you could miss it."

That may have been the day, not unlike the one when he boarded a plane to come to Hollywood to see Ned Tanen, that he saw a new life open up to him, one where he didn't have to deal with agents, actors, and studio execs—the "suits" and naysayers—but could spend more time with his family. Because if his films deal with any adult theme, it is the vital importance of family.

1
WELCOME TO HUGHES WORLD

In the 1980s, John Hughes was the most autobiographical of film writers. The films he wrote track his life from his teenage years through his marriage, jobs in advertising, and having kids at an early age. As much as he admired a writer who could pour years of research into a story, John never wrote anything he hadn't personally done, seen, or been a part of.

Thus, the Chevy Chase character in *Vacation* is his dad; *Mr. Mom* recalls his life as a househusband battling a self-propelled vacuum cleaner; and *She's Having a Baby* reflects his experiences as a father barely out of his teens.

Even his movie sets were autobiographical. At a seminar at the American Film Institute in 1985 he told students, "All my interiors are places I've been. The bedroom is my bedroom—but I'll move bed."

In the pictures they did together, producer

Opposite: John Hughes on the set for *Weird Science* in 1985. Right: Chevy Chase in *National Lampoon's Vacation* (1983) written by John Hughes.

> ## "He was a modern Norman Rockwell . . . There was always something touching in his films." —Steve Martin

Richard Vane noticed how they wound up with the same floor plan for every main house: a front door opened to a staircase with a dining room and living room on either side.

"John, why don't we just keep the sets up for the next movie?" he asked.

"His house in Chicago was like all the houses you see in his movies," said Michelle Manning, laughing.

Sixteen Candles, The Breakfast Club, Pretty in Pink, Ferris Bueller, and *Some Kind of Wonderful* all play with similar themes. He may move the characters around—a rich kid becomes a poor one or a princess converts to the school beauty—but the story stays the story of John's high-school years. *Planes, Trains and Automobiles, Mr. Mom*, and *She's Having a Baby* get into his working and married life as an advertising exec and dealing with young children at home.

His stories took place around dinner tables, kitchens, and washing machines, at school and its dances, in places of work or in vehicles conveying passengers to family gatherings.

A Midwesterner, John was mindful of the calendar. He made certain not only that Ferris Bueller took his day off in spring and *Home Alone*'s Kevin was left alone during a December snowstorm, but also that his stories revolved around holidays and important milestones.

The *Vacation* trilogy, along with *The Great Outdoors*, explores the peculiar trauma of family holiday. All three *Home Alone* films plus *Christmas Vacation* celebrate Christmas; *Planes, Trains and Automobiles* and *Dutch* occur at Thanksgiving.

Left (top): Steve Martin and John Candy in *Planes, Trains and Automobiles* (1987). Left (bottom): Jack (Michael Keaton) borrowing a little milk from his daughter in *Mr. Mom* (1983).

DOES SHERMER, ILLINOIS, REALLY EXIST?

The zip code that Anthony Michael Hall's Brian states in the opening of *The Breakfast Club*, 60062, is to an actual town, Northbrook, Illinois, about thirty miles north of Chicago. Northbrook was originally incorporated as "Shermerville" (the name change came in 1923), and one of the roads through town is still named Shermer Road. "John always had a mental image of Shermer," noted P. J. O'Rourke, the editor-in-chief of the *National Lampoon* when John worked there. "I compare it to the world of J. K. Rowling's [*Harry Potter*]—not magical though, but 'Midwesternal.' "

Meanwhile, weddings, proms, and birthdays figure prominently in his stories.

Hughes World has a strongly suburban look. And like Booth Tarkington, John Hughes was an unabashed Midwestern regionalist. Just as lawyer-novelist Scott Turow places his crime stories in a mythical Midwestern Kindle County and William Faulkner's Southern sagas took place in the imaginary Yoknapatawpha County, John's stories of his teenage and early adult life occur in Shermer, Illinois, a fictitious suburb of Chicago.

John grew up in two places: the Detroit suburb of Grosse Pointe and the North Shore suburbs above Chicago. It was out of these twin communities that he created in his head the town of Shermer in every detail, right down to those railroad tracks with families living on right and wrong sides.

"He once told me not only did he know all these characters in Shermer," continued O'Rourke, "but how they knew each other, who lived where and, even though it was not in any movie, who were cousins. He had a mental map of the place. It was a fully realized universe."

Above: Most John Hughes films had a suburban look and feel like this diner shot in *Sixteen Candles* (1984).

Tarquin Gotch, a Brit who supervised music on many of John's films and later ran his company, put it this way: "I felt I was working with the modern Frank Capra in the sense that he examined American life. The word 'bourgeois' has a negative connotation, which I don't intend. But middle-class American suburban life was his subject matter. He revealed it and its issues."

"He was a modern Norman Rockwell," said actor Steve Martin. "In the greatest possible sense he was a sentimentalist. There was always something touching in his films; he couldn't resist emotions."

Shermer is a suburb dominated by young people. Adults put in odd cameo appearances. These are strange creatures that forget the birthdays of their young, issue orders yet fail to listen to anything their children say. Even more curiously, in some movies adults almost completely disappear.

"Parents and adults to me were always like another species . . . I've never forgotten what it was like to be a kid. " —John Hughes

In *Some Kind of Wonderful*, Keith takes the object of his ardent desires, Amanda, to a very swank adult restaurant. There, a wine bottle chills in an ice bucket beside the table—this for its two diners, both underage high-school seniors.

John's writing kept a narrow range of focus. He understood the basic social structure of teenage life, as well as the recurring problems of puberty. He also knew well the economic disparity in the two communities in which he lived and in the public school systems of Grosse Pointe and Northbrook, Illinois.

John relied on stock characters—the sensitive geek, sympathetic punk, obnoxious preppy, annoying older brother or sister, peripheral parents, eccentric uncles—though they tended to be slightly off-center. It was the white, middle-class

suburbs filtered through a *National Lampoon* sensibility.

The geek was often his hero. A geek, he would say, is a guy who has everything going for him but is too young to know this. By contrast, a nerd is a nerd for life.

John remembered, as few adults truly do, what it was like to feel grown up yet have someone tell you what time to come home.

"Parents and adults to me were always like another species," John said of his childhood. "I never lost that connection. I've never forgotten what it was like to be a kid and look at adults."

"John had the sensibility of being a teenager," said actress Ally Sheedy. "I work with kids now and know something about being around seventeen-year-olds who know everything and know nothing.

"Every possibility is open to them—they have that kind of freedom. They can make the world into anything they want it to be. John tapped into that and was not particularly willing to let go of it."

John was lucky in one sense. He entered moviemaking at a time when Hollywood was overflowing with very young, talented actors.

The era of the so-called "teenpix," a category of films created to exploit the PG-13 rating instituted in 1984, was in full blossom, which had clear antecedents both during the early 80s (*Little Darlings*, *Valley Girl*) and in previous decades (American International Pictures's beach party movies, for instance).

"It was the time of the teen movie—*Fast Times at Ridgemont High*, *The Outsiders*," remarked producer Tom Jacobson, one of John's best friends. "When casting, we saw everyone—all the guys in that age group."

So even in smaller roles you might find John and Joan Cusack, whom John knew from the Chicago area, as well as Robert Downey Jr., Gina Gershon, Kristy Swanson, Dweezil Zappa, and Charlie Sheen. Larger roles went to up-and-comers such as Alec Baldwin and James Spader.

The talent pool featured others such as Emilio Estevez, Jami Gertz, Phoebe Cates, Sean Penn, Kevin Bacon, Matt Dillon, Mary Stuart Masterson, Jon Cryer, Rob Lowe, Elizabeth McGovern, Demi Moore, Ralph Macchio, Virginia Madsen, Mare Winningham, Andrew McCarthy, and many more.

Not all made it into a John Hughes production, but nearly all auditioned.

Above: Jon Cryer (top left), Matt Dillon (top right), and Demi Moore (bottom) were just a few of the talented young actors in the 1980s who would audition for roles in John Hughes films. Cryer, of course, was cast as "Duckie" in the Hughes hit, *Pretty in Pink* (1986).

Yes, it was a good era to be writing for a young cast. Yet John always wrote with an eye, and more importantly an ear, for timelessness. Meaning the jokes aren't based on pop-culture references, which become less funny with each passing year, and his dialogue eschews contemporary vernacular. He essentially made up his own slang.

"If you copy slang . . . by the time your movie comes out people don't talk like that," he said.

Sample Hughes insults: "You stain." "Mutant!" "You're a disease." "You little fungus."

"I've never bagged a babe," Hall confesses to Ringwald in *Sixteen Candles*. We know what he means but who ever spoke that way?

And this from Estevez to Nelson during the marijuana scene in *The Breakfast Club*: "Yo, Wastoid, you're not going to blaze up in here!"

The predominant note, though, which is rare for Hollywood films, is Midwestern. "I didn't realize how Midwestern I am until I spent time in California," John once said.

Knowing this world inside out, he got the details right. "Details were very important to John—sets, wardrobe, props—because they all spoke to character," said Jacobson. "He would keep things grounded, only pushing things slightly beyond the ordinary."

"My movies are popular because they're familiar," said John. "Armageddon doesn't interest me as much as a good family fight."

"John tended to sail very close to the wind of fact," noted O'Rourke. "He was realistic, a naturalist when not exaggerating to make something funny. The beauty of the *Lampoon* appealed to

John: there is verisimilitude in a parody of a cereal box—it was a mock-up of the way an ad agency would do it, not like *Mad* magazine parody.

"There is an immense sense of detail and perfection of his movies," he continued. "John was meticulous about that stuff."

The details were all there in the screenplay. Marilyn Vance, who designed costumes for many of John's films, called their collaboration "a match made in heaven. I was a visual person to begin with so we connected because he was the best storyteller ever.

"You see the character—he gives it so much life—on paper. In *The Breakfast Club*, in the opening where they all pull up in their cars, every little thing determines who these character are, what the families are like."

In *Home Alone*, every physical gag was written out with careful precision in the script itself. No one was coming up with stunts on the sets.

He got criticized for sentimental endings, but he wrote them deliberately. He insisted that when you're young, you want things to come out right but they never do. He meant for his films to depart from reality and say, "This is what I would want to feel." Life doesn't always come out that way. But movies can.

Life did come out perfect in John's own case, though, a fact he celebrated in *She's Having a Baby*, a valentine to his wife and a memoir of the early days of a marriage. Everyone who knew the couple thought theirs was about as perfect a marriage as can be.

"They were madly, beautifully, and romantically in love," said Mia Sara, who played a version of Nancy Hughes as Sloane in *Ferris Bueller*. "He definitely thought he was the luckiest guy in the world."

The only trouble was that *She's Having a Baby* failed to find an audience.

"It was the only truly autobiographical film [of his career]," said Gotch, "and when it wasn't a hit at the box office, this is one of reasons why in his autumn period, if I can use that word, John resorted to doing *101 Dalmatians*, doing sort of iconic stories and got away from this autobiographical material. I think the failure of that film in some strange way knocked the stuffing out of the autobiographical genius of John Hughes."

Which meant that Hughes World would change forever.

Opposite: Opening scene of *The Breakfast Club* (1985) when Claire Standish (Molly Ringwald) gets dropped off for a day of detention. Right: John Hughes and wife Nancy Ludwig attending the premiere of *Pretty in Pink* in 1986.

THE BLIZZARD

When the Great Blizzard of 1979 hit Chicago, John had dual careers. His day job was as a creative director at the Leo Burnett Company, a Chicago advertising agency. Servicing the Virginia Slims cigarette account, he took weekly trips to Philip Morris headquarters in New York. So he seized the opportunity to visit the *National Lampoon* offices at 59th and Madison in hope of a writing assignment.

John was already an established freelance writer at *Playboy*, where he did interviews and humor pieces, plus he was a gag writer for several well-known stand-up comics, including Rodney Dangerfield and Joan Rivers. But in the late 1970s, *National Lampoon* was ground zero in America for irreverent, angry, smart—and smart-assed—comedy.

At the peak of its popularity, twelve million people a month read the magazine. Millions more listened to its *Radio Hour* and attended its stage revues, both featuring young comics such as brothers Bill and Brian Doyle Murray; a diminutive Gilda Radner; an actor-writer-director named Harold Ramis; a manic buffoon in John Belushi; and a tall, gangly clown named Cornelius "Chevy" Chase.

Opposite: Two police officers on Michigan Avenue during the Great Blizzard of 1979 in Chicago. Right: In his early writing days, Hughes was a gag writer for comic greats like Joan Rivers and Rodney Dangerfield.

their first sexual experiences, run-ins with teachers, zits, and that cranky sister. It reminded them to laugh and even ridicule not only politicians, religious leaders, and consumer products, but also themselves and their own foibles.

Unlike *Playboy,* which spoke in one voice—that of founder and publisher Hugh Hefner—the *Lampoon* trumpeted many voices. Every contributor and artist was his own master.

Editor-in-chief Tony Hendra invited John into his office and explained how one became an editor. It amounted to writing filler. John was fine with that. So John became a contributing editor.

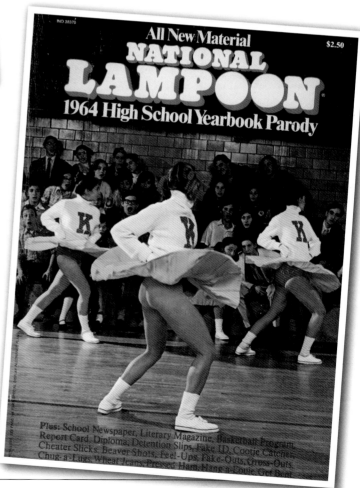

The *Radio Hour* was a precursor to *Saturday Night Live*; indeed, many *Lampoon* writers and actors later moved on to that iconic TV show. Then, in 1978, *Animal House,* the first *National Lampoon* movie, opened and became one of the most popular comedies of its era.

If that wasn't enough of a magnet for the budding comedy writer, there was this: For all its hipness, the magazine's secret ingredient was nostalgia. As exemplified by its legendary *1964 High School Yearbook Parody*, the *Lampoon* reminded readers of their high school and then college,

"There were no restrictions at all," he mused. "I could write anything I wanted. It was an enormous outlet. Those on staff were paid [a salary] to write so the guys didn't want to do anything. I got a nickel for every word I wrote so I wrote a lot of words and made a lot of nickels."

In P. J. O'Rourke, then managing editor, John found a fellow Midwesterner of the same age and political persuasion. ("They were the only two political conservatives in the history of the *Lampoon*," laughed Matty Simmons, the magazine's chairman and publisher.) As O'Rourke himself acknowledged, "John was the best person I ever worked with during that period. We were on the same wave length."

"I shared P. J.'s amusement with and affection for the unpretentious Middle America of our mutual origins," said John. "By the time I departed Leo Burnett, P. J. had educated, trained, and conditioned me to write quick and often—and to look for humor where others hadn't."

John first collaborated with O'Rourke on one of the *Lampoon's* landmark special projects, a follow-up to its high school yearbook parody. This was a send-up of a small-town newspaper, called the *Sunday Newspaper Parody*.

"John had a million ideas and I would say yes to as many as I had room for."

—P.J. O'Rourke

O'Rourke worked out the basic structure of the sections, basing them on the *Toledo Blade*, but needed help with the bulk of the newspaper, meaning the news stories and features.

Simmons suggested that he recruit John, the *Lampoon's* newest contributor. "He got it immediately," recalled O'Rourke. "After all, it was his trademark—that Middle American universe."

John and O'Rourke wrote the bulk of the copy, as well as the black-and-white advertising.

So the February 12, 1978, issue rolled out with "Dacron, Ohio's *Republican-Democrat*," complete with comics, a magazine, women's pages, and color ad supplement.

The banner headline for a town that proclaims itself "The Motor Home Capital of the World" warns about the continuing rampage of a serial criminal, the Powder Room Prowler, still at large despite his trademark of high heels and a bag over his head.

The parody became the *Lampoon's* second biggest-selling issue. And the two men had become friends for life.

When O'Rourke was named the *Lampoon's* editor-in-chief later that year, his first phone call was to John. O'Rourke offered him a full-time staff job for a lot less pay than his copywriting gig.

"You bet!" came John's swift reply. His only stipulation was that he remain in Chicago and commute to New York for editorial meetings. Neither O'Rourke nor Simmons checked to see if John actually quit his other job.

"I didn't think he quit—nor did I care," said an emphatic O'Rourke. "He was so damn productive. We would talk on the phone. John had a million ideas and I would say yes to as many as I had room for."

In fact, he did not quit his other full-time job, at Leo Burnett. To fuel these dual careers, though, John worked virtually non-stop. He

Left: Cover of the hugely popular *Sunday Newspaper Parody* from *National Lampoon* (written mostly by Hughes and O'Rourke).

wrote at night and on weekends. He wrote while riding the commuter trains in and out of Chicago. He even wrote while supposedly working on ad agency accounts.

On occasions when forced to leave his office unattended, he carefully stashed his *Lampoon* copy in a wastebasket covered by the morning's newspaper and sometimes a leftover coffee cup and cigarette ashes, all cleaned off when he took it home in an interoffice envelope at day's end.

When he needed to attend a *Lampoon* editorial meeting, John would show up at work in Chicago, leave a jacket over his chair and a cup of coffee on his desk, and then race to catch the hourly shuttle flights from O'Hare to La Guardia. There he grabbed a cab to take him into Manhattan across the (then) 59th Street Bridge to the *Lampoon* offices. Hours later, in the afternoon, he re-appeared at Leo Burnett in time to throw out the cold coffee and go home.

It was a good life for a man with a reputation as a workaholic. He had two jobs and one wife, a small son—another on the way—and a mortgage. Then came the snow.

The blizzard began Saturday, January 13. By the end of Sunday, 18.8 inches had fallen. Snow and cold continued into February, resulting in frozen tracks on the "L" and Metra systems.

John was trapped at home with his pregnant wife and three-year-old son. Thus, he had ten days to write without having to fool his boss.

For a *Lampoon* vacation-themed issue, John had already gotten an okay to write a story about the days when families took car holidays without seat

Above: Frozen train tracks during the Great Blizzard of 1979 meant that John Hughes had ten free days to write. He began penning a story he called "Vacation '58," which would eventually turn into a blockbuster family film starring Chevy Chase.

belts or worries over second-hand smoke. He had no story but did have a Rand McNally *Road Atlas*, on which he plotted a route from Detroit to the most distant location in the continental United States—Disneyland in Anaheim, California.

Never believing himself to be a prose stylist, John decided to write the first-person story through the eyes of a twelve-year-old so no one could question the writing.

"Hughes was haunted by his father's difficulties and determined that he would never slack off."

In a bedroom converted into an office, he typed the first sentence of "Vacation '58": "If Dad hadn't shot Walt Disney in the leg, it would have been our best vacation ever!"

In the story, the Griswold family begins its journey to Disneyland in a brand-new Plymouth station wagon from their home in Grosse Pointe, Michigan.

John Hughes had in fact spent the first dozen years of his life in that affluent Detroit suburb. Born February 18, 1950, in Lansing, Michigan, the second eldest of four children and the only son, John saw his father, also named John, struggle in a variety of auto company and sales jobs to support his family.

Above: Hughes was left alone on a family road trip as a child, and he re-created that early memory into the biggest comedy of all time, *Home Alone*.

Friends and colleagues later would point to that struggle as a key motivator in the son's tireless work ethic. Part of his drive and productivity was this fear of failure. He was haunted by his father's difficulties and determined that he would never slack off.

"His relationship with his father—I think that informs him," said producer Lauren Shuler Donner. "I know having a father who was a failure in business is a bit of a voice right behind your ear that haunts you a little bit."

When John was seven, his family did indeed take him on a station-wagon vacation. Since his sisters and their girlfriends got the seats, he found himself in the back with the picnic baskets. It proved the perfect place to throw tantrums.

"Would you like to leave?" his mother finally asked.

"As a matter of fact, I would," he replied.

She stopped the car. Calling her bluff, John got out. The station wagon drove off with the little girls' anxious faces pressed up against the glass. The car went round a bend and its taillights disappeared.

At this point, John became aware of the sounds of owls, coyotes, and other wild critters. The station wagon returned after a few minutes.

"Oh, mother, you're back," he said, his confidence now considerably lessened.

"We can leave if you like," she said.

"No, no, no," he replied.

John would later, of course, reproduce this left-behind memory in *Home Alone*.

He may even have recorded that intense conversation with his mother in a notebook. Because from the time he was in junior high, John filled journals with observations, ideas, characters, thoughts, bits of overheard conversations, jokes, and insights. John never went anywhere without a notebook on his person.

In 1962, when his dad got a job selling roofing material, he moved the family to Northbrook, Illinois, north of Chicago. Again, John found himself the son of a struggling middle-class family in another wealthy suburban community. This touched off within him many of the class issues and anxieties that filled his 80s comedies.

Left: While in pre-production on *The Breakfast Club*, Hughes sent Emilio Estevez and Judd Nelson undercover at a local high school to observe (see page 26).

Above: John Hughes also wanted to be an artist, similar to the Keith Nelson character (Eric Stoltz) in *Some Kind of Wonderful.*

Nelson recalled. "There was a jock hall and a freak hall. Jocks did not go into freak hall. Lines were not crossed; they were entrenched. It was good for me to see how heavy those lines of social demarcation were."

In high school, John developed his lifelong antipathy for teachers and other school authority figures. He flunked gym class in his senior year. A gym teacher didn't like John's attitude due to his cavalier approach to the school's dress and grooming code. Indeed, he claims he almost didn't graduate because his hair touched his collar.

While John achieved some level of triumph over this gym nemesis when he actually beat the aging jock at handball—the one sport John, to even his own surprise, excelled in—his ultimate triumph came when he based school vice principal Richard Vernon in *The Breakfast Club* on this teacher.

John clearly never forgot the teachers and staff members who lorded over the thin-skinned youth. While showing the cast of *Ferris Bueller* around the northern Chicago suburbs, he took Jeffrey Jones, who was to play Ferris's flustered principal, to meet his old vice principal.

"This is the guy I want you to pay close attention to," he told Jones before they stepped into his office.

After the usual pleasantries, the VP, a man in a sharply pressed business suit and of stiff paramilitary bearing, turned around to fetch something. John nudged Jones, who followed John's eyes.

As the VP's coat momentarily flew opened, Jones saw a holster with a gun fixed to the guy's belt. He couldn't believe his eyes: the VP was actually packing a gun. He instantly understood what John had in mind for Principal Rooney.

John saw how high school students suffered from categorization—the popular cliques, the jocks, the nerds, and so on. He thought of himself as an outcast at Glenbrook North High, a school seemingly dedicated to its athletes. But it was as an "outsider" that he got to observe it all.

While in pre-production on *The Breakfast Club*, John arranged for Emilio Estevez and Judd Nelson to go undercover at a local public school to give the actors a sense of his high-school days. Estevez was immediately recognized from *The Outsiders*. But Nelson blended in for part of a day.

"I hung out in the hallways where you got an absolute sense of strong class distinctions,"

"The guy was 'Sign up for the Army quick before I kill you!' " laughed Jones.

He would muse about his "bad kid" label later in life to friends and reporters, but this helped him to create Bender in *The Breakfast Club.* The character was based on a fellow student. He was a horrible guy, John admitted, but nevertheless he liked to hang out with him and get insulted. John felt curiously privileged to be in his company.

In 1967, when he turned seventeen, John worried about his future. Up until then all he wanted in life was never to get a haircut and to have a great stereo.

His father provided a reverse role model. The elder John Hughes had wanted to be an artist. In fact, he did paint—but in the basement. He was worried about what the neighbors would think. He would write stories and build things, but a real guy couldn't admit to a creative impulse. A real guy went to work, nine to five. A real guy joined the rat race.

John too wanted to be an artist. He wanted to be Picasso or Michelangelo but couldn't paint. He wanted to be Bob Dylan or John Lennon but lacked songwriting skills. Music did give him solace though.

Despite having few friends at school, he did find one his sophomore year, a British foreign exchange student, who had access to the latest U.K. pop. While everyone else was listening to *Rubber Soul,* John was listening to "My Generation" and "The Ox" off the Who's album two years before it was released in the States. So he came home at night and sat at his bedroom window, listening to albums and reading British music magazines.

If people made fun of him, he'd think to himself: That's okay. Picasso would like me.

"I didn't want to belong because I couldn't belong," he later told a journalist.

In *Some Kind of Wonderful* you get John's wishful self-portrait of the artist as a young man. Eric Stoltz's Keith Nelson isn't much bothered by this status in school. His passion is to paint and perhaps to go to art school. He couldn't care less where he fits into the school's social strata. Not John at seventeen, but John as he wished he were at seventeen.

Above: Hughes went to school with a rich kid that drove an Alfa Romeo every day. He would later create the smarmy *Pretty in Pink* character "Steff" (James Spader) based on that same guy.

One rich schoolmate taunted John all the way through high school. His older brother had an Alfa Romeo. He parked it outside with the top down in the rain. Walking by, John would notice the rose wood buckling on the dash.

He couldn't imagine how kids could live like that. He wasn't a part of that world. That schoolmate became the rich jerk in *Pretty in Pink* (memorably played by a young James Spader).

John recalled his first movie, taken to see around the age of nine, was *The Bridge on the River Kwai*. Later, in high school, he told *The Hollywood Reporter*, "I would find a movie I liked and go see it

Above: Ferris Bueller (Matthew Broderick), Sloane Peterson (Mia Sara), and Cameron Frye (Alan Ruck) fixated at an art museum in *Ferris Bueller's Day Off* (1986).

for three weeks. I was never a movie buff."

He saw *Blow-Up* about twenty-five times, mostly to watch the scenes of the groupies' orgy, Vanessa Redgrave take off her shirt, and David Hemmings's photographer roll around in sex play with two girls in his studio.

He certainly noticed the scene where Hemmings blows up a photograph that may show a murder. Antonioni then cuts back and forth between the photographer and the photo—using closer shots and larger blowups until we see arrangements of light and shadow, dots and blurs.

He directly copied this in *Ferris Bueller's Day Off*. At an art museum, Cameron becomes transfixed with Georges Seurat's *A Sunday Afternoon on the Island of La Grande Jatte*. He stares into the painting, isolating a family with a small child in its middle.

John then cuts back and forth between Cameron's eyes and ever-increasing close-ups of the painting until that child appears to scream amid the dots and blurs.

Several times he saw *Rebel Without a Cause* and could easily sympathize with James Dean's torment over his incommunicative parents. When he saw it again as a husband and parent, he found himself instead sympathizing with Jim Backus's father.

When he graduated high school, John left home for the University of Arizona. He went through four majors in two years but knew he would never graduate. To do so in those days at Arizona meant you had fulfilled your R.O.T.C. (Reserve Officer Training Corps) requirements, a college program that trains students to become officers in the U.S. military. With hair now down his back, he was even more out of place amid the school's tennis-sweater jocks and pick-up trucks with rifle racks than he was in high school.

"It's a big party school, a big fraternity school," he said. "The anti-war movement was very small, and the cops were very tough."

Besides, he was spending serious money in telephone calls. While painting homecoming murals before graduating from Glenbrook North, he had met a tall blond named Nancy Ludwig. He fell hard and was determined to stay in touch via long-distance phone calls and repeated trips home.

After two years he packed it in and returned home. He would tell journalists his epiphany came while listening to John Lennon's "Working Class Hero." In 1970, he married Nancy. He was twenty and she was nineteen.

Nancy and John lived in a converted boxcar. Rent was only $110 a month but even that was too much. The couple then wound up living in his parents' basement for eight months.

He worked in a warehouse, a printing lab, and in direct mailing—an experience that would pay off hugely when he later used direct mail to promote his movies. Meanwhile, he was writing jokes, short stories, and poems on the side.

Things did pick up. John's dad was a salesman, working at companies such as Procter & Gamble, so John thought a career in sales or advertising might be up his alley. He got an entry-level job as a copywriter at Needham, Harper & Steers.

Above: George Seurat's *A Sunday Afternoon on the Island of La Grande Jatte*—the painting that captivates Cameron Frye (Alan Ruck) in *Ferris Bueller's Day Off* (1986).

Right: Just like the character Jake Briggs he created, in *She's Having a Baby*, Hughes had also been a successful advertising exec before leaving the field to write full time.

John has fun with this moment in his life in *She's Having a Baby*, when his alter ego, Jake, turns in a résumé to a prospective employer so full of such transparent B.S. that he is hired on the spot, outrageous lying apparently being part of the job requirements for successful copywriting.

In 1974, John found a better job at the prestigious Leo Burnett. He went to work in daylight and came home well after dark. Occasionally, he stayed up all night doing variations on an ad idea.

He started at $8,500 a year, doubled his salary within six months and doubled it again a year after that. At twenty-seven, he became one of the company's youngest creative directors.

Energized by coffee and cigarettes, he sat at a typewriter and knocked out ad campaigns for dozens of accounts. Two memorable ones were the Edge credit-card shaving test, where an actor demonstrated the close shave one gets from its shaving gel by scraping a charge card under his jaw, and the Sugar Corn Pops spots for Kellogg's that starred Big Yella, a pint-size cartoon cowboy.

He also produced a number of commercials, which is where he first learned to deal with actors, a job he liked immensely. And when no one was looking, he scribbled jokes on a blotter.

He submitted gags to several of the mainstream comedians, Henny Youngman, Rodney Dangerfield, Phyllis Diller, and Joan Rivers. As

"I was almost twenty-nine, and I realized if I didn't move soon, I'd be so deeply entrenched in corporate business life . . . that it would be difficult to leave." —John Hughes

he would later do when sitting in his Hollywood agent's office, pitching titles and story ideas from reams of single-spaced two-sided paper, he bombarded these comics with sheaves of neatly typed gags.

His first paying job as a writer, though, was to ghostwrite a comic strip.

The Berrys was a family comic strip created and drawn by Carl Grubert, who had a background in Chicago advertising as well. Running in newspapers from 1942 to 1974, the strip chronicled the

lives of the Berry family—the parents, a daughter, son, and baby brother.

"The creator had a stroke so his daughter asked me if I would come in and write the strip," said John. "But I was not a draftsman so I took old strips and wrote new jokes to it. It was a great exercise but was not successful."

Below: *The Berrys* was a popular Chicago newspaper comic strip drawn by Carl Grubert. John Hughes briefly stepped in to write the strip when the creator suffered a stroke.

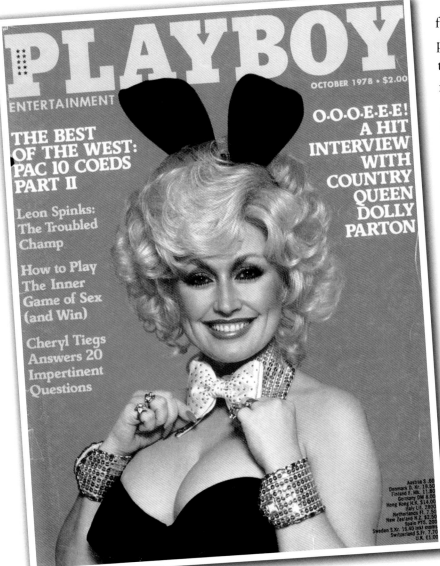

PLAYBOY

ENTERTAINMENT

OCTOBER 1978 • $2.00

THE BEST
OF THE WEST:
PAC 10 COEDS
PART II

Leon Spinks:
The Troubled
Champ

How to Play
The Inner
Game of Sex
(and Win)

Cheryl Tiegs
Answers 20
Impertinent
Questions

O·O·O·E·E·E!
A HIT
INTERVIEW
WITH
COUNTRY
QUEEN
DOLLY
PARTON

Above: Hughes conducted *Playboy's* first ever "20 Questions" interview with Cheryl Tiegs in October 1978.

While taking the train and then a bus to work, he developed the habit of eavesdropping. He would often miss his stop, causing him to be late because he would ride down the South Side listening to conversations. Thus, he collected these moments in his notebooks, and some would later find their way into his stories and then his movies.

Along with gag submissions he started freelancing for *Playboy*. He wrote humor pieces and did interviews. John conducted that magazine's first ever "20 Questions" interview in the October 1978 issue with model Cheryl Tiegs. ("I found her to be a warm, intelligent woman who is so beautiful that I'm sure she would stop an elephant's heart at thirty paces," he wrote in his introduction.)

Meanwhile, John watched his colleagues in advertising turn incredibly bitter and frustrated. Many wanted to be writers and artists.

"As you move up in the agency, they use you less and less for what you're good at," said John. "I was a good writer and they kept moving me up into administering things, which I'm not very good at. I was almost twenty-nine and I realized if I didn't move soon, I'd be so deeply entrenched in corporate business life and country club memberships and that sort of stuff that it would be very difficult to leave."

He portrayed this dilemma in *She's Having a Baby*. Unlike others at the ad agency who have grown bitter selling soap rather than writing the Great American Novel, Jake sees himself as the *rara avis* of advertising: "You're looking at the rare individual. I'm busting out!" he shouts to frustrated colleagues.

John was doing likewise.

"Everybody in my family has always been a businessman," said John. "So creative was—an advertising executive. That was acceptable because you worked at a job and a company and you

"What if I'm sixty-five and retired with all my stock, my profit-sharing, my money, and I'm sitting on the porch thinking I should have been a writer." —John Hughes

sold products. But you were able to think up stuff and were 'creative.' So it took a long time for me to accept the fact I was actually earning a living as a writer."

As he wrote "Vacation '58" he was mindful that "the dark side of my middle-class, middle-American, suburban life was not drugs, paganism, or perversion. It was disappointment. There were no gnawing insects beneath the grass. Only dirt. I also knew that trapped inside every defeat is a small victory, and inside that small victory is the Great Defeat."

By the time he packed "Vacation '58" off to New York, John had made a decision.

"What if I'm sixty-five and retired with all my stock, my profit-sharing, my money, and I'm sitting on the porch thinking I should have been a writer—I wonder if I could have done it?" he said to himself.

He mentioned this to Nancy, who agreed with his decision.

When the snow abated, he returned to work and bid farewell to his co-workers. He was going to become a *real* full-time staff member at the *Lampoon* for what he joked was roughly half his Christmas bonus at Leo Burnett.

"Vacation '58" was ultimately bumped from the vacation issue to an annual edition comprised of pieces that didn't make their intended issues. By then, though, unbeknownst to John, Simmons was thinking that the story would make a dandy *National Lampoon* movie.

THE LAMPOONER

One day early in his new, and this time real, full-time gig at the *National Lampoon*, John happened to be talking with Tod Carroll in the editorial offices when Matty Simmons emerged from his office. He summoned the two editors inside. When they sat down, he astonished them with an unlikely assignment. "I'm producing a new *Jaws* movie," he told them. "You two are going to write the treatment." *Jaws 2*, a sequel to the smash hit Steven Spielberg movie, had come out the year before, getting bad notices but making good money for Universal. It strained credulity, though, that Chief Brody, played again by a highly reluctant Roy Scheider in the sequel, would engage any shark in a third movie.

Simmons explained that it would be called *National Lampoon's Jaws 3—People 0*.

It seemed that Simmons had lunch the day before at the Friars Club with his old friend David Brown, producer—along with his partner Richard Zanuck—of, among other movies, *Jaws* and *The Sting*. Brown had expressed a strong interest in doing a movie with the *Lampoon*. Everyone did in the months following *Animal House*.

Without thinking, Simmons blurted out that title. When Brown chuckled, the publisher and now-movie producer ad-libbed a scenario: Peter Benchley, author of the original *Jaws* novel, goes to his pool for a swim. He jumps in and

Opposite: Hughes began working full time at *National Lampoon* in the late 1970s after abandoning his successful advertising career. Right: Though never produced, Hughes co-wrote the *Jaws 3* parody with fellow *Lampoon* editor Tod Carroll.

disappears. Then a shark fin slowly circles in the surface of the pool. The entire story would be that of the shark pursuing the filmmakers shooting a third movie.

Surprisingly, the producer of *Jaws* liked it. He and Zanuck were having dinner that night with Ned Tanen at the Rainbow Grill and would pitch the spoof to Universal's president.

Moments before he summoned the two editors into his office, Simmons had gotten off the phone with Brown. Tanen liked the pitch too. He had a go-ahead.

Simmons wanted both John and Carroll (who later wrote *O.C. and Stiggs* and *Clean and Sober*) to write the movie. It would be their first film.

While the two went to work from a story outline Simmons had hurriedly dictated after his luncheon while his idea was still fresh, a cast and crew rapidly came into place. Surprisingly, Richard Dreyfuss signed on. Then *Animal House*'s Stephen Furst came aboard to play a star gone to seed, while Mariette Hartley would be a tough studio exec.

Meanwhile, John was getting his first taste of the "development" process—and it was bitter. A draft would come in, Simmons and the suits gave notes and it was back to the drawing board. He found this affected his writing.

It wasn't, John discovered, about, "Is this a good script?" It was more, "Is this something that they'll make?" The former apparently was the wrong question to ask, but it was the only question he could conceive of.

The Hughes–Carroll draft submitted in August created many of its best jokes by aping scenes in the original movie, such as the opening beach bonfire sequence, only this time the celebrants are studio execs and starlets.

When the head of production gets killed by a shark, associates argue at his memorial service over how many "minutes of silence" to give the late executive. Should it be five minutes, like a previous deceased studio exec got? Or ten minutes as another one recently had? Since other important meetings occupy the day's schedule, the decision is made for five minutes today and another five tomorrow.

Other than spoofing Hollywood, though, the script ran out of gags before it ran out of pages. Nevertheless, pre-production went forward. At this point somewhere between $1.5 and $2 million had been spent on the picture.

In late fall, Tanen called Simmons into his office. He was pulling the plug on the production, he told its producer. Simmons became furious and demanded to know why. Tanen wouldn't tell him who had ordered the shut down or why. (It was Sid Sheinberg, president and chief operating officer of MCA/Universal, the executive who sponsored Spielberg's early career in film. "What the fuck are you doing?" he shouted at Tanen when he got wind of the project. "You're making fun of our most esteemed film!")

In retrospect, it was strange that *Jaws*' producers had been so eager to mock one of their greatest triumphs.

John arrived at the *Lampoon* at the moment it was getting into the film and television business. So nearly every writer was a hot property. Many had movie projects. Beyond the glamour, the difference in pay between writing for the magazine and the movies was profound.

John soon found himself on this lucrative treadmill, which tended, he soon learned, to involve turning out one horrible script followed by another.

Above: *Delta House* cast members (left to right) James Widdoes, Bruce McGill, John Vernon, and Stephen Furst in 1979. Right: Michelle Pfeiffer scored her first TV acting role in *Delta House* as "The Bombshell."

Meanwhile, at the magazine itself, John did like the deadline writing. He was often among five or six writers and editors putting out an issue every month. Plus, he got involved in additional projects where he got to learn how to write in different areas, making jokes about all types of things and parodying various styles.

Sexual naughtiness would play an element in his writing, including early screenplays, eventually culminating in a rebellion by the women involved in *The Breakfast Club*.

Universal decided it wanted a TV spin-off of *Animal House* so *Delta House* was born. ABC approved the series, which aired in 1979. John wrote four episodes and co-wrote a fifth. Despite a writing staff of *Lampooners*, including Doug Kenney, Harold Ramis, Chris Miller, Simmons, and Carroll, the series never took off. ABC cancelled the show after thirteen episodes. Its only claim to fame may be a young actress cast as the Bombshell, named Michelle Pfeiffer.

Despite his protestations that real writers worked at magazines and wrote books, not screenplays, O'Rourke did attempt a screen collaboration with John. Based loosely on their Sunday newspaper parody, *The History of Ohio Dawn of Time to End of the Universe* fell into "a mutual area of interest," O'Rourke noted. "We never really got it to work and finally abandoned it. But it was fun to work together."

Meanwhile, O'Rourke wanted to shift the magazine's focus to longer, *New Yorker* style pieces. Plus, he was constantly under the gun with deadlines, budgets, and personnel conflicts while Simmons was out in Hollywood trying to make movies.

"It was not a pleasant place to work," he said. "You can't gather humorists together in one place and expect them to get along; it's like a sack full of cats. John was a huge exception to that. He got along with everybody. From his experiences at the ad agency he knew how to deal with people. I did not always."

O'Rourke left the *Lampoon* in 1981.

That same year, Don Simpson, president of production at Paramount Pictures, phoned Simmons. It seemed the studio owned the film rights to Alex Comfort's *The Joy of Sex*, the popular 1972

sex guide apparently purchased more with an eye to the best-seller lists than its screen-worthiness. The book contained no actual story to adapt to the screen.

Simpson pitched this: why not *National Lampoon's Joy of Sex*?

Why not? Simmons wrote an outline detailing a man's sex life into his thirties. John wrote the screenplay while John Belushi came aboard to star. Three days before production, on March 5, 1982, Belushi died of a drug overdose in West Hollywood.

The film was eventually made with another script altogether. Simmons paid back $250,000 to make certain the movie came out without the *Lampoon* name attached.

Another John Hughes project did, however, bear that moniker.

NATIONAL LAMPOON'S CLASS REUNION

When John attended his high-school class reunion, he saw how shockingly little everyone had changed. When the former classmates all got back together, they were the same people and belonged to the same cliques.

This gave him an idea for a raucous, broadly played farce. He quickly hammered out *Class Reunion* and then showed it to Simmons. John hoped

From the people who brought you "Animal House"

NATIONAL LAMPOON'S

CLASS REUNION

No class
has less class
than this class.

ABC MOTION PICTURES
presents
NATIONAL LAMPOON'S
CLASS REUNION

Starring
GERRIT GRAHAM
FRED McCARREN
MIRIAM FLYNN
STEPHEN FURST
SHELLEY SMITH
and MICHAEL LERNER
Special appearance by CHUCK BERRY
Original Music by PETER BERNSTEIN &
MARK GOLDENBERG
Written by JOHN HUGHES Directed by MICHAEL MILLER
Produced by MATTY SIMMONS

DOLBY STEREO   Read the Dell Paperback

R RESTRICTED   ABC MOTION PICTURES

Above: John Hughes' first cinematic screenplay was
National Lampoon's Class Reunion (1982).

he would produce it as a *Lampoon* movie. Simmons passed. It wasn't very funny in his opinion.

John pleaded with Simmons to let him at least use the *Lampoon* name, then a sure-fire selling point for the script. Simmons relented, which he later regretted. John got the film set up at ABC Motion Pictures, the network's newly formed theatrical subsidiary.

Shortly into production, Brandon Stoddard, the ABC film executive supervising the project,

fired the producer and asked Simmons to come aboard to produce. Since the *Lampoon* name was on the picture and production was going poorly, Simmons reluctantly did so.

The movies in the 1980s were awash with two disreputable yet highly lucrative subgenres—the teen sex comedy and slasher horror films. So there is some inspiration in John's decision to combine and then kid these two subgenres. Little of that inspiration, however, went into the making of *National Lampoon's Class Reunion* (1982).

A spoof of horror-movie tropes and clichés, *Class Reunion*, which stars Gerrit Graham and Michael Lerner, traffics in the rude, snarky humor of *National Lampoon* satire. But the film is undone by its low budget and the even lower common denominator aimed for by its mostly limp gags.

The movie concerns a reunion of former students a full decade after graduation. John's screenplay sets up any number of potentially amusing situations—a constantly dazed pair of dopers, the supreme egotist, a perpetual virgin, the handicapped student, the school tramp, and a *Carrie*-like girl gifted/cursed with magical abilities—all of whom are eventually overshadowed by the specter of a deranged alumnus, driven mad by a high-school prank, returning to exact revenge.

The main problem, at least as realized on the screen by director Michael Miller, is that little is done with these rote characters, all members of Lizzie Borden High's class of '72.

Right: Misty Rowe, Zane Buzby, Mews Small, Fred McCarren, and Gerrit Graham were some of the stars in Hughes' comic horror flick *National Lampoon's Class Reunion* (1982).

The film's central figure, as much as the film has a central figure, is one soon to become familiar in the Hughes canon: the outsider. Poor Gary (Fred McCarren) is remembered by absolutely no one. Not even his best friend can place him. No nametag is even available to him. So his name is scribbled on his jacket with a marker pen.

Soon enough, all of the school's outside doors are locked, and deranged Walter Baylor (Blackie Dammett) is bumping off one ex-classmate after another. Which doesn't prevent the party from continuing, or Chuck Berry putting in a surprise appearance to sing his novelty song, "My Ding-a-Ling."

There's a tiny bit of the risqué, with an occasional bare breast, the adventures of the actress Mews Small's accident-prone blind girl, and Chip's

acknowledgement that he has thought of Carl as a farm animal. Otherwise *Class Reunion* walks on the mild side, with actual horror-violence going no further than soft smacks to the head, hardly the makings of a slasher parody.

The slapstick action is indifferently staged and no character development reaches beyond initial introductions. Miller glosses over situations with comic potential—such as the alum with fangs or a "Medieval Sciences" room stocked with torture devices. The film, which opened during the October 31 weekend, barely got past the $10 million mark when all was said and done. *Class Reunion* was deemed a box-office disappointment by *National Lampoon* and its distributor, ABC Motion Pictures.

When leaving a cinema near his home, John had the unnerving experience of the owner yelling at him. He had booked the feature for a month, thinking it was going to be another *Animal House*. So John had his first screen credit—and first humiliation.

MR. MOM
"When you're down you're not necessarily out."

One day, an ambitious young Hollywood producer put in a blind call to John. She had noticed his byline on his *Lampoon* stories and thought they were very funny—and that he should write screenplays.

She discovered she had come late to that party as he had a deal with ABC Motion Pictures already. Plus, he was writing another screenplay, *Debs*, a satire on Texas debutantes, for Aaron Spelling Productions.

Nevertheless, Lauren Shuler pitched him an idea, which he did not warm to; he then tried to bring her aboard his Spelling project, which didn't happen. But the upshot of their conversations over the telephone was that a bond had formed. As with O'Rourke, their Midwestern background did the trick.

"He's from Chicago and I'm from Cleveland. My father eventually went bankrupt and his father had [financial] problems too, and somehow we just connected," recalled the producer, who now goes by her married name of Lauren Shuler Donner.

During one call, he regaled her with the challenges of being a househusband when Nancy went out of town. He had never done grocery shopping and had no idea how to operate a washing machine. His way to change fouled diapers involved dishwashing gloves, tongs, and a mask.

Encouraged by her laughter, John mentioned he had eighty pages of a screenplay inspired by these events in a drawer. Would she like to read it?

When Shuler finished reading those eighty pages, she knew she wanted to make *Mr. Mom*. On his next trip to Los Angeles, he came by her office. Both writer and producer did *Mr. Mom* "on spec," meaning they worked for free until the

Above: John Hughes penned the comedy *Mr. Mom* after his own laughable failures as "househusband" when his wife, Nancy, had to go out of town.

project got set up. They didn't even have a written agreement with each other.

After his early screenwriting experiences on assignment, this was how John preferred to work. If someone paid him to write a script, then that person could infuse the writing with his or herjack own ideas. But if John went to producers with a completed script, he saw it as a take-it-or-leave-it proposition. Do you like the script the way it is? If not, fine, no money down, no obligation. John didn't like to collaborate with producers or to get producers' notes.

Since John had an association with Spelling, a TV mogul with six hours of programming a week

on ABC at the time, he brought Spelling aboard. So *Mr. Mom* got set up at Spelling and Sherwood Productions, with Twentieth Century Fox distributing. Ted Kotcheff (*The Apprenticeship of Duddy Kravitz*) was set to direct.

The young writer and producer, neither possessing the kind of industry "juice" to stand up to show-business lions, would later regret these associations.

Sherwood was a production company run by David Begelman, a disgraced Hollywood studio executive who had been involved in an embezzlement scandal in the 1970s. Spelling was a veteran of television but a movie neophyte. Plus, he had never made comedies, and thus, he was insecure. Consequently, both men feared failure more than they sought success.

"They were so terrified—it obstructed everything they did," said Shuler Donner.

When she secured the services of a brilliant production designer, Lawrence G. Paull, it was a real coup. Paull had just done one of the most visionary science-fiction films ever made, *Blade Runner*. Yet at the time of its release, *Blade Runner* was not only a flop, but hugely expensive, a combination loathed by Hollywood suits.

"David Begelman didn't want any keys [department heads] who were associated with flops," she remembered. So Paull got bounced off the project.

Spelling soon got rid of her director as well. He saw one of Kotcheff's recent comedies, *Who Is Killing the Great Chefs of Europe?*, and didn't fancy the film. So he replaced Kotcheff with Stan

Dragoti, who'd had a hit a few years earlier with the Dracula spoof *Love at First Bite*.

Begelman and Spelling also hated working with a screenwriter who was not in L.A. John would fax in new pages from Chicago quickly but his physical absence irked them.

So while she was out of town to scout locations for her next film, *Ladyhawke*, the two men fired John and brought in two female TV writers to pen without credit the final shooting script. Shuler Donner was very upset but could do little against such industry veterans.

"Spelling and Begelman were powerful players," she explained. "John and I were newbies. He had done *Class Reunion* and this was my first feature."

So if one wants to speculate about John's later antipathy toward Hollywood, this early brush with the town is a good starting point. A man many remember as a fierce hard-baller and a convicted thief ran John off his second project.

While *Mr. Mom* has a happy ending from a Hollywood point of view—*Mr. Mom* ($64.8 million) actually outgrossed *Vacation* ($61.4 million) at the national box office in 1983—it's hard to know what might have happened had John and Lauren Shuler made the film they had wanted to make.

Certainly, John's first draft—dated April 25, 1982—and a second draft—dated July 7, 1982—reveal a much different kind of film, one with much darker undertones and sexual themes.

John's original screenplay actually portrayed a disastrously dysfunctional suburban family. As the title promises, the story is that of parents who undergo role reversals—when the husband is laid off from his engineering job at a Detroit auto plant and his wife lands a job at an advertising agency.

While early scenes emphasize the comedic aspects of man vs. household and a new girl in an ad agency bursting with too much testosterone, later scenes turn sharply bleak.

The wife is, frankly, a bitch.

After years of apparent bitter regret over a "degree that I've never used," Caroline is soon coming home drunk at one o'clock in the

Above: The original draft of *Mr. Mom* was much darker than the movie that was eventually produced.

Above: Caroline (Teri Garr) was originally scripted to have an affair with her boss, but that was cut from the final movie.

morning, complaining about Jack's bad cooking—"Shitty tasting torte," she remarks—casting aspersions on his virility, AND having an affair with her philandering boss.

Jack kicks her out of the house. He then hits a "meat market" bar, picks up a hot number named Vicki, and takes her home for torrid sex, which gets interrupted by his uncomprehending kids. Vicki screams "perverts!" at the entire family and runs shrieking from the bedroom.

Eck. We're definitely not in Hughes World. More a rather nasty *Lampoon* spoof.

The story ends with a chastised Caroline meekly asking Jack to let his wayward wife come home. Startlingly, he acquiesces but insists the roles remain reversed. She will keep her job (and apparently that boss) while he remains a house dad.

"I like this just fine," he insists.

This was not the story either John or Shuler Donner wanted to make. So a rewrite focused more on the out-of-work guy and his loving family and softened Caroline significantly.

The couple has more civilized conversations about the role reversals. Jack, speaking from experience, tells his wife, "You're not giving yourself to your family because you're too busy giving them [at the job] everything else."

Caroline no longer has an affair with her boss. Instead, when he makes a pass, she belts him across the face. Jack still kicks her out—he believes the lies of the boss's wife— but again takes her back with the proviso that the role reversals remain permanent.

His one demand: "No wisecracks about my cooking."

The second draft contains more comic business than the first, including a grocery shopping expedition gone even more seriously awry. The screenplay underwent more changes after this draft before John's dismissal. Shuler Donner recalled a comic bit, pitched to her by John while the two ate in a restaurant, where Caroline, still unused to the company of adults, cuts a steak into tiny bites for her boss over lunch.

The final movie, though, betrays the TV roots of Spelling and his new writers. Situation comedy dominates and the supporting roles are caricatures. The couple's three children are little more than witnesses to dad's housekeeping fiascoes. None of John's empathy for young people, so acute in his future comedies, is on display.

Michael Keaton and Teri Garr, two of the screen's major comedians in that era, starred in the PG-rated film. They display plenty of charm and warmth, yet the story demands that they spend much of their screen time in separate scenes.

In early scenes John mischievously plagues his hero, Jack, with a series of non-stop crises. Within

Below: Though they didn't share a lot of screen time together in *Mr. Mom*, Michael Keaton and Teri Garr were two major comedians of the era that shared an easy on-screen warmth.

one six-and-a-half minute sequence, a TV repair woman, exterminator, and plumber show up simultaneously—and apparently without Caroline alerting him to these appointments—while an overloaded washing machine in the basement is on the brink of exploding, a vacuum nicknamed Jaws is running amok upstairs, smoke fills the kitchen, and the baby is devouring a can of chili.

While certainly the film's funniest extended sequence, Dragoti merely sets these debacles in motion without any comic rhythms in the editing, or rising tension as one crisis spills into another.

Indeed, the whole film feels mechanical, without any of the inspired bits of comic business director Harold Ramis and star Chevy Chase cooked up in *Vacation*, a film released a week after *Mr. Mom* in July 1983. Consider, for instance, an early dialogue scene in *Vacation*, where Beverly D'Angelo is scraping food off dinner dishes and handing the plates to Chase, who gives each dish a quick wipe and puts it back on the shelf. Subtle physical gags like this run throughout *Vacation*, while *Mr. Mom* plods on, one lumbering step in front of the next.

True, John didn't supply a narrative filled with much comic stimulus. One would expect the househusband to get hooked on soap operas, play poker with the other housewives—the one inspiration here is that store coupons substitute for money—and get dragged by these women into a male strip club.

As one would also expect, Caroline must dodge advances by her libidinous boss (Martin Mull), dream up the slogan that saves a big account—"The Tuna with a Heart!"—and come home unexpectedly to catch an oversexed neighbor (Ann Jillian of TV's *It's a Living*) in her bedroom.

The marriage never feels in any more jeopardy than the house is from Jaws. The only infidelity happens in Jack's imagination, and this is awkwardly staged like one of his beloved soap operas.

The third-act rescue of Jack from a life of household drudgery, with his former boss (Jeffrey Tambor) begging him to come back, feels phony and forced. Even worse, the movie reneges on its mildly enlightened role reversals when it insists that women really do prefer vacuuming and laundry to the challenges of the workplace, while men belong out of the house Monday through Friday.

VACATION
"Getting there is half the fun."

In 1982, Simmons had lunch with Mark Canton, a new production executive at Warner Bros., who had worked with Ramis on *Caddyshack*. He very much wanted to make a *Lampoon* movie. Despite a turn-down from Paramount, Simmons always felt John's "Vacation '58" would make a great comedy. He handed a copy of the story to Canton.

When Canton convinced studio heads Robert Daly and Terry Semel to acquire the project, Simmons asked John to do the screen adaptation.

In "Vacation '58," a comic memoir of a family car trip with just enough exaggeration and outrageous misfortune to snuggle comfortably into the naughty pages of the *Lampoon*, John caught exactly the right tone of Huck Finn–like innocence in its narration by one of the family's sons.

Minor problems begin when everyone oversleeps the day of departure. (Oversleeping would become a common device for John's *Home Alone*

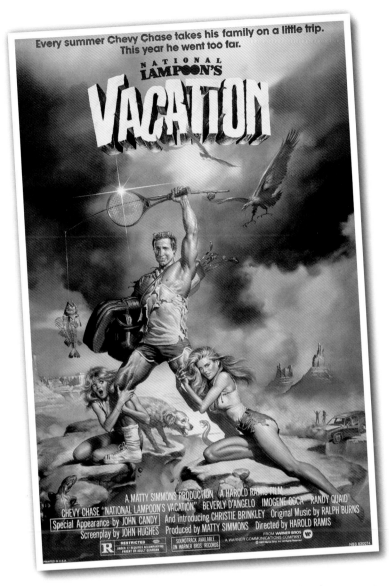

Every summer Chevy Chase takes his family on a little trip. This year he went too far.

NATIONAL LAMPOON'S **VACATION**

A MATTY SIMMONS PRODUCTION · A HAROLD RAMIS FILM
CHEVY CHASE "NATIONAL LAMPOON'S VACATION" BEVERLY D'ANGELO · IMOGENE COCA · RANDY QUAID
Special Appearance by JOHN CANDY · And introducing CHRISTIE BRINKLEY · Original Music by RALPH BURNS
Screenplay by JOHN HUGHES · Produced by MATTY SIMMONS · Directed by HAROLD RAMIS
FROM WARNER BROS · A WARNER COMMUNICATIONS COMPANY

Above: The Herculean movie poster for *National Lampoon's Vacation* (1983) by fantasy artist Boris Vallejo.

screenplays.) There is a minor escalation when Aunt Catherine telephones to suggest swinging by Wichita to pick up Great Aunt Edythe and driving her to her son's home in Tucson, since the Griswolds are going in that "general direction" anyway.

All-night driving binges find Dad, Clark, falling asleep at the wheel and driving up on sidewalks and running over bikes. Dad insists he is unfamiliar with Illinois traffic signs.

Things go from bad to worse with the deaths of the great aunt and her dog. Then a tow-truck operator and mechanic take the family for every cent they've got to repair the Plymouth when Dad takes a wrong exit and drives off a small cliff. It's a small cliff, mind you.

Later, Dad, seriously short on cash in those days before ATMs, is forced to rob a motel, then successfully outrun highway patrol cars only to drive the family station wagon into a military missile testing range at the Yuma Proving Ground. While one missile does knock the car over and waken the baby, Dad gets the station wagon through the test range so he can yell triumphantly at startled guards, "You better hope to God that the Russians aren't flying Plymouth station wagons, 'cause they're invincible!"

The family laughs hard, right up until a bunch of drunken American Indians rob the Griswolds of their stolen money and many of the station wagon's parts. When the family does make it to Anaheim, sufficiently behind time that only one day is left for Disneyland, they discover the amusement park is closed for repairs.

Now in complete meltdown, Clark proceeds to purchase a gun, get a map to movie stars' homes, and track down Walt Disney.

"I'm Clark W. Griswold, and you owe me!" he tells the great man, just before firing a shot into his leg.

So there it was: a short story that doubled as a complete film treatment. The comic incidents, mix of dark humor, family squabbles, and unpredictable outside forces was ready-made for a *Lampoon* movie.

But with Chase signed to play Clark Griswold

Above: The Griswold family's infamous pea green "Wagon Queen Family Truckster" (which was based on a 1979 Ford LTD Country Squire). Five Trucksters were made specifically for the film.

to entice fans of *Saturday Night Live*, John needed to reconfigure his story. Not only must the focus shift to his character, but Dad could no longer be a man so easily angered and frustrated. Instead, Chase is benignly oblivious to much of the chaos that surrounds him. His sunny optimism brightens the dark events that rain down on this family.

John considerably deepened the roles of other family members. He gave the mother, Ellen, both a maternal side and a sexuality that makes it clear that, aside from quarrels over auto routes, Mom and Dad are a very happily married couple, eager to close bedroom doors whenever a chance arise. Ellen shines a romantic-comedy light on Clark, letting audiences know he is a good guy, loved no matter what he does.

John reduced the number of kids to two and beefed those parts up considerably, so the characters could be played with enough juvenile sagacity that an audience might wonder whether Mom and Dad were raising the youngsters—or the other way around.

John clearly enters a comfort zone in *National Lampoon's Vacation*, a world of parents and children, domestic catastrophes, dogs that bite, and elderly aunts that bite even worse. One senses his

> **"The family vacation comedy is fairly common these days, but in 1983, it was pretty much an untried genre."**

joy as he turns his comic sights on such a familiar world that locates its laughs in characters.

Clark Griswold proved to be one of Chase's best movie roles, one that he would continue throughout *Vacation's* three sequels. Working with his *Caddyshack* director, Ramis, he plays Clark as a man almost "stoned" on family life. He never notices when his son chugs a can of beer, and he tends to downplay moments of danger.

He prefers to view a wrong turn taken in St. Louis that lands the Griswolds in an African-American ghetto as a teaching opportunity that will acquaint the family with places in America they wouldn't normally see. Moments later, when

Below: Dana Barron (top left), Anthony Michael Hall (top right), Beverly D'Angelo (bottom left), and Chevy Chase (bottom right) making treasured memories as the Griswold family in *National Lampoon's Vacation*.

a gunshot rings out, he calmly suggests that everyone roll up the car windows.

This sequence features clichéd black characters that steal the station wagon's hubcaps and extort money from Clark in exchange for directions back to the highway, directions that are never forthcoming. This no doubt replaces the longer sequence of the Indian attack in the original story. Neither episode would stand up to scrutiny in today's more socially conscious climate.

"I'm not proud of it," Ramis would later say of the scene.

The movie also gives the father an actual profession, albeit a dubious one. He has spent the last fifteen years of his life, he says in an offhand remark, to "develop newer and better food additives." Hmm …

For Clark's wife, Ellen, Ramis cast the beautiful and talented Beverly D'Angelo. As well as being a singer, D'Angelo is an exceptional actress who has never gotten her due from critics or the industry. But Hollywood knew her to be reliable and consistent, able to play second fiddle to Chase but never get lost in the background.

She is aboard *Vacation* as a facilitator, reactor, and minder to the rest of the cast, helping to set up and support all the gags and gamely fulfill the film's need for gratuitous bare breasts in a lame *Psycho* joke where Chase substitutes a banana for a butcher knife.

She is, in other words, a straight man with curves.

Fourteen-year-old Anthony Michael Hall (in braces) and sixteen-year-old Dana Barron play the Griswold kids, Rusty and Audrey. As the movie progresses, the young actors carry more and more of the comedy load.

The scenes where the Griswolds visit their fiercely inbred relatives, a sequence that moves the comedy further to the dark side, and others where Dad seeks to engage his son in "man-to-man" chats find the youngsters demonstrating superb comic timing and getting the most out of line readings.

The family vacation comedy is fairly common these days, but in 1983, it was pretty much an untried genre. The film's success owes much to the fine cast—including the superb TV and film comedienne Imogene Coca as Aunt Edna, Randy Quaid as poor, white-trash layabout Cousin Eddie, and Miriam Flynn as his long suffering wife—as it does the novelty of situating R-rated humor into a family comedy.

The frequent use of the "F-word" in front of youngsters, especially when Dad goes into full meltdown phase, and mild hints of incest and a not-so-mild hint of animal abuse in the fate of Aunt Edna's beloved pooch, mischievously undermine the sanctity of the American nuclear family, making *Vacation* very much a *National Lampoon* product.

Little Miss Sunshine (2006) owes much to John's comic inspiration.

John was, of course, forced to eliminate Disneyland and its late founder from the finale. Instead he found a stellar substitute in a fabricated Walley World, with its mascot changed from a Mouse to Moose (specifically Marty Moose) and its creator from Walt Disney to Roy Walley, nimbly played by 1940s film star Eddie Bracken (made up to look rather like Uncle Walt).

The film's original ending saw Clark buy a gun and stalk Roy Walley in his San Marino mansion, where he forced Roy to entertain his family by doing a song and dance. But that ending bombed with test audiences. After investing seventy-odd minutes on the road to Walley World, viewers wanted to see the place.

So Ramis and Simmons asked John to create a new ending. The cast was called back for reshoots and John Candy was added as a befuddled park guard. The new ending sees Clark essentially hijack Walley World by taking the guard hostage and forcing him to open the various rides to his family. (A telltale sign of the reshoot is that in the intervening months Hall had grown about three inches and towered over his co-star Barron.)

The new ending performed much better with test audiences, causing Warner Bros. executives to breathe a sigh of relief.

Candy brings delicious comedy to his role as the funniest kidnapped victim since Gene Wilder

Below: John Candy's cameo as the Walley World security guard wasn't in the original script.

Above: Chevy Chase and Christie Brinkley (in her debut film role as The Girl in the Ferrari) take a stroll by the hotel pool in *National Lampoon's Vacation* (1983).

in *Bonnie and Clyde*. From his opening deadpan line—"Sorry, folks, park's closed. The Moose out in front shoulda told you"—Candy is every frightened little boy forced on to rollercoaster rides of increasing daring, only to discover that he loves being kidnapped. His is a brilliant last-minute spark of virtuoso comedy that gives the ending a genuine kick, although John would always prefer his original ending.

John's other new addition is the Girl in the Ferrari. In his first draft, John had a teenage girl, the same age as Rusty, meet the family on the road. Ramis decided she should be a gorgeous woman instead to bring the focus back to Chase.

This mysterious blonde (undoubtedly modeled after Suzanne Somer's Blonde in T-Bird from *American Graffiti*) is played by supermodel Christie Brinkley, who gets "introduced" to movies in the title credits. She materializes in a red sports car throughout the movie, unseen by other family members but teasing poor Clark's libido something fierce.

Vacation was a huge hit and, of course, created a franchise. D'Angelo felt that a "massive" amount of the credit belonged to Ramis.

"I felt his absence in all the others [*Vacation* sequels]," she said. "He was a hands-on, amazing collaborator. He was old school: he set up everything, looked at a scene, [would] suggest a tweak and knew what would work. He had acerbic wit but [was] so kind."

The one-two punch of *Vacation* and *Mr. Mom* made John a big man on the Hollywood campus. A young screenwriter out of Chicago had solo writing credits on two of the industry's top-grossing films of the year.

By now John was grinding out scripts and treatments faster than most writers get ideas. *G.I. Jones* was a musical comedy about a kid in the army, peeling potatoes in the kitchen, who falls in love with a general's daughter.

Patagonia was an Indiana Jones–style movie, while *Spy vs. Spy* played as an espionage comedy. None got past the first draft but, increasingly, John was not enjoying the *Lampoon* experience. He was chafing over what he perceived as "some kind of indentured servitude" to Simmons.

After *Vacation*, John quit being a *Lampooner*. For one thing, even before *Mr. Mom* and *Vacation* came out, he already had deals for *Sixteen Candles* and *The Breakfast Club*. Deals for him to write—and direct.

4

THE COMING OF BOOTH TARKINGTON JR.

John loved to describe his early appearances in Los Angeles as that of a Booth Tarkington Jr., a Chicago rube with literary gifts lost in a land of gold chains, red Ferraris, and big sideburns. He would insist that the first day he entered the I. M. Pei–designed bastion of CAA—the powerhouse Creative Artists Agency—in Beverly Hills, he was mistaken for an IRS agent in his "poplin suit and rep tie."

The truth of the matter was actually not far off. Michelle Manning does remember his appearing in Ned Tanen's office with "his Eddie Bauer tote bag and L.L.Bean apparel." His longtime costume designer Marilyn Vance recalled first visiting John in his modest house on the outskirts of Chicago, where ducks played prominent parts in pillows and tapestries, and a plaid couch sat in the living room.

Yet she also remembered his transition to Hollywood styling under the influence of his *Weird Science* producer, large-than-life hipster Joel Silver.

Opposite: Judd Nelson, Molly Ringwald, Emilio Estevez, Ally Sheedy, Anthony Michael Hall, and John Hughes on the set of *The Breakfast Club* (1985). Right: John Hughes in 1987.

"John Cusack was to play Bender and Virginia Madsen was going to play one of the two girls."

Soon enough, he was buying expensive clothing at the high-end L.A. fashion house Maxfield; collecting art, photography, and Roseville pottery for his Brentwood home; and driving a black Porsche. Not a red Ferrari, mind you, but still a Porsche.

"There was a comic side to this—Mr. America from Chicago temporarily enthralled by Joel Silver, Maxfield blue clothing, and early twentieth-century pottery," said Sean Daniel, then a Universal senior executive. "John had ambivalent feelings about life in Hollywood and in the industry. He was trying to live it, if you will, but it wasn't him."

But let's return to that Midwestern writer with a swelling reputation and L.L.Bean apparel. Tiring of the travails of a screenwriter in the film industry, he hatched a plan to create an entry point into directing.

It was a two-pronged effort and, as luck would have it, both endeavors paid off. John left CAA for its stalwart rival ICM and its president, Jeff Berg. He asked Berg to help him make the leap into directing.

John thought if he could write something that could be filmed very inexpensively, perhaps in a single location with a handful of actors, then all he needed to worry about were the performances. From his days producing commercials at Leo Burnett, where he mainly dealt with actors and food, he knew that would play to his strengths.

So he wrote a script called *Detention* about five high-school students suffering through a Saturday of detention in the school library—five kids in one room. A group of Canadian dentists agreed to finance this low-budget project but, eyeing a possible TV sale, they demanded he hire a few stars from sitcoms. One was Jimmie Walker, then known for playing J.J. on the series *Good Times*, to play Bender. Since their suggested actors were closer to thirty than high-school age, John said no.

Seeing where this was going, John had a contract drawn up where it would be virtually impossible for him to lose control. He would get little money for directing but control was more important at this point. Then A&M Records got involved.

The record label founded by musician Herb Alpert and recording executive Jerry Moss had formed a film division, A&M Films, in 1981 under Gil Friesen. A&M Films agreed to put up $750,000 to produce *Detention*. In the winter of 1982, John started casting in Chicago for a non-union production. John Cusack was to play Bender and Virginia Madsen was going to play one of the two girls. The next step was to recruit from a very talented pool of actors at Northwestern University.

It never happened.

While developing *Detention*, John sent *Sixteen Candles* to ICM. When Tanen's new production company agreed to Berg's demand that its writer would direct, John had no choice but to grab the studio picture. But he didn't want to lose *Detention*.

As he went into pre-production on *Sixteen Candles* for a summer shoot, John faced an unnerving task. Instead of a low-budget non-union indie where he had total control, he found himself at the helm of a $6 million ship that featured a large cast of adult and young actors, multiple locations, and many moves by a union crew with huge trucks and equipment. Despite being surrounded by Tanen and a veteran crew, the production was a lot to manage for a neophyte director.

John mentioned how this was not at all what he imagined his debut film to be like to Manning. He told her about *Detention*, a film he still wanted to make next.

She pointed out that it made no sense to go from a $6 million studio production to an indie costing under $1 million. She read *Detention*, and

then sent it to Tanen. He knew Friesen, so the two companies agreed to partner on *Detention* as a studio film. A call was placed to Berg.

John now had two films set up back-to-back as a director. This took much of the pressure off him on *Sixteen Candles*. Were that to fail, he still had a movie set to go that winter.

SIXTEEN CANDLES
"Quit feeling sorry for yourself. It's bad for your complexion."

One of the pros Tanen hired to help his new director was casting director Jackie Burch. She did discover, though, that two of the film's principal actors were already cast in John's mind.

Right: Movie poster for *Sixteen Candles* (1984) which was both written *and* directed by John Hughes.

Earlier, at a general meeting at ICM when the agency first agreed to represent John, agent Hildy Gottlieb had given him a bunch of 8x10 headshots of actors. Among them was a freckle-faced, red-haired teenager who looked like Becky Thatcher in *Tom Sawyer*. As legend has it—and for once the legend is true—he put that photo of Molly Ringwald up on a bulletin board above his word processor when he wrote *Sixteen Candles*.

When John finished the script, Gottlieb set up a meeting with Ringwald and her mother. John liked her a lot, but since she was his first interview he continued to read young actresses in L.A. and New York, only to come back and read Molly again. No one had come close. She got the lead role.

Ringwald seemingly was born for show business. At age six, she recorded "I Wanna Be Loved by You," a music album of Dixieland jazz with her father and his group, the Fulton Street Jazz Band. At ten, she was chosen to play Kate in the Los Angeles production of the musical *Annie*. In 1980, at the age of twelve, she performed as a lead vocalist on two Disney albums.

In her first film, Ringwald had co-starred in Paul Mazursky's *Tempest* (1982)—she received a Golden Globe nomination—but John claimed he never saw the film until after *Sixteen Candles* was shot.

At this point John had seen a rough cut of *Vacation*. He felt that Anthony Michael Hall had stolen his scenes from Chase, so he had Hall in mind when writing "the geek" in *Sixteen Candles*.

Burch brought Hall in to read. Although shy at the first reading, he and the director quickly found much in common. "When John and

Left (top): John Hughes wrote the character of Samantha Baker in *Sixteen Candles* with a head shot of Molly Ringwald hanging above his desk. Left (bottom): Molly Ringwald was nominated for a Golden Globe in 1982 for her debut film role in *Tempest* directed by Paul Mazursky.

Left: Actor Gedde Watanabe fooled the casting director of *Sixteen Candles* by auditioning for the role of Long Duk Dong with a heavy Korean accent. Watanabe had in fact been born in Utah.

accent, yet was genuinely funny, pretty much what Burch knew her director wanted. When Wantanabe called her on the phone a couple of days later, she didn't recognize his voice.

"This is Gedde," he told her.

"Where's your accent?" she demanded.

"Well, I was kind of born in Ogden, Utah," he said.

The Japanese-American actor had, in fact, been doing serious theater in New York, including Shakespeare in the Park. Adapting the accent of a Korean friend, he decided to pretend not to speak English for his audition.

When she had finished laughing, Burch told him to do the same thing for John when he auditioned. He did and got the role.

Finding Watanabe's "sexy girlfriend" was a happy accident. A friend took Burch to a play so far off Broadway that it was in New Jersey. There she saw a six-foot actress named Debbie Pollack. She didn't even have an agent.

Burch made sure John had trained theater actors in key roles, such as Blanche Baker, daughter of Oscar-nominee Carroll Baker, who played the older sister. For Ringwald's father, John wanted veteran Paul Dooley, but the actor expressed reservations about such a peripheral role. John wrote a new scene for him between his character and Ringwald's that convinced him. More importantly, it proved to be a crucial scene in the final film.

When its legion of fans fondly recalls *Sixteen Candles*, it's usually as a Molly Ringwald picture

Michael got to know each other, magic happened," said Burch. "He was what John was like in high school almost. He pleasantly surprised even me."

For the role of the jock, Burch brought in a newcomer, Michael Schoeffling. He was green and shy, certainly not a typical school athlete, and mumbled his lines. So he was initially ruled out, only to get a call back as John and Burch liked the sensitivity in his facial expressions. He wound up getting cast.

Finding someone for the role of an Asian exchange student perplexed Burch until a twenty-eight-year-old Asian actor walked into a New York casting session with the apparent drawback of not speaking English.

Gedde Watanabe read the lines with a heavy

Above: Anthony Michael Hall playing Farmer Ted, one of John Hughes' most masterful characters, in *Sixteen Candles*.

or that comedy about a pouty teenager having the single worst day of her life.

It is neither.

Rather, it's an expertly crafted ensemble comedy with crowded multi-plot action and a brisk pace. Ringwald's Samantha Baker just happens to be at the fulcrum of this action.

While all the characters and situations of a teen comedy are present, John's screenplay stands them on their heads.

In no teen comedy does the wallflower get her ideal guy. Instead, she is given a life lesson: she is made to understand she must see beyond looks and status to the inner essence of a person. Meaning she'll probably wind up with a geek.

In no teen comedy is that ideal guy a jock. Jocks are made the object of derision by (usually non-jock) filmmakers as revenge for slights real or imagined suffered in high school. Yet John gives the jock an insight into the soul of a wallflower while he ditches the prom queen.

And in no teen comedy are dads allowed to show empathy for their kids. Nor are break-ups to go without heartaches, outsiders supposed to find happiness, or, absurdity of absurdity, does a geek score with the hottest girl in school.

Ridiculous.

So John throws out all the models; he reverses all expected norms. Even the notion of an entire family forgetting a child's birthday is far-fetched, although in the context of another child's impending nuptials, it's perhaps believable.

As good as Ringwald is as the ignored Sam, demonstrating that at sixteen she is fully a professional actress with sharp comic timing and physical grace, her character is not John's greatest achievement in *Sixteen Candles*. Rather, his most original and fully realized character is the one referred to alternatively as the Geek or Farmer Ted.

As played by Hall, this is a supporting role only in the sense that Bottom in Shakespeare's *A Midsummer's Night's Dream* is a supporting role. The Geek is a true original, a clown rather than a fool or jester. He is a wise clown though. He is as shrewd as he is kind, but he is not a wit. He doesn't know he's funny.

> **"Hughes' most original and fully realized character in *Sixteen Candles* is the one referred to alternatively as the Geek or Farmer Ted."**

Every exigency finds the Geek ready: his response is always admirable. He is also the favorite of his fellow geeks, the Dip Shits; he admits to Sam that he is, in fact, the "King of the Dip Shits."

While he has an enormous crush on Sam, the moment he discovers the real object of her affection is Jake Ryan (the impossibly handsome Schoeffling), he immediately tells her, quite truthfully, that Jake had just asked about her. He wants Sam to be happy even at the cost of his own unhappiness.

He is gentle, mild, and good-natured, yet sees himself (quite absurdly) as a lothario. He can mix mean martinis and put moves on girls like an old *roué*, yet has to admit to Sam, in the film's most touching scene, "I've never bagged a babe."

Hall, then gangly with an oversized head and his body as yet unformed, becomes a WASP version of Woody Allen. As in Allen's depiction of his younger self in movies such as *Annie Hall* and *Radio Days*, the Geek is insatiable in his sexual curiosity, sophisticated in some things and innocent in many more. The Geek hasn't grown into the man he wants to become—but he no doubt will.

Hall plays the Geek with so much nervous energy that his body actually hops when he speaks. While *Sixteen Candles* purports to tell Sam's story, the Geek is her narrator, commentator, and facilitator.

Unlike nearly all teen comedies in that or any other era, John cast many actual teens. So the differences between freshmen and seniors are striking: They seem like different species.

These physical differences further underscore the absurdity of the skinny, "utterly forgettable" Sam ending up with Jake, or the gangly Geek, his teeth still in braces, ending up with Haviland Morris's prom queen, Caroline. (Morris was, in fact, twenty-four, as was Schoeffling, when the film was shot.)

This is acknowledged in one of the film's earliest scenes, where Sam examines herself in the mirror after awakening on the morning of her sixteenth birthday. "Chronologically, you're

Below: The King of the Dip Shits (Anthony Michael Hall) showing off the prize (Samantha Baker's underwear) to his fellow geeks in *Sixteen Candles*.

Right: John Cusack, Anthony Michael Hall, and Darren Harris redefining the word "geek" in *Sixteen Candles*.

sixteen today," she tells herself. "Physically, you're still fifteen." She sighs. "Hopeless."

The linchpin for the comedy is the Baker family forgetting its middle daughter's birthday. Indeed, several of Sam's lines begin with, "I don't believe this …" or, "This has got to be a joke …"

This is not a case of John forgetting he is repeating himself in his dialogue, but rather the filmmaker laying out the comical absurdity of his tale from start to finish.

In her second major screen role, Ringwald gives a performance that many still see as emblematic of her early success in movies. On camera she's a tease: She pouts, frets, forgives, exalts, smiles, laughs, and screams like any sixteen-year-old drama queen. Every emotion simmers beneath her volatile surface.

In the film's key scene, she's seated inside a dismembered car chasse in the school auto shop with Hall; she shifts moods and attitudes any number of times. She is beginning to see the nice guy inside the Geek, even as she fends off his ineffectual advances.

John cuts away from her final reaction shot, though, just after the Geek asks, for the sake of a bet he made with the Dip Shits, if he might borrow her underpants for ten minutes. The brilliance of this cut is that it lets the audience supply her reaction. By this time we're getting used to her unpredictable, though often generous, behavior. So it's left to our imagination.

The film's first act piles on characters and incidents with neither chaos nor confusion. John superbly ushers each set of characters into his two main venues, home and school, with nonchalant ease.

The Baker family's harried morning ritual introduces its members—Dad (Dooley), Mom (Carlin Glynn, mother of Mary Stuart Masterson, who will later star in *Some Kind of Wonderful*), snarky brother Mike (Justin Henry, grown older and rounder after *Kramer vs. Kramer*) and the three daughters. Sam, of course, comes between Ginny (Baker), the focus of all the family's attention, and Sara (Cinnamon Idles), who is promptly forgotten for the rest of the movie.

This sequence establishes the two main plotlines: Ginny's wedding the following day to her dubious fiancé, Rudy (John Kapelos), and the total eclipse of Sam's Sweet Sixteen due to a long shadow cast by frantic wedding preparations.

Mike, a perpetual brat, lets Dad in on a third, and ultimately crucial, issue in what unfolds over the film's forty-eight hours: Ginny is having her period.

"That should make for an interesting honeymoon," Mike winks to his father.

Throughout the movie, Mike serves as a Puck-like figure, a mischief-maker. He comments on all the action rather than participating in any of it. John also gives Mike the film's best zingers.

School introduces the fierce social strata in which Sam must operate: the Geek, who comes on to her on the school bus ("Am I turning you on?" he asks as she doesn't even disguise her hostility); Jake, her dreamboat; his steady (and her rival), Caroline, the school hottie; and assorted background characters.

Notice the complete absence of any school-teachers or staff members. The only teacher who appears on camera does so in study hall, where he sits just in front of a blackboard containing a message that points directly to him: "Total Idiot."

The background characters mostly function as running gags, especially the Cusack siblings,

neither well known at the time. Joan says nothing really—she murmurs to herself—yet wears a neck brace that leads to physical comedy involving a water fountain and beer drinking.

John Cusack is one of the Dip Shits, a crew of fellow geeks into headgear and computer software. Their best gag involves a party scene where they inadvertently knock over a pyramid of beer cans painstakingly constructed by thick-necked seniors, possibly the only skill these guys will ever master.

John Hughes finishes his introductions to the characters when Sam returns home from school and confronts both sets of grandparents. Throughout this and many of his films, John delighted in casting veteran character actors in such roles.

Edward Andrews and comedienne Billie Bird play Sam's paternal grandparents. A simple "How are you?" from Sam elicits from this pair a litany of physical woes that all fall under the category of Too Much Information.

Her maternal grandparents are played by musical comedy performer and songwriter Max Showalter, and Lucille Ball's protégé, Carole Cook. Grandma Helen greets her by examining Sam and announcing to her husband: "She's finally gotten her boobies! They're so perky!" To which Grandpa cheerfully notes, he'll have to look for a magnifying glass. Grandma moves in for a grope.

Moments later, out of earshot of the grandparents and as one of her many asides to the audience, Sam mutters: "I can't believe my grandmother actually felt me up."

John remembered what it was like to be a kid and look at adults, which is why he had the grandparents in underwear. During the shoot, Andrews couldn't understand why John wanted to shoot him in his underwear, or why he kept directing him to hike the pants a little higher up. As people get older, John noticed, they tend to wear their pants higher.

Sam loves her grandparents, but they are almost like creatures from another planet, which is why John put *The Twilight Zone* theme music in their introductory scene.

THE **LONG DUK DONG** CONTROVERSY

The final character and only bridge between home and school is one that has become controversial. This is the foreign exchange student, Watanabe's Long Duk Dong. Critics held their noses at this Asian stereotype in opening-day reviews and have been doing so ever since. Bad enough that Dong is a mishmash of Chinese, Japanese, and Vietnamese, with a vaguely phallic name. But at every mention of his name did the soundtrack have to bang a gong?

Dong can be seen, charitably, within the Elizabethan tradition of the jester. But the role really shades closer to a less noble tradition in American films and theater.

Racial and ethnic jokes were a staple of American cinema going back to its earliest days. The silent clowns were never above anti-Semitic or anti-black gags; nor was Preston Sturges. The Jewish entertainer Al Jolson never apologized for doing much of his act in black face.

Right: There was a lot of criticism over the character of "Long Duk Dong" who was seen as an Asian stereotype for many reasons, including the fact that a gong would ring out whenever someone mentioned his name on screen.

These things were never benign, at least not to audience members whose ethnicity was being ridiculed. As far as Asian caricatures are concerned, Long Duk Dong doesn't offend nearly as much as, say, the Japanese landlord Mr. Yunioshi in Blake Edwards's *Breakfast at Tiffany's* (1961), made all the more appalling by being played by a white actor, none other than Mickey Rooney.

Watanabe himself saw the exchange student as being a fun-loving outsider who actually gets a "sexy girlfriend" and thoroughly enjoys his exposure to American culture.

"It was in the 80s and there were no role models at that time, especially in movies. I was the only [Asian character] out in a movie," he explained. "When I did it, I had no concept about what people would think about it. I thought it was just play and so did John. Both of us had to be educated about it down the road."

John's own grandparents hosted foreign exchange students. He noticed they especially liked the Asian ones who were so unfailingly polite and helpful. To John they were patting themselves on the back for hosting the students, yet "what they really got was like free labor. So the minute [Dong] gets away from them he goes completely berserk, cuts loose, and proves that he isn't what they thought he was."

There's actually a worse racial joke in *Sixteen Candles* that is seldom commented upon. This comes when Samantha is discussing with a girlfriend her ideal guy, who would pick her up at school in a Trans Am. She adds the word "black," which the girlfriend mistakes for the guy, not the Trans Am.

"A black guy?" she asks incredulously.

When this false impression gets corrected, a look of relief floods her girlfriend's face.

The reception to Long Duk Dong might have greatly improved had John not cut an extended sequence, shot over two days, of Dong performing a song at the big dance. Dong jumps up on stage and raps about what he likes about America, while all the kids get into his performance.

"If that scene had been left in, it would've had been interesting to see how the reaction to my character might have changed," said Watanabe. "To this day it just kills me [that it was cut]."

John puts Samantha on a journey into womanhood. Along the way she sees drawbacks, such as her sister's abrupt marriage to a boy whose only qualification for matrimony is that he's totally enamored of his bride. But Sam also realizes womanhood's potential happiness, with the attention she gets not only from Jake, but the Geek himself.

Samantha is the most beguiling character John would ever create. Her exaggeration of her own calamities and self-absorption are no reflection of character flaws, but rather of the extreme melodrama of the teenage years.

Meanwhile, the Geek's nighttime odyssey with an inebriated Caroline ends the complete absurdity of *Sixteen Candles* on its most absurd note of all.

From the point that Jake "gives" his drunken

Above: Caroline (Haviland Morris) realizes she's sitting in a parking lot next to a dorky freshman (Anthony Michael Hall) with her hair inexplicably chopped off.

incapable of either responding to or remembering the event takes *Sixteen Candles* into areas its author had no intention of visiting. Indeed, he gives us no evidence that any such act ever took place. Rather he is again playing with absurdity.

If *Sixteen Candles* has a flaw it's in how the third act gets taken up with the wedding and the slapstick surrounding Ginny taking muscle relaxants to relieve her menstrual cramps, thus forcing the movie to abandon its heroine at a crucial time. As originally written, the sequence went on even longer, with a lost wedding ring as part of the chaos, a comic cliché fortunately dropped while in production.

girlfriend to the Geek, somehow expecting a kid without a driver's license to get her home in his parents' Rolls—leading to a moment where John breaks the fourth wall, as he will later do in *Ferris Bueller*, and lets the Geek speak directly to the audience: "This is getting good!"—the movie loses track of this very odd couple.

They wake up together in the Rolls in a parking lot, neither one certain of what transpired over the rest of that night and early morning. Memories are cloudy but Caroline is pretty certain they "did it." Prodded further on this point by the Geek, she is also pretty certain she did enjoy it. Both are fully clothed and neither one a reliable narrator of what really happened.

The idea of sexual intercourse with a woman

Sixteen Candles was made on such a modest budget that when the big dance sequence was staged in a stifling Niles Township East High gym—summer heat had pushed temperatures well above 100 degrees—the production company made a decision not to spend money on air conditioning.

Against high expectations, the film grossed only $23.7 million domestically, which disappointed Universal. Yet the film became a most successful ancillary title, proving to be a must-have as a VHS and later DVD rental for successive generations of teenage girls on sleepovers.

John built his reputation on what he achieved in *Sixteen Candles*—the ability to fuse elements of zany humor with three-dimensional characters, and to use a soundtrack brilliantly. Under the music supervision of Jimmy Iovine, the movie put to work theme music from movies and old TV shows such as *Peter Gunn*, *The Twilight Zone*, *The Godfather* (for the new in-laws), *Dragnet*, and even Sinatra's version of "New York, New York."

THE BREAKFAST CLUB

"When you grow up, your heart dies."

"Collaboration" is a word tossed around a good deal in Hollywood, even when true collaboration is seldom realized within the film community. But by becoming a studio movie, *Detention*—the title was soon changed to *The Breakfast Club*—gave John a chance not only to cast from an unbelievable talent pool of young actors, but also to collaborate with these youths to flesh out a raw script that most film people frankly saw as little more than a dull group-encounter session for children. It would also allow John to collaborate with veteran editor Dede Allen, which was to have a lasting impact on his career.

In his mind, John had cast three of his five young roles while in post-production on *Sixteen Candles*. He knew he wanted Ringwald and Hall, so they were on board. He also knew he wanted an actress who had read for Ringwald's older sister in *Sixteen Candles*. While that hadn't worked out, John still admired Ally Sheedy from her work in *Bad Boys* (1983), a gritty teen crime film.

He sent the script to her in England, where she was shooting *Oxford Blues*, then followed up with a phone call. He told her he wanted her to play Allison, a character that has no lines for the first half hour of the film.

Surprisingly, the actress loved the idea.

Like Ringwald, Sheedy had enjoyed a precocious childhood. Both a published novelist and a dancer with the American Ballet Theatre by the age of twelve, Sheedy was a veteran actress at twenty-two, having played a recurring character on *Hill Street Blues* and starred in *Bad Boys* and *War Games*.

Some of the ideas of how Allison "acts up"

Right: The iconic movie poster for *The Breakfast Club* (1985), a film that John Hughes had originally called *Detention*.

In the audition process, Estevez was reading off-camera with someone else but John found himself looking instead at Estevez. Afterward, he approached Estevez and asked him if he would play Andy.

"Well, I'd really like to play Bender," said the actor.

"I think that you're the only guy in the world to play Andy," said John.

Estevez agreed.

Which left Bender. For this role, John had to find someone who could play a pretty reprehensible guy, a guy who says cruel things repeatedly for a long time. And he doesn't get redeemed until the very end.

Back when John was going to do the film

Left: Actress Ally Sheedy played the role of Allison Reynolds in *The Breakfast Club*. Below: Emilio Estevez originally auditioned for the role of Bender, but John Hughes was convinced he'd make the perfect Andrew Clark.

without speaking came from John's script, but others were ad-libbed inventions by Sheedy herself. Working closely with John, she said, "I just made up things as we were going along."

"Allison is communicating all the time," noted Sheedy. "It doesn't feel like she's not talking."

(Burch and Manning said Ringwald at one point wanted to switch roles with Sheedy, but it's not clear that John gave this more than a moment's thought.)

The Breakfast Club became a major casting call for young actors on both coasts. Emilio Estevez came in to read for the role of Bender. At that time, John was having difficulty finding the right actor for Andy, the wrestler. What John was looking for was tricky—a seemingly bland character whose motivation in life is to be like everybody else. So John needed just the right actor to play that role.

independently, he had cast John Cusack in the role. But Burch, returning from *Sixteen Candles* as his casting director, fought this. She thought Cusack projected too much of a conservative Midwestern kid. She wanted cool, smart, volatile—and threatening. She thought she had just the guy.

Meanwhile, John, Burch, and co-producer Manning saw many actors, including Sean Penn, Nicolas Cage, and Rob Lowe. Everyone in that age range wanted Bender.

The role was still uncast when Burch's guy, a twenty-five-year-old with a prep school background, philosophy as a college major, and the Stella Adler Conservatory as his true education, entered Universal's casting offices in New York.

He came in to the outer office wearing a trench coat and boots. Waiting for his name to be called, he roamed the room recklessly, at one point snatching a stapler off the desk of Manning's assistant and banging it on the desk. Others in the office grew concerned. Security was called. An officer walked in just as an assistant poked a head out of the inner office door to call out: "Judd Nelson?"

Great, just in time, the nervous actor thought to himself.

"He was totally Bender during the interview," Manning recalled. "Jackie knew him but I didn't. You knew he was acting but even after he did the scene he stayed in character."

John and Manning brought him back several

Above: Judd Nelson showed up to the audition wearing a trench coat and boots, and his unpredictable behavior prompted a call to security at the Universal casting studio.

more times but continued seeing better-known actors. Yet John kept saying, "What about that Judd Nelson guy?"

Finally, Universal flew Nelson to L.A. for a final audition. He walked into a room on the lot with five stools sitting in the middle, four of which were occupied by the other actors already cast. More

Right: Judd Nelson didn't break character when the camera stopped rolling, an acting technique that nearly cost him the role.

than a dozen decision-makers sat along two of the walls. Ever in character, Nelson strode into the room with a Walkman blasting "Holidays in the Sun" by the Sex Pistols. He was asked to sit on the empty stool and to please turn down the music.

But what got him cast in the movie's final major role nearly cost Nelson the job a week into production.

When people first meet Nelson, the son of a Maine attorney and a fellow attorney and state assemblywoman, they usually are impressed by his intelligence and passion for acting.

"Judd is really free physically and has got this really quick mind," said Sheedy. "He's all over the place, making weird connections here and there—he is not your typical actor showing up for work."

"Judd Nelson would come in in the morning

with incredible comments," John said later. "He read the script every single night for six months. He had a fix on that character I couldn't get because I had to watch five of them."

"John and Judd were on the same page—they had similar senses of humor," added Sheedy.

Yet once production began, Nelson, a man who in reality was nothing at all like Bender, stayed in character the whole time.

"In the movie he treats Molly badly," said Manning. "But when you break for lunch, you still shouldn't treat her badly, and he was doing that. Molly was John's muse, for lack of a better word. So he was protective of her and it hurt him the way Judd was treating her outside of the scenes."

This continued for over a week. John, who characteristically delegated unappetizing personnel issues to others, asked Manning to fire Nelson.

Manning called Tanen in L.A. to ask what she should do. Tanen insisted that with a week of filming completed, firing was not a good option.

"Get his manager out there and have her smack him around," he said.

Mind you, Nelson's manager was his live-in girlfriend, Laurie Rodkin, who now owns a jewelry chain in Los Angeles. She flew to Chicago and, whatever she told him, the issue vanished.

"Then he was great," said Manning. Whatever "Bendering" Nelson felt he needed to do for the remainder of the shoot took the form of pranks played by him and Estevez at the Westin O'Hare Hotel.

For his part, Nelson said this: "The story says

we [detainees] all reach a mutual understanding by the end of the film. My initial thought was the furthest I can go from that common ground, the distance [my character would] travel would be that much greater. But I may have started too far outside at the beginning."

If ever a movie should have been shot on a Hollywood soundstage, it was *The Breakfast Club*. Five characters in a single room needed no location shooting, hotel bookings, or per diems for cast and key crew. But John had other ideas. He didn't want to leave his family in Chicago, and he was adamant about doing the movie out of town since he felt the ensemble nature of the piece would benefit from everyone being in the same hotel.

Sure enough, a family atmosphere soon developed among the cast in the triangle of the Westin

EUROPEAN DISASTER

While in pre-production on *The Breakfast Club*, John received a phone call from Matty Simmons, chairman and publisher at *National Lampoon* magazine. After the success of *Vacation*, Simmons knew he had to have a sequel. So he came up with the idea for *European Vacation*: the Griswold family wins a quiz show and gets a bargain-basement trip to Europe, a continent filled with as many national stereotypes as possible.

He then banged out an outline and sent it to John. Without much enthusiasm, John wrote a script, sent it off, and understandably forgot about it. Now Simmons was demanding a rewrite. John explained he was in the middle of pre-production for his most important production yet and didn't have the time.

"I blew my top," Simmons admitted. "He had been paid $500,000 to write a script. You sign a deal to write a movie, you finish. I lost my temper, which probably hurt me more than it did him. 'How do you do this to me, the one who brought you into this fucking business?' I said. 'How do you screw me?' "

The two didn't talk again for years. And since Hall was cast in *The Breakfast Club*, Simmons had to recast the Griswold kids as well.

O'Hare Hotel, the Hughes family home, and a library set constructed in the gym of the shuttered Maine North High School nearby. In late winter and early spring, the cast had nowhere to go unless John invited them to dinner at his house or took them into the city to hear blues at a nightclub.

In the rehearsal period, he would give each of his young cast members a weekly cassette tape of mixed music styled for their individual tastes. When Hall, who was staying with his mother and younger sister, had his sixteenth birthday, the whole cast went to Chuck E. Cheese's. (John gave him a bass guitar.)

Closed down two years before, Maine North High had, due to its ugly cement-block structure, inspired an urban legend that the Mob was involved in its construction. The atmosphere was oppressive: so much, including the school hallway sets, was jammed into the high-school gym, not to mention the editing facility.

Opposite: The production of *The Breakfast Club* was incredibly collaborative. Hughes (bottom right) would frequently sit with the cast and get their feedback on the script, making changes based on their ideas. Above: When deciding on where to sit in the library for the day, Hughes let the actors choose their spots based on their characters' personalities.

As the set was being constructed, John and his young cast went into "rehearsal" mode. This for John was an opportunity for everyone to get to know each other and to make changes in the script. In this case, though, the cast deconstructed it.

When John happened to mention a first draft of the screenplay, Estevez asked him how many drafts he had.

"A few," John answered.

"Can we read them?" asked Estevez.

He brought out every draft of his script. Everybody read through them and cherry-picked what worked best for his character.

"John sat on the floor cutting and pasting, and the next morning he brought in a new draft of the script," said Manning. "He'd stayed up all night, drinking coffee, smoking cigarettes, and listening to music not released in the U.S. yet. He just power-wrote."

For instance, Nelson recalled that Estevez's monologue about taping a student's butt together—which explains why Andrew got detention in the first place—actually came from an earlier draft. So the script was essentially rewritten even as the set was built.

At the first actual rehearsal of the opening scenes—held in another section of the school with tape on the floor and a few tables and chairs to roughly indicate the set—everyone initially sat at the same table. Nelson turned to his director and said, "I'm not sitting with them. I don't like them."

"Where would you like to sit?" asked John.

Nelson looked at Hall. "I know Michael comes in before me so wherever he sits, that's my seat." "That okay?" John asked Hall.

"It's okay with me," said Hall.

"I'm not going to sit with any of them either," chimed in Sheedy.

"Where do you want to sit?" asked John.

"Way in the back, as far away as possible."

"Fine," said John.

And so the cast and John choreographed the movie's opening moments, where wary students, who barely know one another, take seats in the deserted library in accordance with their prejudices and preconceived notions.

"Hughes encouraged collaboration, which was great," said Nelson. "I thought all directors would be like that. I didn't know how rare it is for directors to like actors. For most directors, actors are necessary evils."

"I felt more and more open to do whatever I wanted to," agreed Sheedy. "John was open to everything. It was a pretty incredible atmosphere to work in."

That collaboration continued into dinner. John would have the cast and others over for dinner at his house many nights. Dessert consisted of a raid on the freezer, which was full of Dove ice-cream bars. One such evening, as the Dove Bars were being consumed, his two young actresses, joined swiftly by Manning, ganged up on him. They strongly objected to one aspect of the screenplay—the gratuitous female nudity.

The movie was going to be highly claustrophobic if John didn't break up the talkathon in the library. So during that Saturday of detention, the school's synchronized swimming team was to come by to practice with an extremely sexy gym teacher. Escaping momentarily from the oppressive scrutiny of Mr. Vernon, the youngsters would sneak out of the library and find a peep hole into the women's locker room. There they spy the curvaceous teacher topless. For lack of a better term, it was another of John's *Porky's* moments.

The auditions for the role had been mortifying enough for Manning and even for John. Burch had made each actress take off her shirt. John was horrified but Burch insisted, "Well, we have to see if they're going to work!"

Karen Leigh Hopkins, who would later find success as a film actress and screenwriter, was cast in the role.

But one by one, over those Dove Bars, his female cast revolted. This is really sexist and misogynistic, they hammered at the writer. Why would you do this?

In a true collaborative spirit, everyone had a voice and John listened. That night, after everyone drove back to the hotel, he sat down to write.

The next morning, John came in with a new version of the screenplay, where a janitor replaced the gym teacher. This was heartbreaking news for Hopkins, but John was ecstatic when none other than Rick Moranis agreed to play the janitor.

John was a big fan of the SCTV veteran, who was one of Canada's most famous "hosers" as one-half of the Bob and Doug McKenzie comedy team. He had also just come off the smash movie *Ghostbusters*. Then Moranis showed up on the set.

His hair was severely cut, gold caps were on his teeth, and he insisted on playing everything in the accent of a Russian immigrant. As he mugged in front of the camera, the other actors exchanged glances and mouthed a collective, "What the fuck?" to each other.

"John was horrified as well but it's Rick Moranis—he idolized Rick Moranis," recalled Manning. "I knew when the dailies got to L.A. the very thing we were sitting there thinking but *not* saying, Ned Tanen would say."

Sure enough, she got the call.

"What the fuck was that?" Tanen all but screamed into the phone.

"Well, Rick came and that is his interpretation of the janitor," Manning reported.

"No, we're not going to do that," he stated.

The Russian caricature would pull the audience completely out of what was really a serious movie.

"Ned said we're not doing that," Manning reported to John.

"Well, I can't fire Rick Moranis," responded John.

"Then I guess I have to," said Manning.

And she did. John called on another Canadian, John Kapelos, who of course played the fiancé in *Sixteen Candles* and was in Chicago working at Second City. Kapelos come in to play the role—and did it as written. No Russian accent.

John would later add a final touch to the character of Carl the janitor by posting a photo of him in a hall display case dedicated to the school's graduates; thus, Carl went to the very school where he now works as a janitor. In the movie, he's the eyes and ears of this institution. Yet Carl once was a wise ass. Just like Bender.

HIGH SCHOOL FASHION SHOW

Above: Chrissie Hynde of The Pretenders (seen here in 1983) had an androgynous style which influenced at least two of *The Breakfast Club* characters—Bender and Allison.

John worked with costume designer Marilyn Vance for the first time on *The Breakfast Club*. She wound up being John's longest collaborator. She would continue working on his productions and remain in close contact with him after he abandoned Hollywood.

They had an affinity that John never experienced with anyone else on a set, save for John Candy. "He marched to his own drum," she admitted. "He was a lovely, well-mannered person, but he didn't embrace people, let's put it that way."

Vance's costumes pop out in a Hughes film, and he knew this. He loved what she did and how she defined his characters. Another factor in their long friendship and collaboration is that she worked in one of the few areas where he never felt competitive. In writing, directing, producing, editing, music, marketing, and promotion he was as good as, if not better than his collaborators. But his sewing was probably as bad as his vacuuming.

Unknown even to the costume designer was a subtle connection to Chrissie Hynde, the leader of the rock/new wave band the Pretenders, in both Sheedy and Nelson's look.

"I wanted Allison to look like those cool young women who hung out with beat poets in coffee houses, listened to poetry, wore black eyeliner, and smoked hugely," said Sheedy. "The only other person who looked like that then was the Pretenders' Chrissie Hynde—that pale, dark, androgynous rock-singer look."

Meanwhile, Nelson wore all sorts of custom buttons on his jean jacket underneath the overcoat, but the one that meant the most to him was a Chrissie Hynde button. "I wanted to make sure I wore that one," he said. Eventually, the movie would have a third connection to Hynde in its iconic final song.

Ringwald rebelled against her look. Despite her youth, Vance found her to have "a very commanding way about her. I think John was one of the only people who had true control over her. The clothing I had set up at the beginning was Daddy's Little Girl with lots of money, and in browns and pink.

"But she decided she was not a sweet little fussy girl who wore a beret and boots and short skirts—the spoiled brat type. She wanted to be more sophisticated. So we wound up changing her up—not her colors but a longer Ralph Lauren skirt with a beautiful brown belt over it and higher boots, a more sophisticated feeling. John felt, that's okay, let's go for it."

The two would clash again on *Pretty in Pink*. The film was shot in thirty-four days. Originally planned for twenty-eight, the production was behind schedule almost from day one. A week into shooting, Dede Allen arrived in Chicago.

Dorothea Carothers "Dede" Allen was a Hollywood legend. Along with having edited such classic films as *The Hustler*, *Bonnie and Clyde*, and *Dog Day Afternoon*, she was renowned for her creativity, revolutionizing the way movies were cut and helping to bring such European techniques as

"Hughes encouraged the actors to ad-lib, and he would let the camera roll no matter what . . . If they screwed up, he just kept rolling."

overlapping sound and emotional jump cuts into American films.

She would mentor the young John Hughes in visual storytelling. John had developed a habit that would continue through his filmmaking career of shooting a lot of footage. On the group session at the end of the movie alone, he shot an extraordinary two hundred thousand feet of film. He encouraged the actors to ad-lib, and he would let the camera roll no matter what the actors did. If they screwed up, he just kept rolling. There was no interruption. John would force them to think on their feet.

Which, of course, meant massive amounts of footage to assemble.

After the crew wrapped for the day, John saw Allen every night for two to three hours. Sometimes it would take an hour to run the dailies because John shot so much film.

They never discussed individual cuts. Rather, they discussed the characters and story. She was constantly challenging him: is this what a particular character would do? Sometimes he admitted it really wasn't.

She would force him to pick takes when all he wanted to do was to fall asleep. "It was like having your mom there," he would later joke.

But he learned from her: "Nothing matters so much as communicating what a character is," John explained. "If the shot's a little out of focus or it isn't framed just right, that doesn't matter if it's

COSTUME DESIGN BOARDS

Costume designer Marilyn Vance (below) created a costume design board for each character in the film, either cutting out a face or figure from a magazine or sketching one herself to give that character a "look." The original design boards (see opposite page) became those characters.

Allison Reynolds (played by Ally Sheedy):
Black was not happening at the time according to Vance, but that was Sheedy's character. So her purse, fabric, and cashmere sweater, supposedly her father's, were black. She was a dark character.

Brian Johnson (played by Anthony Michael Hall):
For Hall's character, Vance chose green and khaki pants and regular turquoise blue and white sneakers with two different color socks. "Nike made me those three-toned sneakers for Michael," she adds.

Claire Standish (played by Molly Ringwald):
Vance explains she didn't want to make Claire "hard" so she went with a pinkish look accented by a brown leather jacket.

Andrew Clark (played by Emilio Estevez):
Vance went with royal blue for the team jacket, figuring blue to be the school color. She adds, "Then we cut those T-shirts to make him bigger and more muscular."

John Bender (played by Judd Nelson):
Bender, of course, is a renegade, anti-fashion guy (as was Jon Cryer's Duckie in Pretty in Pink). Vance reveals, "I still get emails today about Bender—where did that overcoat come from? A thrift store! We cut the shirtsleeves off, beaded it up, and made sure the plaid matched."

Above: Esteemed costume designer Marilyn Vance (center), who worked on several Hughes films, including *The Breakfast Club* and *Pretty in Pink*, seen here with Jon Cryer (right) and producer Lawrence Gordon (left). Vance still receives fan mail and inquiries today about the costumes she did for *The Breakfast Club*.

The Breakfast Club

Cathy

The Breakfast Club

The Breakfast Club

Brian

Andy

The Breakfast Club

John

The Breakfast Club

Clockwise, left to right: The original costume design boards for *The Breakfast Club* starting with Allison Reynolds (Ally Sheedy), Brian Johnson (Anthony Michael Hall), Claire Standish (Molly Ringwald), Andrew Clark (Emilio Estevez), and John Bender (Judd Nelson).

Above: Anthony Michael Hall and Molly Ringwald pretended not to be a couple during the filming of *The Breakfast Club*, but no one else on set was convinced.

Yet Allen knew how to take a cut of, say, Molly turning around to yell at Judd in an early scene and place it in a later one where it would do more good.

"It's all Dede—it's one of the reasons the film works as well as it does," said Sheedy. "She was a genius. She was putting together film in another room, then coming in and telling John what shot she needed or didn't have."

Fredell Pogodin, the unit publicist, recalled looking at the dailies and noticing how limited the visual options were: "It could have been very static, mostly monologues and talking heads. That [the final film] is so much more is attributable to Dede. She worked magic."

For his part, John acted more like he was part of the cast. He sat right next to or underneath the camera, often cross-legged and close to the actors. "He was right there, so filled with glee that he was getting to make this movie. He was joyous," said Sheedy.

The one person who was anything but joyous was the script supervisor, Bob Forrest, who had worked at that job going back to the early 1950s. It is commonly believed that the experience led to his retirement shortly after production wrapped.

A script supervisor follows the script for the director on the set to verify the actors' lines are correct, make notes of action, wardrobe and hair, and check the matching of details as the sequences of scenes are photographed. If a line of dialogue does get changed, he must write it down so the editor will understand that in Take Two a new line was said.

However, when a director lets actors stray so much from the script or, worse, lets five people talk all at once, the only detail he can get right is the tearing out of his own hair.

saying what you want it to say about the character. You must get down to absolutely the barest minimum that you need to tell. Don't put in anything gratuitous. Question everything; challenge everything. We would spend an hour on whether we should use this line or this line."

The film was shot in continuity, meaning in the actual order of the scenes in the script, a highly unusual thing for any movie, but possible in a film with really only a single set and five actors who never had days off.

He complained bitterly to Manning. "I got him a microcassette recorder," she said. "The poor guy gave up trying to keep notes and would just sit with a recorder on and write it all out afterwards. Every day he was going to quit."

Then, in the second half of the shoot, the Molly-Michael thing began. After being inside that cement block all morning, when the cast broke for lunch, they would try to get away. One afternoon, as Sheedy ate with Manning, she looked out a window and murmured, "Oh, that is sweet."

Manning followed her gaze and saw Hall and Ringwald sitting under a tree, having a picnic.

"Oh, no. This isn't good," she told herself. "They can't do that."

The two then pretended for the remainder of the shoot that they weren't a couple, but no one else was convinced. It certainly gave Nelson and Estevez further motivation for teasing.

The first cut of *The Breakfast Club* ran nearly three hours. "It's a great version," John would later say. "Dede and I would have [released] it if we had our druthers."

But Universal wasn't going to allow that to happen. First of all, no one in the front office liked the project. The film was produced by the previous head of the studio, and there is never any love lost between a former president and a current one. And then there's the fact that theater owners hate long movies—you can't schedule as many screenings, and thus, you sell much less popcorn.

So Dede and John went to work.

One of the major trims was to excise a long speech by Ringwald explaining why she was in detention in the first place.

"It's a wonderful piece of acting," John would say, "about how she ditched school to go shopping at Neiman Marcus by borrowing a driver's ed car

that had two steering wheels. She went to McDonald's, had lunch, and on the way back no one was driving since both were eating so they hit a mailbox. She's laughing hysterically. Emilio has a deadpan look. 'You had to be there,' she says, and he says, 'Yeah, you had to be there.' "

"DON'T YOU (FORGET ABOUT ME)"

Meanwhile, Manning was sent off to England to find a band to record the theme song.

Keith Forsey was an early pioneer of disco, who worked with legendary producer Giorgio Moroder on Donna Summer's club records, as a drummer, and on the song "Flashdance… What a

Above: Chrissie Hynde convinced her husband, Jim Kerr (center) of Simple Minds, to do the song "Don't You (Forget About Me)" for *The Breakfast Club* soundtrack.

Left: "Don't You (Forget About Me)" is perfectly juxtaposed against the film's closing scene where the Criminal pairs up with the Princess and the Basket Case finds love with the Jock.

Feeling" from the movie *Flashdance*, as a co-writer.

"Someone said to John, 'Get Forsey to score your movie and it'll be like getting Moroder,' " said Manning. "So Forsey wrote this song and did a demo. It was perfect for the movie."

Manning and record producer David Anderle flew to England to find a band to do the song. They wound up stuck there for a month.

"We had a cut of the movie and had this song, and David Anderle was going around London showing the tape to bands," recalled Manning. "All were passing. English schooling is so radically different they couldn't come to grips with the story. Everyone said, 'Where's the headmaster?' "

Then Chrissie Hynde—an influence on Sheedy and Nelson, remember—totally got the movie. But she would have to commit to a music video. Since she was pregnant, she refused. However, she was married at the time to Jim Kerr of Simple Minds.

"She told Kerr, 'You have to do this movie,' " said Manning. "David Anderle said, 'Perfect— that's an A&M act. They're on our label!' I was just happy to finally leave London."

Manning and Anderle returned to L.A., only to hear that Simple Minds had passed. Tanen thundered at A&M's Gil Friesen that A&M needed to tell its band to do the song.

In a rebellious mood, Simple Minds sent a track to L.A. designed as an emphatic Screw You.

"It was the same song but horrifying," said Manning. "They had changed the song to make it 'their own.' "

So A&M forced Simple Minds not only to re-record the track, but to do it exactly like the demo. Everything, including the orchestrations, was to be the same.

Not only did the film's closing track, "Don't You (Forget About Me)," words and music by Forsey and Steve Schiff, break Simple Minds into the U.S. market, it became the band's only U.S. no. 1 single, in April 1985.

While the songs in the film are not especially cutting edge, the way John juxtaposed them with his scenes is. Just think of that final song going against Nelson's fist pump of triumph.

"Those lyrics really work for the picture," John told a journalist. "It's saying, 'Just don't forget about me. You don't have to love me, just don't forget about me. Don't leave me out in the cold. I just don't want to be obscure.' Which I think is a good battle cry at sixteen."

The first thing one notices looking back at *The Breakfast Club* across a couple generations is how remarkably good the cast is. The demands of John's screenplay are daunting, but the cast plays these roles brilliantly without ever getting outside their characters or finding actorish ways to make comments about their foibles.

Each role is, deliberately, a high-school stereotype. All are serving detention on a Saturday so they're stuck with each other for nine hours under a nightmarishly authoritarian teacher. Like the inmates in *One Flew Over the Cuckoo's Nest* or the jurors in *Twelve Angry Men*, there is no exit for these five. As they sullenly face one another over a very long day, they have nothing to lose but their false identities.

The Breakfast Club represents the darker side of Hughes World, all those things John normally pokes fun at—only this time he's serious. The issues these detainees face include child abuse, peer pressure, self-loathing, insecurities, overwhelming parental expectations, and sheer neglect.

The Breakfast Club is anomalous in John's career. It is his one film that could arguably be called a drama, albeit a very funny one.

Left: The incredibly talented cast—Judd Nelson, Ally Sheedy, Emilio Estevez, Molly Ringwald, and Anthony Michael Hall—helped make the film as memorable as it was.

Above: Emilio Estevez and Ally Sheedy after Allison has been "made over" by Claire in the film. Sheedy admits it's not her favorite part of the movie.

We sense John is after big game here, confining everyone to close quarters, then one by one delving deep into each psyche and background to understand why everyone is "acting out." Only a superior cast could pull this off and overcome the pretensions of the screenplay.

In the voiceover narration at the film's beginning, John lays out how each individual is viewed by fellow students, parents, and faculty. This then is a cross-section of John Hughes's student body: a brain, athlete, basket case, princess, and criminal. Implied is the understanding that no one, possibly including the individuals themselves, looks beyond these superficial labels.

The trick in John's screenplay is to let these types talk and talk until gradually the layers of false identity get peeled away to reveal what they share in common, not what sets them apart.

To ease into his drama, John fills the first act with sparkling comedy, much of which stems from the mutual animosity between the detention teacher, Richard Vernon (Paul Gleason), perhaps angrier about how he is spending his Saturday than any of the students, and his five disgruntled charges. Whatever qualifications or ambitions Vernon once had as a teacher, they have long since burnt out due to troublesome students, job frustrations, and low self-esteem masquerading as adult contempt.

So, before the five detainees can direct their poisonous bile at each other, they collectively employ this against the common enemy in a serious game of one-upmanship between the two camps. Mr. Vernon has no hope of winning this game.

The comic byplay is among the finest in John's screenplays and concludes when John Bender (the Criminal) asks Mr. Vernon: "Does Barry Manilow know you raid his wardrobe?"

Thus, John lets comedy and light moments of idle boredom among the kids smooth the way for the more earnest soul-searching to come. These young people really don't like each other, an animosity based on little personal knowledge, but rather each one's sense of his or her status within the school and their perceptions of the others. They feel they don't belong in the same room together. They regard one another mostly with sneers, except for the insecure Brian, who so carefully guards his own welfare he has no time to form concrete opinions of others.

Of these young actors, only two of them—Ringwald and Hall—were actually teenagers when the film was shot. Ringwald, with a few biographical alterations, could easily be Samantha Baker a year later as she pouts and fusses in her very first scene. She is Claire (the Princess), furious over the whole injustice of Saturday detention for someone of her stature.

Meanwhile, Hall plays Brian (the Brain), not as geeky as Farmer Ted, but rather lonely and insecure. This guy certainly does not make mean martinis or think girls will fall for him if only subjected to the full force of his charm offensive. Intelligence at his age is a burden, something that sets him apart from others.

"Memorably, Sheedy's Allison (the Basket Case) says nothing for the first thirty-three minutes."

Above: The talented Ally Sheedy uses quick laughs, facial expressions, and rapid eye movements to make her point as Allison in *The Breakfast Club*, a role which is silent for more than a half hour.

> **"Nelson, the eldest actor at age twenty-five, brings a brooding sensuality to the role . . . that is hard for the viewer to shake."**

One thing Ringwald and Hall's characters do carry over from *Sixteen Candles* is their virginity. The crucial difference between the two movies is that it genuinely pains them to admit to this condition in *The Breakfast Club*. While uncertain whether he or she is ready to experiment sexually, each sees being a virgin as detrimental socially, a stigma if word were to get out. As long as that status remains shrouded in mystery, outward appearances can be maintained.

Nelson, the eldest actor at twenty-five, brings a brooding sensuality to the role of the juvenile delinquent that is hard for a viewer to shake. Before any second-act revelations, we sense his molten anger. Every smartass wisecrack carries enough venom for a colony of wasps.

He dresses the part—loose-fitting clothes, fingerless gloves, denim jacket—and he carries a switchblade. Such is the force of his sarcasm that, as much as the others dislike one another, they often band together against Bender.

Estevez, twenty-two and already with major credits such as *Tex*, *The Outsiders*, and cult classic *Repo Man* behind him, plays Andrew (the Athlete) in contrast to most jocks in youth movies. Right away, we sense Andy's sensitivity to others, especially Claire, whom he instinctively protects from Bender's bullying. Even his knee-jerk aggressiveness when provoked pains him. He is fighting the role assigned to him in the school hierarchy—and, we later learn, his father.

Memorably, Sheedy's Allison (the Basket Case) says nothing for the first thirty-three minutes.

She gasps, giggles, sneaks peeks at her fellow inmates (and quietly hides the switchblade), but otherwise occupies the last seat in the library housing the detainees, wrapped up in her dark shawl, layers of clothes, and personal anxiety. When she does finally speak, though, try to shut her up. She taunts the Princess into admitting her virginity by making up outrageous lies about her own sex life. Once out of her shell, she is utterly disarming yet tough as nails. Since her parents ignore her, she carries this to the next logical plane: she assumes everyone at school ignores her too and acts accordingly.

She runs through more physical tricks than a vaudeville comedienne: weird sounds, darting eyes, funny grimaces, and cut-short laughs. She is an actress playing an actress. She's conning the breakfast club into accepting her role as a recluse, but maybe she's conning us too. The script ultimately undermines her, but Sheedy is never undermined: she's dazzlingly alive until a cop-out ending.

When Claire finally does pay attention to Allison—she gives her a makeover by brushing her hair back and replacing her makeup with Claire's princess style—the Basket Case becomes every shy, excited teenage girl and flowers before the slack-jawed detainees. While a hopeless cliché—the ugly duckling turning into a swan (and, oddly, looking much duller and more ordinary than in her goth get-up)—Sheedy has the instincts to pull off the film's most comic role. Nevertheless, Sheedy admitted her makeover "is not my favorite part of movie."

The film's key sequence comes in a group confessional that is part Truth or Dare and part AA meeting. Here, all five finally give up their false IDs. Each has a soliloquy that explains his or her behavior.

It is to John's credit as a director that so artificial a game plan comes off without feeling forced or contrived. However, neither he nor his actors can overcome the shortcomings of these "explanations." It's open season on parents and teachers. "Blame the adults" explains everything.

The Athlete admits he "tortured" a scrawny, younger kid so that he could get his old man "to think I'm cool." The Criminal has a home life from hell and an old man into physical abuse.

Meanwhile, the Basket Case's parents do something even worse: "They ignore me."

Brian is alone in stepping outside himself and admitting, "I don't like what I see." He takes some of the onus on himself. Claire prefers to point to peer pressure, of having to live up to her impossible school reputation. Finally, she too falls back on faulting parents who give her things rather than love.

As yet another quarrel breaks out among the gang of five, Andrew has an epiphany: "My God, are we going to be like our parents?"

The Princess: "Not me. Ever."

The Basket Case: "Unavoidable. It just happens."

The Princess: "What happens?"

The Basket Case: "When you grow up, your heart dies."

If we need any proof of this, Mr. Vernon is forever lurking on the edges of the film, his heart as dead as it gets.

The film opens—at the suggestion of Sheedy—with an epigraph from David Bowie's "Changes":

"And these children that you spit on/As they try to change their world/Are immune to your consultations/They're quite aware of what they're going through …"

Yet in the film's final moments, as parents pick up kids—with John himself playing Brian's father—the Athlete kisses the no-longer enigmatic Basket Case while the Princess gives the Criminal her earring. All these changes are suddenly over. Everything has gotten resolved and these kids have come to the realization they can blame other people for their traumas and longings.

STUDIO REACTION

Universal's new chair of the motion picture group and Ned Tanen's successor, Frank Price, and his longtime associate and marketing head, Marvin Antonowsky, never got John Hughes. They resisted *Sixteen Candles*, but Tanen's deal with Universal gave him enough "juice" to get the film made on a tight budget and schedule. After previews, the two grudgingly admitted the studio might have a winner in *Sixteen Candles*.

But the two resolutely hated *The Breakfast Club*. They didn't see its entertainment value and didn't know how to sell it. The exchanges between them and Tanen became so heated that at one marketing meeting, Tanen overturned a table.

"Antonowsky was being such a dolt," recalled Sean Daniel, the Universal executive overseeing the film.

So much of the release campaign ended up not with the studio marketing department, but with Nancy Gallagher of Seiniger Advertising. Howard "Howie" Deutch of Kanew, Mager & Deutch of New York cut the trailers.

Above: The actors in *The Breakfast Club*—along with several other young talented actors at the time—became grouped as the "brat pack," a term they hated across the board.

"There's no way I'm ever going to end a movie on a negative note." —John Hughes

The Breakfast Club opened strongly on February 18, 1985, with an enormous per-screen average and a box-office gross of over $5 million in its opening weekend. It played well in major cities but dropped off in rural areas. It was gone in three weeks in the South.

John figured the R-rating and lack of stars hurt a little. Plus, the song wasn't in stores until a week or so afterward.

"I think [Universal] should have platformed it a little bit more but I don't know if the studio had a lot of confidence in the movie," he said. "It should not have gone into 1,100 theaters—bang, let's go. But that was not my decision."

By now, John and his young actors were attracting the attention of the nation's top critics and film journalists. It comes with the territory for a film starring five of Hollywood's top young actors and a box-office gross of $45.9 million.

A *New York* magazine writer coined the nickname "Brat Pack" for actors who appeared in *The Breakfast Club* and, soon afterward, *St. Elmo's Fire*, produced by Shuler Donner. The "founding" members included *The Breakfast Club* cast along with Rob Lowe, Andrew McCarthy, and Demi Moore. Whether intended or not, the term swiftly acquired a pejorative connotation that swept a group of actors enjoying success in youth movies into a convenient but silly phrase for media savants that implied entitled yet undeserving celebrity.

The "brats" were unfairly portrayed as hard-partying actors with the world at their feet, whether deserved or not, rather than a talented collection of young actors who in some instances worked together in films. Understandably, the actors hated the term and reportedly even stopped socializing together.

Writing in the April 8, 1985, issue of *The New Yorker*, Pauline Kael in her review of *The Breakfast Club* found that John's dialogue has "an easy, buggy rhythm" in those moments when the kids are killing time or being funny. Hughes "does have talent," she noted, "but in *The Breakfast Club* it's tucked in around the edges of his schematic plot."

She complained that the writer-director "has gone the group-therapy route this time and has also fallen back on the standard device for appealing to teen audiences, the device of *Rebel Without a Cause* and *Splendor in the Grass*: blame adults for the kids' misery."

"Young audiences," she mused, "have always been suckers for this kind of flattery."

The review that incensed John the most occurred in *People* magazine where, he grumbled to an interviewer, "the guy said that I don't so much depict kids as I enshrine them, that I believe their problems are more serious than nuclear war. And on the cover of his own magazine: 'Teen Suicide: Why Are Our Children Dying?'... If a kid has a problem so serious that he's willing to take his own life, that is a problem as serious as nuclear war."

As for the film's happy ending, he vowed, "There's no way I'm ever going to end a movie on a negative note."

He never did.

HOLLYWOOD BOUND

In the midst of making *The Breakfast Club*, John got the idea for his next feature, a broad, slapstick sci-fi comedy once again to star Hall. Certainly, *Weird Science* came out of the zeitgeist of teen/science movies in the early 80s such as *WarGames, Real Genius, Short Circuit*, and *Zapped*. Yet *Weird Science* wound up being a fairly minor Hughes comedy, although it did decent enough at the box office for his winning streak to continue.

WEIRD SCIENCE
"Gary, nobody likes us."

The startling thing is how prescient the movie is in its exploration of themes more common to science fiction today—themes about computers, virtual reality, and artificial intelligence. Without stretching too far, one can even say *Weird Science* anticipates Spike Jonze's dazzlingly innovative *Her*.

The set-up is pure Hughes: two geeks, about as unpopular as high school boys can get, engineer

Opposite: John Hughes on the set of *Weird Science* in 1985. Right: Movie poster for *Weird Science*, a film written and directed by John Hughes.

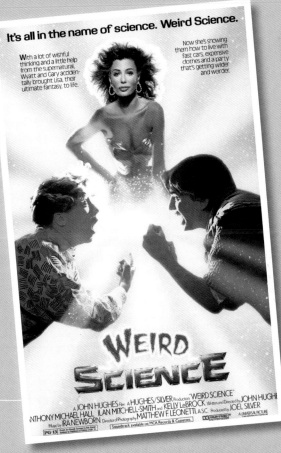

It's all in the name of science. Weird Science.

With a lot of wishful thinking and a little help from the supernatural, Wyatt and Gary accidentally brought Lisa, their ultimate fantasy, to life.

Now she's showing them how to live with fast cars, expensive clothes and a party that's getting wilder and weirder.

WEIRD SCIENCE

A JOHN HUGHES Film A HUGHES/SILVER Production "WEIRD SCIENCE"
ANTHONY MICHAEL HALL ILAN MITCHELL-SMITH and KELLY LeBROCK Written and Directed by JOHN HUGHES
Music by IRA NEWBORN Director of Photography MATTHEW F. LEONETTI A.S.C. Produced by JOEL SILVER
A UNIVERSAL PICTURE
PG-13
Soundtrack available on MCA Records & Cassettes.

Above: Kelly LeBrock starred as Lisa, the digitally crafted girlfriend for loners Gary (Anthony Michael Hall) and Wyatt (Ilan Mitchell-Smith).

But John lost Wright when her manager got her a role in the daytime soap opera *Santa Barbara*. Next, Kelly Emberg was cast. A model and cover girl, Emberg's main claim to fame at that time was as Rod Stewart's girlfriend.

There was only one problem: "She couldn't act," said Vance.

By now desperate, John sent Burch out to find someone who was "gorgeous and can act."

She found LeBrock, an American-born British model who, the year before in her acting debut opposite Gene Wilder in *The Woman in Red*, showed she could act.

Hall, in a bizarre hairdo that seems somehow to float above his head like a shaggy halo, is Gary, friendless other than for his secret sharer and equally friendless buddy, Wyatt Donnelly. This co-conspirator Wyatt is played by Ilan Mitchell-Smith. John had seen the young actor the previous year in *The Wild Life*, an Art Linson-directed comedy written by Cameron Crowe, and perhaps was attracted to his high-pitched voice.

The two pair well together, two sides of the same coin essentially, with Wyatt being the computer whiz and more hysterical of the two.

The film's weird science scene—making no bones about borrowing from the *Frankenstein* movies that inspire the boys' idea—is played for tomfoolery. The home-computer transmogrification of sexual fantasy into corporeal reality looks like a bad videogame from that era.

Wyatt first designs female dimensions that suit the boys' fevered imaginations—superb breasts but

the perfect woman in a computer only for her to materialize in the flesh-and-blood form of Ford supermodel Kelly LeBrock. As easy as it is for the boys to concoct this sentient being—who soon acquires the name of "Lisa"—it was difficult to cast. The original choice for the role was then-unknown Robin Wright.

"She was not voluptuous but still hot for young boys," commented casting director Burch.

not too big, mind you—then cutouts from *Playboy* and *Time* magazine are fed into the computer. A photo of Albert Einstein is sufficient to give their perfect woman the perfect brain while a Playmate of the Month supplies the perfect body.

Then they hack into a government computer for additional power. This somehow pulls in enough electrical energy to cause Shermer's electrical grid to go haywire as the boys' overloaded PC sends Wyatt's two-story house into shock, with electrical appliances blowing up and more furniture shaking than in *The Exorcist*, until—*voilà*—their dream girl waltzes through an exploding door.

Naturally, she is not what the boys ordered. Or at least not what they think they ordered. With full pouty lips, cropped T-shirt, and panties that hide very little, LeBrock is indeed a fantasy come true but … she is clearly her own woman, with brains and a complete understanding of the circumstances of her "birth."

She says she will do whatever they command since they created her, but the way she says this lets them, and us, know there are limits. So goodbye pornographic wet dream and hello to another Hughes meditation on Geekdom.

Initially, however, neither the boys nor John seem to know what to do with her. Despite being the creation of the two young men, Lisa is still the adult and the one who's in charge. Since she wants to party, the trio go off in search of one in a fin-tailed Cadillac with fake IDs, all courtesy of Lisa's unaccounted-for magic.

They wind up in a nightclub that seems a cross between a risky dive bar and a hip blues club. Whatever the case, their appearance in the doorway causes the entire place to go stone silent, jaws dropping as much for Lisa's shocking beauty as for her unlikely companions.

The film's funniest line comes at the prompting of John Kapelos, in his third straight Hughes film, who asks Lisa what she's doing with these two very young men.

"It's purely sexual," she replies.

John finally does come up with something to do with his exotic temptress, and it's pretty banal. Lisa becomes a social coach for the boys,

Right: Gary and Wyatt are caught with their pants down in *Weird Science*. (Note: a young Robert Downey Jr. plays one of the school bullies, as seen in the background.)

coaxing them to greater feats of daring within high-school society to the point that a pair of cute girls will, as Gary puts it, actually like them for what they are.

In other words, there's got to be a life lesson here.

None of which prevents John from indulging in flat-out slapstick, much of it coming from yet another of his marathon teen parties while parents are absent.

Lisa's invitation to a *soirée*—loaded with more promise than she ever intends to deliver on—to two older bullies (one played by Robert Downey, who as yet wasn't using "Jr." in his billing) results in the entire student body showing up, apparently unaware the house belongs to the unpopular Wyatt.

So the comic push-me/pull-you of the long sequence finds Lisa goading the boys into displays of their true selves so the cute girls will ditch the lame bullyboys and fall for the reluctant duo.

This involves more weird science, the source of which is never explained, any more than is Lisa's British accent is. The party ends with maximum destruction, a whirlwind that sucks all the furniture out of the living room (and clothes off one coed—John simply can't resist a little raunchiness), parents in a family photo who inexplicably come to life, and a nuclear missile ramming up into Wyatt's bedroom. John never attempts to provide logic to any of this.

The boys' mettle gets proven when Lisa somehow summons a mutant motorcycle gang from hell to invade the party.

Here, John borrowed from the Mad Max movies. Not only does he costume the bikers to resemble the apocalyptic gang from those films, he actually hired Australian actor Vernon Wells to spoof his role in *Mad Max 2: The Road Warrior* (1981) as the homicidal motorcycle gang leader.

Above: Chet Donnelly (Bill Paxton) might just be the meanest oldest brother on screen in *Weird Science*.

Gary does stand up to them—by pulling out a gun, a real one actually, and not the authentic-looking water pistol he thinks it is—and the gang beats a hasty retreat. The girls swoon and the house is, thanks to more weird science, restored to its normal state moments before Wyatt's parents arrive home.

So the idea that inspires the comedy, the creation of the "perfect woman" by geeky boys, pretty much gets abandoned before the halfway mark. But not before John tiptoes up to a few creepy scenes of the twenty-four-year-old LeBrock kissing and slightly fondling two fifteen-year-old boys. (Imagine how audiences would react if the sexes were reversed!)

Undoubtedly the best thing about *Weird Science* is Bill Paxton, who plays Wyatt's older brother, Chet. Beyond physical and mental abuse, Chet delights in extorting money and valuables from Wyatt in exchange for his silence about Wyatt's activities. Lisa revenges all of this when, as the movie winds to a close, she turns Chet into a toad resembling a Star Wars creature.

Perhaps its dominant image, after that of LeBrock's initial appearance, that is, occurs when the boys first indulge in weird science with bras tied on their heads.

"By the way," Wyatt asks, "why are we wearing bras on our heads?"

"Ceremonial," says Gary, as if that explains everything. Perhaps it does.

John had this to say in *Interview* magazine: "A nerd will be a nerd all his life. When we did 'The Nerd Book' at *National Lampoon*, the nerds got picked up as if there were a lot of them at every school—and there aren't. Maybe two. There are many more geeks. A geek is a guy who has everything going for him but he's just too young. He's got the software but he doesn't have the hardware yet. When you're a freshman boy, the junior, sophomore, and senior boys take all the girls. You don't fit in your body, your feet are too big and your head too small. If you talk to any girl other than your mother or older sister, you think they're going to hit you."

PRETTY IN **PINK**

"Love's a bitch, Duck. Love's a bitch."

Above and right: Promotional poster and DVD for *Pretty in Pink* (1986).

While *Weird Science* was filming in Chicago, Tanen had news for his director that would stun him: Tanen was giving up producing to return to the executive ranks as head of Paramount Pictures.

"You're leaving the movie?" asked a bewildered John.

"No, I'm going to work at Paramount but Michelle will come over every day. I'm still the producer and will still go to marketing meetings."

Then he added: "The first thing I'm going to do at Paramount is sign you to a big overall deal."

The initial Paramount deal, inked in March 1985, was a typical one for that era, a first-refusal deal for two years, meaning John would move to the Paramount lot, where all his expenses would be paid, and the studio would have first look at all of his projects. If they did refuse, he could pitch them elsewhere.

Just over a year later, in June 1986, Tanen and Paramount not only renewed and re-negotiated the contract, the studio gave John significantly more creative control. By then, Hughes Pictures had rechristened itself Hughes Entertainment and was ensconced in Paramount's Building C, unofficially renamed the Hughes Building.

Jack Rapke (John's agent) called Michael Chinich, who as Universal's head of talent had worked with John on *Sixteen Candles* and *The Breakfast Club*. He asked Chinich to come to Paramount to run the company.

As John hatched plans to move his brand into television, recording, and publishing, he knew he would have to turn directing chores over to others. He had grown comfortable with Howard Deutch, who had cut the trailers for *Sixteen*

"I am not a really a hip guy. I just don't fit in." —John Hughes

Candles and *The Breakfast Club*, so he had no hesitation in offering him a directing gig.

He sent Deutch two scripts—*The New Kid*, about a teenager's experiences in a new high school in Arizona, and *Pretty in Pink*. Deutch preferred the latter. John did have to fight to put a guy who had only directed music videos on the picture. But the studio quickly gave its own new kid what he wanted. *Pretty in Pink*, budgeted at $7 million, was green-lit and set to roll in June.

"After *The Breakfast Club*, John was exhausted and needed someone else he was comfortable with to direct," said Deutch. "He had very ambitious plans and in my opinion could have been another Walt Disney. If he was able to deal with Hollywood politics, he could have built an empire."

What he did do, however, was the one thing he told everyone he would never do—move to Los Angeles. He couldn't be a Hollywood mogul in Chicago.

He rented the Brentwood house of actor Donald Sutherland briefly before he found a house to buy in the same West L.A. neighborhood. While he maintained a two-story colonial house in Northbrook, he and the family spent most of the next four-and-a-half years in Southern California.

In press interviews, he continued to play the Booth Tarkington Jr. card: "I didn't realize until I spent a lot of time in California just how Midwestern I am. When I look at the 'hipper things,' I am not a really hip guy. I just don't fit in."

Above: John Hughes in a *Miami Vice*-style jacket on the set of *Pretty in Pink* (1986).

Yet his Brentwood house was decked out in the postmodern Italianate style of the Memphis Group: spray-painted walls featured whites, blacks, and grays—with crazy globs of orange dots. His office at Paramount continued the Memphis theme with flashes of peacock blue, silver, and yellow in the reception. Inside, near a black leather sofa, his deck was a slab of gray marble and his coffee table fake cement upon which sat two massive plastic-foam rocks.

A *Women's Wear Daily* reporter described his startlingly altered appearance thusly: "Hughes … is wearing black Gianni Versace, set off with a blue splash of a tie. He has a round face and shaggy beige hair, steel-rimmed glasses, and a reputation for being prolific but somewhat difficult."

Which is not to say his anti-Hollywood pose

> ## "His was a heavy heart, deeply sensitive, prone to injury—easily broken."
>
> —Molly Ringwald on John Hughes

was an act. "He didn't love being here, nor the people," said Vance.

While he hated parties—indeed he never went to any—what he loved was being at his home with family and a few close friends.

"He was a pretty private person but on evenings and weekends, you might hang out at his house where there was a pool and basketball court," said Matthew Broderick. "He loved to talk and be part of a group of four to five people. Maybe in the hot tub with Nancy, Jennifer (Grey), and Howie Deutch. It was hilarious, great fun—a small group and thousands of cigarettes. I don't see him at a big party."

He did miss Chicago—or to be accurate, Northbrook. Every month or so the family went "home," where he could go to the Cypress Inn for a fish fry on Friday night and sit with people who didn't really care what he did.

In a way, he was right: Most filmmakers of his status, whether they're aware of it or not, sink into a cocoon of isolation. Their routine is to drive from home to studio to premiere to home to a set. They spend the day conversing with like-minded people, discussing movies, ideas, and actors, then wonder why all their movies start to look alike.

John had few industry pals. The one trendy thing he genuinely liked was dining at Spago.

"Hey, they've got good food," he would insist.

When he needed a fix of home amid the sun and palm trees, he visited the Forum in Inglewood to take in a Kings hockey game. A longtime fan of the game—the Detroit Red Wings were still his team despite being a Chicago Blackhawks season ticketholder—he said the Kings in their purple-and-gold era made him feel like he was back in Chicago.

Deutch went to work on *Pink*. He wanted Ringwald for the lead but ran into strange resistance. As studios do, Paramount wanted the flavor of the month—Jennifer Beals, star of the studio's *Flashdance*, was a current favorite—and John, surprisingly, was no longer pushing his "muse."

"I went to Molly and begged her to do it," said Deutch. "[The role] was written for her; it was Molly. She was John's muse—very important to him in *The Breakfast Club* and *Sixteen Candles*, but eventually that [relationship] started to fade. He didn't fight me on it. They were still colleagues but not as loving and close as it was. She wanted to do the picture once I went to her so it was not pulling teeth."

What caused John to shut off contact with Ringwald and, soon enough, Hall? Several factors emerge—not the least of which was a pattern that cast a dark shadow over John's entire film career.

In Ringwald's case, her celebrity—her face on *Time* magazine's cover as "Hollywood's new teen princess" based largely on work in his films—bothered him greatly.

He refused to cooperate with the article and was annoyed that Ringwald quoted him liberally. To that same *Women's Wear Daily* reporter, he fumed: "She said that I said she is a box-office draw. I didn't say any of that stuff."

As for her being on the cover, he groused, "I mean, God, there are so many things going on around the world."

Left: Molly
Ringwald as
Andie Walsh in
Pretty in Pink.

Then, too, Ringwald and Hall saw an understandable need to work in films other than those by John. Which meant they weren't always available to act in his films.

"When actors would pass [on offers] those rejections were very, very difficult for John Hughes," noted Rapke. "Any type of criticism was a very hard thing for him to deal with."

In a *New York Times* op-ed piece she penned days after his passing, Ringwald referred to Sheedy's iconic line in *The Breakfast Club*— "When you grow up, your heart dies"—then wrote that a "darker spin" could be gleaned from those words: "His was a heavy heart, deeply sensitive, prone to injury—easily broken. Most people who knew John knew that he was able to hold a

grudge longer than anyone—his grudges were almost supernatural things, enduring for years, even decades. Michael suspects that he was never forgiven for turning down parts in *Pretty in Pink* and *Ferris Bueller's Day Off*. I turned down later films as well."

Strangely, the dark side to John escalated along with his success.

Again, Rapke, the agent who tried to shield him from his own folly: "I think he suffered tremendously and that would manifest itself in different ways—being cold, aloof, distant, angry. If left to his own devices, I think he would have blown up even more of his relationships than he did."

One major difference on the set of *Pretty in*

Right: Molly Ringwald originally wanted a strapless, Madonna-style dress to wear to the prom scene at the end of *Pretty in Pink* instead of the hand-made dress she wore in the final cut.

Pink, though, was John's unwillingness to tolerate Ringwald's tantrums. Once again, she clashed with Vance over her look.

In the film, her character is a poor kid. So she wears thrift-store clothing but changes things up. Her clothes have their own personality, just as she has her own identity. For a dance, she takes two dresses and puts them together into one.

"She hated a dress I came up with," said Vance. "She wanted a strapless dress with a big skirt. She wanted to look like Madonna.

" 'But that's your character,' I said. 'I'm going by your character, not Molly Ringwald.' So I went to talk to John. After all, he created this character. John said of course that's what she is. So she wore it. Reluctantly."

Vance outdid herself with *Pretty in Pink*. The characters' wardrobes *are* the characters' identity.

Indeed, as the film opens, Molly does a reverse striptease. We watch in close-ups as her Andie Walsh puts on war paint and an outfit to dazzle the town. She pulls nylon stockings up high, high, high on her thighs, zips the back of her skirt, rummages for the right earrings, does her eyes and lips, and then dons a pale pink blouse.

She sports large oval glasses, frizzy red hair, and ruby red lipstick to contrast with her alabaster skin and long earrings. *Voilà*, she is a modern-day Jane Austen heroine, who knows her own mind—and taste in men.

Everyone notices this outfit. It starts in the morning. Her dad (the estimable Harry Dean Stanton) wonders how much her "latest creation" set her back. Fifteen dollars for the used shoes and she made the rest herself, she replies.

Later at school, her longtime male chum calls

it a "volcanic ensemble," which he defines as "hot, dangerous." But the snooty rich girls wonder where she got her clothes: "The Five and Dime Store?" they taunt. (This, of course, is all too accurate.)

So the stage is set: some appreciate her beauty and wardrobe creativity; others fear to stray from rigid class perimeters in taste and style.

Her suitors similarly dress their parts. From the upper class comes the evil, chain-smoking Steff (James Spader) and his best friend, good-guy Blane (Andrew McCarthy). They favor perfectly coiffed hair, blow-dried into place. Light blue, white, gray, and beige are coordinated among their sports jackets, linen suits, pressed shirts, and slacks—a preppy look, in other words.

Andie's other suitor is a great Hughes misfit, this one going by the name of Duck or Duckie,

"Our relationship was not the best."

—Jon Cryer on Molly Ringwald

although he will also answer to Phil Dale (Jon Cryer). Aware of his geekdom but seeing it as no real obstacle, Duckie is head-over-heels when it comes to Andie. He pursues her with an ardor even she cannot completely deny (although she does try).

The Duck follows Andie's eccentric dress code—only he follows it out the window. His dark hair, when not covered by hats, piles up high and curls over his forehead. An army insignia turns up on a sports jacket. Sloppy shirts fight the patterns of his coats.

Left: Molly Ringwald had hoped they would cast Robert Downey Jr. in the role of Duckie Dale instead of Jon Cryer.

One outfit finds him in dark glasses, black hat, a white T-shirt under an open maroon flannel shirt, leopard-spotted shorts held up by suspenders, and scuffed-up Keds. It's a fashion statement, all right, but what that statement is beyond iconoclastic individualism is hard to say.

The bizarre costumes were "great for me as an actor—so flamboyant they did a lot of the work for me," said Cryer. "In acting school you put on a mask and it's surprising how your body conforms to the character of that mask. It's how we as humans are, so costumes like those from Marilyn were a gift."

But Cryer does admit, "That rockabilly swagger is totally misplaced on me."

Ringwald was cool to this young stage actor in his first major film role. Cryer, a

twenty-one-year-old New Yorker, felt understandably vulnerable making *Pretty in Pink* in Hollywood.

"Our relationship was not the best," Cryer said of Ringwald. "Later I found out she was uncertain about [the producers] casting me. She wanted Robert Downey Jr. But once I was cast she told everyone, 'Oh, well, he's my gay friend.' Which is interesting because I'm not gay, nor did I intend the character to be." Cryer now can laugh: "So I want to stand up for effeminate hetero guys. We do exist and that's who Duckie is."

Pretty in Pink was the first of many Hughes written-and-produced films that John did not direct. The question that always loomed over such productions—and indeed caused many directors to shy away—was, what degree of control does John exercise when not actually in the director's chair?

It depended on whom you asked.

"He was very, very supportive but not around that much," said Deutch. "He was on the set the first day in the record store and didn't like some design things, which we changed."

Cryer said he leaned on his neophyte director, not John: "Howie and I were incredibly close during the shooting. It was the first breakthrough movie for both of us so we felt scared in a similar way. I felt we bonded over that."

Yet John's fellow producer, Shuler Donner, insisted that "Howie was brand new and John, let's say, was guiding the movie. He ghost-directed it. He wanted Howie to do it but Howie was lost until he got his footing in the last two weeks."

"John stood next to Howie for the whole movie," said Chinich. "He basically did everything—he cut it and sold it. *Pretty* was a success because John directed the movie."

Below: John Hughes was always extremely involved in his movie soundtracks, and *Pretty in Pink* gave The Psychedelic Furs its first international exposure.

Whatever the case, Deutch went on to direct two more films for John and has enjoyed a successful career in film and television production.

Everyone does acknowledge that the soundtrack was pure Hughes, and a lot of it was English imports. He wanted the Psychedelic Furs' song "Pretty in Pink" associated with Andie. This would give the band its first international exposure. He also wanted songs by the then-little known New Order.

"Ninety percent of the soundtrack are John's choices," said Deutch. "He laid New Order's 'Elegia' against the shot of James Spader looking at Molly coming to school. I pride myself that I'm a music guy—I knew cutting-edge bands. I never heard of New Order. But I was thrilled when I saw how that music and shot worked."

Calamity only struck after the movie wrapped. Test audiences hated *Pink's* ending.

In John's original ending, Andie and Duck dance together at the prom, implying they wind up with each other. In an acknowledgment of their status as fellow outsiders, they cautiously step out on the floor to dance to David Bowie's "Heroes."

About sixty-five percent of the cards from test audiences came back negative. Audiences, especially young girls, hated the ending: The girl has got to get the "cute" guy (McCarthy). That meant they wanted Andie to end up with a rich kid.

"Which I was very much against and Ned Tanen was against but John was, oddly, more open to that than I would've thought," said Shuler Donner. "I thought he would have a proprietary thing for his ending, but he realized people come to a movie to be entertained and if that's what they want then okay."

So in John revision's, Andie shows up solo at the prom, as does Duckie, just as in the original.

Above: Andrew McCarthy wore a wig when they re-shot the final scene in *Pretty in Pink* because he had already shaved his head for a different role.

However, Blane also shows up solo. He never had a date he "forgot" about. Duckie even helpfully points out to Andie that Blane came alone. So true love triumphs over class—and the Duck's feelings.

The new ending, shot six months after production wrapped, found McCarthy in New York doing a play for which he had lost weight and shaved his head. So he had to play the new scene in a terrible wig.

While never fully accepting the altered ending, Cryer now says, "I was okay with it. Plus Andrew in that wig lightened my spirits a bit."

Above: James Spader (Steff) is convincing as local "richie" and Blane's smarmy best friend in *Pretty in Pink*.

Meanwhile, John did give Duck a consolation prize. After giving up the love of his life, a hot chick beckons to Duck. That hot chick? Kristy Swanson, who would later star in the *Buffy the Vampire Slayer* movie.

The film was shown to test audiences with both endings. The cute guy won hands-down.

Only a couple of years separate the release of *Sixteen Candles* from *Pretty in Pink*, yet in that short time Ringwald had blossomed from a cute though coltish sixteen-year-old into a sophisticated, sharp-looking woman who catches the eye of her school's most eligible boy.

Ringwald anchors *Pretty in Pink* as the highly believable focus of male attention. John's script surrounds her with three distinctive male characters—well, four if we count her dad—as she radiates balmy charm and smashing good looks with undeniable confidence.

The issue John's screenplay is grappling with is that of class in America—a heavy subject that John ultimately fumbles. He casts the issue in such black-and-white terms with much of the dialogue being so "on the money" that the theme never develops any resonance. It's as if merely demonstrating that class distinctions exist in

Middle America, and doing so in a very superficial manner, is sufficient for his dramatic purposes.

Three male students fixate on Andie during a spring day of their final semester at Meadowbrook High, a school mostly of "richies." Steff's approach to her is crude and easily parried. Seeming surprised, he can't understand why Andie is any different from the other girls who succumbed to similar propositions from him.

"I have some taste," she tartly explains.

He recoils, declares her "a bitch"—a lame retort that possibly reflects his lack of practice in snappy comebacks to female rejection—and immediately becomes her mortal enemy.

The handsome Blane initially settles for longing gazes at Andie, looking for the right opportunity to make a subtle move.

Meanwhile, Duckie makes his feelings clear to everyone but Andie. He makes plain in his soliloquies and asides to the viewer that he loves Andie too much. In a charmingly old-fashioned ploy, he even visits Andie's father to make his intensions known.

"I'd like to marry her," he explains, but must admit he hasn't told her this. He's "laying the groundwork."

That groundwork gets torn up when Blane develops the courage to ask Andie out. It's an awkward date, though, as he shows up late, then takes her in his BMW to Steff's house where a rich kids' party is underway. Here the film lays the snobbery on thick, with Steff in complete Iago mode. They finally leave but Andie becomes even more upset when he tries to drive her home.

"I don't want you to see where I live, okay?" she snaps.

The film's major problem is that there isn't much at stake in this romantic triangle. The key issue is who will take Andie to the prom, which given the ages of the characters—everyone is months away from university—feels insufficient. The film does end with that prom where Duck does as his name implies and gets out of the way for the better man. By this time, though, we've grown so fond of Duck—especially when lip-syncing to Otis Redding's "Try a Little Tenderness"—that we want a more complicated or ambiguous ending.

Meanwhile, is Blane McDonnagh really the right dude for our Andie?

"His name is Blane?" exclaims a shocked Duck. "That's a major appliance. That's not a name."

Below: Duckie (Jon Cryer) performing his iconic rendition of Otis Redding's "Try a Little Tenderness."

What kind of values allow Blane to have such impossibly snide and vulgar friends, based seemingly on mutual wealth? Who on earth are his parents? He even jokes they believe in "arranged marriages." At one point Steff smirks, "I've seen your mother go to work on you … it's vicious."

More than any other John Hughes film to date, *Pretty in Pink* takes place in a world without parents. School seniors hang out at the cocktail lounge CATS (with Andrew Dice Clay as its chatty bouncer), smoke cigarettes in school (even gym), and drift through a town and its parties, dances, clubs, and businesses, where seemingly no one over thirty exists.

Annie Potts, as Andie's co-worker of the record store Hot Trax (modeled after a Chicago record store) in one crazed hairstyle after another, is the only "older" woman in the film. Yet she shares Andie's belief in experimental attire and in her giddiness when a prospective boyfriend materializes. So age here means nothing—she's a teenager at heart.

Above: One of the original movie posters for *Ferris Bueller's Day Off* (1986).

FERRIS BUELLER'S DAY OFF

"When Cameron was in Egypt's land . . . Let my . . . Cameron . . . go."

Tensions ran high in Hollywood executive suites in 1985 as March approached. The Writers Guild of America was threatening to go on strike over the home-video market, which was then small and primarily consisted of distribution via videotape. No one knew how long a strike would last. So any screenplay in the works would be on permanent hold for the duration.

Which meant Tanen, having just signed his wunderkind to a splashy contract, was staring at a start date for *Pretty in Pink* … and then nothing. So the ink was hardly dry on that contract before Tanen pestered John for another script.

"John finished *Ferris Bueller's Day Off* in three to four days," recalled Tom Jacobson. "He then turned it into studio and they said, 'Go.' We were in pre-production the following week."

John had met Jacobson a few weeks earlier. Paramount production chief Dawn Steel, who was something of a mentor to the twenty-eight-year-old, introduced John to him. She knew

Jacobson, working in production for Simpson/Bruckheimer Films, wanted to establish himself as a film producer.

"We hit it off," said Jacobson. "I think it was that Midwestern thing—I'm from Kansas City. He really liked that and that I was of the young, up-and-coming generation and not the established generation."

Jacobson produced *Ferris Bueller*. As a producer or studio exec, he would have the longest professional run with John other than Marilyn Vance.

The central character, Ferris Bueller, a teenager who, in his last semester of high school, decides to take a day off, had the potential to come off as utterly smug and self-absorbed. While, unlike many of John's geek characters, Ferris is extremely well liked, he could easily be seen as a brat who gets away with everything, a view that his own sister clings to, as a matter of fact. He is vastly experienced at fooling all adult authorities with the singular exception of the school principal.

Audience reaction to such a slick operator was hard to gauge unless John cast that role and that of Ferris's only antagonist with just the right actors.

Matthew Broderick's name came up but he was in a Broadway show at the time and his representatives hesitated at the proposition of the twenty-three-year-old star playing a teenager.

"His reps didn't jump at it," Jacobson admitted. "John wanted people to want to do his movies. He would not chase people. But this was one of the few times he did."

Another issue was the amount of screen time in which Ferris would break the movie's fourth wall and speak directly to the audience. However, Broderick had done the same thing in two Neil Simon plays, *Brighton Beach Memoirs* and *Biloxi Blues*.

"John finished *Ferris Bueller's Day Off* in three to four days." —Tom Jacobson, film producer

John then screened for Broderick the 1966 film *Alfie*, where Michael Caine talks frequently to the audience. The actor quickly became convinced he could pull off the monologues.

"There was probably some pause but not much as I remember," Broderick said of his agreeing to the role.

For the role of school principal Ed Rooney, John met in late July with another stage and film veteran, Jeffrey Jones. While the two didn't immediately hit

Above: Ferris Bueller (Matthew Broderick) can't resist a microphone in *Ferris Bueller's Day Off* (1986).

Right: Mia Sara, Matthew Broderick, and Alan Ruck on the set of *Ferris Bueller's Day Off* (1986).

"Mia Sara's major challenge in the audition opposite Broderick came in hiding the 'enormous crush' she had on the star."

it off—John kept Jones waiting in his Paramount office for three hours—John did pick Jones, who had played the emperor in *Amadeus*, to be Rooney.

Rooney's is the only character to present any sort of impediment to Ferris. He was his foil, the Wily E. Coyote to Broderick's Roadrunner as it were. Without him, *Ferris Bueller* would not be a funny picture.

To play Ferris's hopelessly hypochondriac friend Cameron, John took Broderick's advice and cast an actor who was already a buddy of Matthew's on stage and off. Alan Ruck had played Matthew's best friend in the original Broadway production of *Biloxi Blues*. Though he was

twenty-nine years old, the two made their "friendship" work on stage and no one saw any reason why this wouldn't carry over into their movie.

Knowing each other so well as friends and colleagues before production began was, as John later remarked, one of those intangible things that shows up on film.

For the role of Ferris's girlfriend, Sloane—named after Tanen's teenage daughter, who served as an unofficial teen consultant to John—John went with a beautiful, young actress from Brooklyn. Mia Sara had graduated from high school the year before, the same year she had appeared in Ridley Scott's *Legend* opposite Tom Cruise.

Her major challenge in the audition opposite Broderick came in hiding the "enormous crush" she had on the star of *Ladyhawke* and *Brighton Beach Memoirs*.

Production, which was to begin in September, was divided between Chicago and L.A. due to budgetary concerns and the weather. (The story needed to take place in spring.) A "Midwestern" house in Long Beach, California, served as the Bueller residence for interiors and even some exteriors. All upstairs sequences were filmed on a soundstage.

As usual, John insisted on his own peculiar rehearsal period, which began August 29. Actors hung out with one another and visited locations.

Since everyone stayed at the same Chicago hotel, John would meet his actors in the same room every day to rehearse, which was mostly schmoozing and eating and looking at pictures.

"He was always playing Preston Sturges movies," recalled Broderick.

John drove his four principal actors around in a beige Lincoln Town Car to show them his Chicago and talk about his life there as a high school student. He slammed music cassettes into the car's tape deck to play music he intended for certain scenes. He did admit, though, that he was still searching for music for the film's big parade sequence.

"I want something like Elvis or the Beatles but then I want something Midwestern, kind of schmaltzy," he said.

Jones piped up: "How about Wayne Newton?"

"Who?" said John. Addicted to cutting-edge music, he apparently was unaware of more mainstream performers.

"Well, his song 'Danke Schoen' is about the schmaltziest thing I can think of," said Jones.

"BUELLER ... BUELLER ..."

"When I first read the script, there was the part of a teacher but it was just a voice, not a real role," said Michael Chinich, who use to run John's production company. "Jesus, I said, this is my friend Ben Stein. He's not in the business but he'd be perfect."

Ben Stein, who graduated as valedictorian from his Yale Law School class, had written many books and served as a newspaper columnist and as Richard Nixon and Gerald Ford's speech writer. (He helped craft Nixon's resignation speech.) As a favor, Stein did come in for the voice role and was so good that John decided to turn the camera around and film him. He became a full-fledged celebrity with his appearance in *Ferris Bueller*.

His dull roll call of students' names until he comes to "Bueller ... Bueller ..." with no reply has achieved iconic status. Funnier still is his ad-libbed lecture on the impact of tariffs on trade and economic policy to zoned-out students who comprehend not one word he is saying. This was in fact one of his university lectures on voodoo economics delivered with hilarious deadpan seriousness.

Above: It took four days for Hughes to shoot the infamous phone scene among Rooney (Jones), Grace (McClurg), Ferris (Broderick), and Cameron (Ruck).

A few minutes later, John stopped at a music store and went in to look for a Wayne Newton cassette. While Broderick, Sara, and Ruck stayed in the car, Jones got out to try on sunglasses for sale outside the store. While he was trying on a pair with flips, John came out and saw him.

"Those are perfect for the film," John said.

So he bought three pairs. Not only did Jones now have flip-up sunglasses for Rooney, John had found his parade music.

The only actor who felt uncomfortable with these "rehearsals" was Sara.

"I was very young," she said. "His method of rehearsals was more about trying to get to know you. He and Jennifer [Grey] got along incredibly well. I think on a personal level, I didn't really understand he wanted to be friends. That felt awkward. I felt like a kid and that I didn't belong in the environment he created."

Again, John sat under the camera and always kept it rolling. This way he could stay close to the actors and, as new lines would occur to him, he'd "rewrite" the scene on the fly.

John was among the first directors of that era to have high shooting ratios, exposing much more film (expensive in those days) than his contemporaries. Jacobson estimated that on *Ferris Bueller* he shot at least a million feet of film and printed about 650,000 feet. This was to become a methodology for other writer-directors, such as James L. Brooks.

Spontaneity and improvisation were the goals. John welcomed input from all of the actors and then decided whether he wanted to act on a suggestion. Edie McClurg, playing Rooney's secretary, came up with the delicious idea of pulling pencil after pencil—four in all—out from her bubble hairdo. And John suggested Rooney should be picking at invisible specks of dust on his desk.

"It's a tiny little thing but just right for that guy," remarked Jones.

The sequence between Jones and McClurg as multiple phone calls come in consisted of four pages of dialogue to be shot in two days. John ended up using four days to capture all the physical comedy the actors came up with.

Shooting the upstairs hallway scenes, where Broderick talks directly to the audience, John told the actor to keep his eyes on the camera at all times.

"Never look away and then back even for a moment," he said. "Newscasters look the whole time at the camera. Otherwise viewers would think something else is going on."

One day, while filming Ferris going to the shower as he's speaking to the camera, John suddenly had an inspiration. He went to Broderick and conferred briefly with him, then told his cameraman, Tak Fujimoto, where the actor was going to stop and say new lines.

As instructed, Broderick popped out of the bathroom in his robe, stopped on his mark, and delivered his lines: "What are you guys still doing here? The movie's over. Go home." He turned and walked away.

This, of course, became the very end to the movie.

TWIST AND SHOUT

Fujimoto, who shot *Pretty in Pink*, gave John one of his best-shot films ever. The compositions in the museum sequence give the film visual pizzazz. The camera work for the parade, staged very close to where John worked a decade earlier in advertising, provided editor Paul Hirsch with plenty of remarkable footage to assemble into the film's kick-ass sequence.

The parade was filmed during the Von Steuben Day Parade, an annual German-American event in the Chicago area in mid-September. As the film was fairly low budget—originally $10.8 million, with John going slightly over at $11.2 million—the

Above: Alan Ruck (Cameron) and Matthew Broderick (Ferris) were friends before *Ferris Bueller's Day Off*, which could help explain the funny and easy relationship they shared on-screen.

"The turnout for the fake parade was greater than for the actual one."

Above: The infamous parade scene was everyone's favorite day on the set for *Ferris Bueller's Day Off*. The people in the crowd at the parade were real people, not actors.

plan was to shoot during the actual parade and then the following weekend, shut down several downtown blocks to get the remaining shots. This meant getting people willing to participate as extras for free. Production coordinator Fredell Pogodin went to various AM radio stations to arrange promotions to bring in a crowd.

About 10,000 people showed up. The turnout for the fake parade was greater than for the actual one.

"John was already a successful Chicago native and Chicago is a very loyal city, very patriotic to its own," noted Jacobson.

For everyone who worked on the film, this was their favorite day. Seemingly all of Chicago danced in the streets to "Twist and Shout." The sequence, the *Chicago Tribune* later wrote, "is a mad-cap, upbeat brouhaha that does for the upside of street festivals what *The Godfather II* did for the down."

"Those were real faces, real people," John exclaimed. "That guy twisting up on the scaffolding was no actor. He was a real guy. That was spontaneous and we were lucky enough to catch it … but that's why that shot has a little wobble in it." "It was difficult but insanely fun," said Broderick.

He and choreographer Kenny Ortega had worked out dynamic dance moves for the actor atop a float. But early in the shoot, Broderick dislocated his knee while running through his neighbors' yards for a sequence near the film's end. So the intricate steps were cut.

"Kenny said just do whatever you feel like—make it up," said Broderick. "In some ways it came out funnier. I was a crazy person in those days, very spontaneous."

In a different but no less significant manner than *Pretty in Pink*, *Ferris Bueller* underwent substantial changes following initial test screenings. John took nearly an hour out of a movie he felt was too long.

Of Ferris's sisters, only Grey remains in the final cut. A subplot involving Charlie Sheen and his family got excised, leaving only a final police station scene between him and Grey.

Then test scores were coming back negative about Sloane. John soon figured out why. During the parade, when Sloane and Cameron walk together and talk about their lives, Sloane has a line meant as social commentary about the different opportunities afforded to men and women. But because of the sarcastic tone in its delivery, John realized that audiences weren't getting it, and consequently disliking Sloane.

He cut the line. The next time John screened the movie, her character recommendation level went up ten points.

During a Wrigley Field scene, Sloane said, "Can we go home? I'm not having fun." John cut that line too. He worried some would feel that Ferris forces people do things they don't want to do.

Mostly, though, John recut *Ferris Bueller* to be a comedy.

"The longer version was very good but most of what was excised was more dramatic backstory stuff—a lot of darkness," said Broderick. "The longer version was brilliant and introspective, where the tone gets serious and characters talk about what happens when you get older. More material like in *The Breakfast Club*, that fear of what happens when you reach a stage in life where you're at the top of the world in high school but what comes next?

"*Ferris* has a perfect little shape to it. The other [longer] movie was braver in some ways but [the final cut] is a jewel—like a fine watch. John wanted more fun—and a funny film."

This is an interesting comment. Coming from advertising, where story and imagery are meant to sell a product, John believed the audience was king. "He was making movies for an audience," insisted Jacobson. "He wanted them to relate to his intentions."

So when the darker, more introspective moments were cut—material, as Broderick indicated, more in line with the seriousness of *The Breakfast Club*—he was bowing to his audience.

To return to Ringwald's reminiscences, she believed the two films he made with her and Hall were "the most deeply personal expressions of John's … None of the films that he made subsequently had the same kind of personal feeling to me. They were funny, yes, wildly successful, to be sure, but I recognized very little of the John I knew in them, of his youthful, urgent, unmistakable vulnerability."

So one wonders if, at the height of his success,

John was already pulling back from his own braver, darker vision of life. As Ringwald wrote, "It was like his heart had closed, or at least was no longer open for public view."

Ferris Bueller grossed $18 million in its first dozen days. The domestic box office eventually hit $70 million.

Geekdom was wearing out its welcome even for John. Not high school, mind you, but the student subspecies of the geek. For *Ferris Bueller's Day Off* (1986), John reversed course to focus on the most popular guy in school. He has a great girlfriend and a best buddy who, while not a complete geek, comes close enough in his melancholy, moody aimlessness, and level of anxiety.

This was, in fact, the triangular relationship John often found himself in while in high school with Nancy and whatever buddy he was hanging out with at that moment.

"I was never sure between me and Alan which one was John," said Broderick. "It was the two sides of him I guess."

So in real life, for all of John's empathy for the geek, he identified himself nearly as much with the relatively popular and happy student who did have a girl—his future wife, in fact—and was completely at ease in his friendships with geeks. While Ferris himself is a fictional creation—can anyone be so effortlessly cheerful and able to talk himself into and out of all of life's situations?— John puts a lot of himself into Ferris.

Ferris is someone everybody likes. While prone to mischief, he hasn't a mean bone in his body.

A star almost from the day he turned professional, Broderick was supremely skilled at physical and emotional comedy. He possessed a natural charm and self-confidence that eases an audience into accepting Ferris for what he is: a privileged young

man whose pursuit of happiness, indeed his pursuit of the perfect day, stems not from selfish or narcissistic motives, but rather a supreme *joie de vivre*.

Once he makes his decision to play hooky, he dedicates the day to his friend Cameron, essentially using the day's activities to liberate Cameron from psychosomatic illness caused by a domineering, unloving father. So Ferris's day off is ultimately a selfless act, not a selfish one.

While the role of Sloane has generous screen time—the three are inseparable once they head into Chicago—John doesn't develop the role with the same depth he did for female characters played by Ringwald or Sheedy. Sloane is devoted and loving to Ferris, but perhaps, as a surrogate for John's own wife, he refrained from plumbing this character's depths.

Sloane has no parent issues or school issues or any issues, for that matter. She seems happily well adjusted, which is death in a dramatic role. What can an actress play? Sara can only give Sloane elegance and a beguiling calm in the adventures of the day.

Ferris's day off is every bit as absurd as *Sixteen Candles*. In each, John observes the classical unities of time and place by keeping the action localized and on a clock. *Ferris Bueller* takes place, ostensibly, in less than twelve hours.

The simple act of the school's most popular boy skipping class by feigning illness not only sends shock waves through the school—one rumor has it that Ferris is at death's door—but ultimately causes all of Chicago to celebrate with the young man in a parade sequence that features thousands of extras rocking out to his lip-syncing "Danke Schoen" and "Twist and Shout."

But first he must fool his parents about being

sick. They buy it, despite the fact that Ferris tells us it's his worst performance of being ill. Ferris constantly breaks the "fourth wall" to speak to the audience, even lecturing about his philosophy of life and his worries about Cameron marrying the first girl who lets him into her bed, and how that would be a disaster for him. Your problems are his problems—that's what's so great about Ferris—and having Broderick speak directly to the audience pulls us into his orbit.

Then the trio borrow Cameron's dad's car, which happens to be a fully restored, cherry-red 1961 Ferrari 250 GT California, a car that, tellingly, the dad loves more than his own son. This, we soon realize, is all part of Ferris' plan to free the soul of Cameron Frye.

They zip into Chicago, leave the car with a highly unreliable parking attendant, then visit the Sears Tower, take in a Cubs game, crash a snooty restaurant, visit the Art Institute, and join the parade down Dearborn Street. John keeps their adventures serendipitous and carefree, about as lacking in narrative drive as possible as the trio remain blithely unaware (well, nearly so) of the havoc their absence causes.

For the film's increasingly bizarre comic incidents, John relies on subplots. The most outrageous concerns Principal Rooney. This is Ferris's ninth absence from school this semester and Rooney takes the youth's cavalier attitude about attendance as a challenge to his authority.

"He gives good kids bad ideas," he storms to his secretary, Grace (McClurg).

Abandoning his duties at school just as Ferris abandons his own classes, Rooney stalks Ferris all over the Chicago suburbs in an increasingly strange odyssey, running afoul of a police tow truck and the Bueller family dog. As easily

Above: The character of Sloane (Mia Sara) didn't go over well with test audiences, but John Hughes figured out why and eliminated a few lines that were turning people off of her character.

flattered and angered as he is fooled, Rooney is a lightning rod for negative energy and the source of much of the film's great slapstick.

While seemingly oblivious to his principal's quest, Ferris has anticipated his every move, even rigging answering machines and doorbells to lead Rooney astray.

Above: Jeanie Bueller (Jennifer Grey) finds love at the police station with a local druggie played by Charlie Sheen.

In a similar fashion, Ferris's own sister, Jeanie (Jennifer Grey, who would later become engaged for a while to Broderick), is made just as livid by her brother's fake illness. As the sibling who can get away with nothing, she is furious that not only does her brother get away with everything, but no one is on her side: not her parents, the school secretary, or police. She even manages to get arrested for a "false" 911 call when there was a real intruder in her home!

Another running gag/subplot involves Ferris's clueless parents, Katie and Tom Bueller (played by Cindy Pickett and Lyman Ward, who did, in fact, get married following the shoot). Their activities during the day see them cross paths with their errant son and his companions on numerous occasions without ever making eye contact.

Ferris Bueller is filled with delicious gags, verbal and visual. The scene between Grey and Sheen at the police station is, of course, much funnier today than when the film was originally released. When Sheen answers "Drugs" to her question of why he has been arrested, this is, unfortunately, all too prescient. Yet even the fact that Ferris's uptight sister can connect with a high-school junkie, who offers her sagacious advice before she winds up kissing him and then exiting the station totally flustered, is very funny.

Ferris Bueller finds its core story in a relationship we never even see on screen—Cameron and his dad. What we do see is how mentally screwed up Cameron is.

"He loves his car. He hates his wife," is how Cameron sums up his father. Becoming catatonic when he realizes the Ferrari's odometer is going to give away his son's joy riding, Cameron is only able to snap out of it when he "kills the car."

"I'm just tired of being afraid," he insists. Then, fully liberated by Ferris's influence, he proceeds to kick the Ferrari until the hugely expensive car accelerates in reverse, crashes through a garage window, and falls into a ravine below Cameron's house. The car—and his dad's abuse—has indeed been killed.

MOVIE MOGUL

Ferris Bueller's promotional taglines were "Leisure Rules" and "One Man's Struggle to Take It Easy." Smart ad copy from Paramount's marketing department? No, John came up with those lines. The poster for the film was designed before the movie was shot. So, kudos for this to the studio's marketers? Again, no—John designed the poster.

News about the movie reached a fan base via newsletters long before the movie opened. Yes, you guessed it: John wrote those newsletters, which were mailed from Hughes Entertainment.

"John was an innovative pioneer in movie advertising long before the era of email blasts," said Pogodin. "He would pen those newsletters himself in 'teen speak.' He really understood direct-mail advertising."

John started a fan club for Hughes Entertainment from a database created from fan letters he

Opposite: John Hughes on the set of *Ferris Bueller's Day Off* in 1986. Right: Hughes wrote many of the promotional taglines for his movies, including *Ferris Bueller's Day Off*.

"I've been around big-time directors . . . for forty years and can't say enough about his creativity. It's like a tsunami came to Hollywood and it's never been the same." —Michael Chinich on John Hughes

had received from tens of thousands of kids. From this database his company mailed out everything from newsletters designed and written by John to *Pretty in Pink* buttons and *Ferris Bueller* posters.

"He tapped into youth culture," said Chinich. "He had an enormous following. He did everything on his movies—the music, marketing, posters, everything. There has never been anybody quite like him. I've been around big-time directors and actors for forty years and can't say enough about his creativity. It's like a tsunami came to Hollywood and it's never been the same. There wasn't a thing he couldn't do."

Broderick remembered that, at his first meeting with John as the two walked down Park Avenue in New York discussing their movie, John carried a stack of *Pretty in Pink* stickers.

"*Pretty in Pink* was about to come out so as we talked, he would be putting up on every lamppost these stickers," Broderick said. "It was extra advertising for his movie."

The studio was happy to let him supervise the cutting of his trailers and the design of posters. It was a waste of time and money to do otherwise, since John had final approval and few, if any, could do these things better than him.

This was also a way of avoiding fights, for it was about this time that John began to develop a reputation for an erratic management style and mercurial behavior.

Watching this was Shuler Donner, one of the few with whom he did not quarrel.

"He changed after *Ferris Bueller*," she said. "He became caustic. He became rude. He'd hire somebody to run his company and then decide he did not like him and stop talking with him and that person would leave. The only one with staying power was Tom Jacobson."

So that which had happened to Ringwald and Hall later happened to other actors and to Pogodin, Chinich, studio heads, and directors who helmed Hughes screenplays. Curiously, many of these associates were later brought back into the Hughes orbit, only to be dumped again.

Tarquin Gotch would speak of the John Hughes experience as a matter of extreme shifts in temperature. Gotch first met John through Kelly LeBrock. The two men immediately hit it off, since Gotch was a British A&R man who had signed many of the bands John loved. He helped John out with the soundtrack for *Pretty in Pink*, but *Ferris Bueller* was his first credit.

"When John liked you, the sun shone," Gotch explained. "He was a charmer. Before I knew it, I was an in-house music supervisor for John and we were hatching plans to parlay his tremendous influence with teens at the time, both in films and music, into something fun—a label. It was never about making loads of money; it was about finding bands and bringing them to people's attention. That's what drove John."

John got Paramount to get a work visa and green card for Gotch so he could commute between London and L.A. Gotch continued to manage various bands—the Beat, XTC, the Dream Academy, the Lilac Time—all bands that John liked.

"I realized that my being in England may have been very attractive to John because his mode of writing was to work all night straight through—coffee, cigarette, typing, coffee, cigarette, typing—and listening to music. Because of the time difference he could call up and chat about story and music ideas because to him they were interwoven."

They continued to work together in this fashion until *Christmas Vacation*. Then Gotch suddenly found himself out in the cold.

"With John, when he loved you the sun shone and when he went off you it was a bleak Siberian winter," said Gotch. "I never found out what it was I did or didn't do. No idea."

Then, a year later, John phoned Gotch in England.

The first thing John asked was: "Do you want to be a producer?"

"Yes," Gotch replied.

"Then come and run my company in Chicago," said John.

"John, you fired me," said Gotch. "I haven't spoken to you in a year. This makes no sense."

"I'll pay you a lot of money," said John.

"How much?" asked Gotch.

Gotch then found himself on a plane to Chicago.

"John said I had to give up management of all my bands. So it wasn't an easy decision, actually," Gotch recounted. But he took the job in Chicago and basked once more in the Hughes sunshine. But John's impulsive actions became evident to the entire industry during his next trouble-plagued production.

SOME KIND OF WONDERFUL

"I like art. I work in a gas station. My best friend is a tomboy."

When auditioning for *Pretty in Pink*, Jon Cryer told John he was a big fan of one of his *Lampoon* stories about a kid spy. He thought it was every teenage boy's fantasies rolled into a single story. Later, John told Cryer he was thinking of using that story for a movie script.

Above: Promotional poster for *Some Kind of Wonderful* (1987).

"*Some Kind of Wonderful* was an upside down version of *Pretty in Pink*."

—Michael Chinich

Above: Casting for Some Kind of Wonderful was complicated from the start, especially when the director changed. And then changed again.

By the time John sent an early draft of *Some Kind of Wonderful* to Cryer, not much of the original story was left.

"What started as kid spy thing had morphed into an Ultimate Date thing—a crazy epic night more in the vein of *Ferris Bueller* that included the Blue Angels aerobatic flight team. It was big…and really, really funny," remembered Cryer. Although he wasn't cast in the movie, out of curiosity he asked to read the final shooting script.

"I read it and said, 'Oh, okay, I didn't see that coming. Why do *Pretty in Pink* again?' " said Cryer. The original intent had changed that much.

"*Some Kind of Wonderful* was an upside down version of *Pretty in Pink*," said Chinich. "I thought it was one of John's weakest stories."

In the movie, another teen romantic triangle is spread over the two sides of a town's tracks. A high-school outsider pines after someone seen daily since the third grade. But the object of desire never recognizes this romantic fixation. However, in this incarnation, the outsider/geek is a tomboy with a passion for percussion, and the object of desire, the Molly Ringwald character, as it were, becomes a blue-collar boy with a passion for art.

Meanwhile, this pleasantly rumpled young man, Keith, has a crush on the school's hottie, Amanda. These urges embolden him to overcome his shyness to ask her out. When she throws him for a loop by accepting a date—for reasons that will prove less than pure—this sends the dynamics between the tomboy and blue-collar kid into emotional turmoil.

The kicker is that the hot Popular Girl comes from the same side of the tracks as Keith and Drummer Girl (also known as Watts). She has gained acceptance among the Richies only because of her stunning looks.

In his second film for John as director, Howie Deutch grew frustrated in the casting process. So he made what he thought was an innocent request. John had a screenplay that everyone thought was going to make a great motion picture. *Oil and Vinegar* had a young man and woman driving across country to attend a wedding. It was a talkathon not unlike *The Breakfast Club*, with the two characters lowering their guards and getting into their life stories. Both Broderick and Ringwald were interested in the roles.

"It was a very good script, deceptively simple," said Broderick, although he added there was concern that it might be "too subtle and slight."

Deutch was itching to direct that film. One day he found John on a Paramount dubbing stage, putting the finishing touches on *Ferris Bueller*. He told John that he would much prefer doing *Oil and Vinegar* than *Some Kind of Wonderful*.

John turned to him with a distracted look and nodded his head. "Oh, sure," he said. "Great."

The next day, Deutch found himself locked out of his studio office. John had fired his protégé.

"I was persona non grata," said Deutch. "No one would talk to me. So tail between my legs, I went back to New York and cried on my parents' shoulders. They said you've got to try to get him to forgive you."

To replace Deutch, John hired Martha Coolidge. As the director of such films as *Valley Girl* and *Real Genius*, she too had carved out a niche in teen films. So the industry saw the combination of John and Coolidge as a first collaboration of two heavy-hitters in teen films.

"We had a great time working together—we complemented each other," said Coolidge. "We developed the film, would talk through the material, and the next day he would have fifty pages rewritten. No matter how funny a scene would be,

the angst and character conflicts were serious, not just jokes. And there was a kind of grounded truth to the female characters."

Mary Stuart Masterson was already aboard as Drummer Girl. For her male lead, Coolidge cast Eric Stoltz, who had read for *Valley Girl* and nearly got cast.

"Eric is gifted and sexy, but very pristine looking," she commented. "His red hair and sharp feature made him very clean. So I had him dye his hair color two shades darker and add extensions. The character was not supposed to be handsome. So having unruly, darker red hair zinged him up."

She cast Kim Delaney as Amanda Jones and Kyle MacLachlan as Hardy Jenns, the film's villain. Coolidge was also delighted with her

Right: Eric Stoltz starred as Keith Nelson, an artist from the wrong side of the tracks.

Right: A lovers' quarrel between Amanda Jones (Lea Thompson) and Hardy Jenns (Craig Sheffer) in Some Kind of Wonderful (1987).

locations and storyboards. "It was an easy prep, maybe one of easiest I've ever had. I've never been so ready," she said.

The Monday before the Thursday start, Chinich called her office and asked her to come over right away to the production office.

"I knew something terrible had happened," she said.

It got more ominous. "You'd better sit down," said Chinich. She did, and watched as he took a deep breath.

"We are going make this movie," he said, "but not with you."

Coolidge looked at him dumbfounded. "What do you mean?"

"You're fired," he said, then added: "It was nothing you did."

Soon enough, she found out that Deutch, back in John's good graces, was already on the lot, interviewing replacement actors.

Why did John fire Coolidge and bring Deutch back on to the picture?

Vance insisted that John was unhappy with the screen tests done with the actors Coolidge cast: "I don't think he particularly cared for her vision of characters. I don't think the chemistry was right for John."

"As a collaborator, why not tell people you're not happy?" said Coolidge. "He was involved in the casting and really happy with the cast. I never heard a peep from him."

Deutch said John had re-opened conversations with him through "back-channel diplomacy" a while before—John and Deutch shared Rapke as an agent—due to his unhappiness with Coolidge's vision of his script.

"She had requested him to rewrite and it had become more dramatic," said Deutch.

Coolidge insisted she always loved the script and John's changes were mostly to accommodate casting, locations, and developments during a two-week rehearsal period with actors.

"Martha wasn't fired because she was no good," maintained Chinich. "The movie couldn't have been worse with Martha doing it."

While acknowledging that Vance's account may have some truth, Chinich said, "John was there for the casting sessions." He never said a word.

Lending credence to John's unhappiness with the cast is the fact that he and Deutch immediately replaced Delaney with Lea Thompson and MacLachlan with Craig Sheffer. The two wanted to fire Stoltz, too, but Tanen refused to let them.

Privately, Tanen and Chinich both told Coolidge that they expected the multiple changes, coming just three days before shooting, to ruin the movie.

"Ned told me John Hughes was too important to [Paramount] to let one movie stand in the way of him as a commodity," said Coolidge, who was given another movie (1987's *Plain Clothes*) to make by the studio.

Some crew members did quit in disgust. In shock, Stoltz called Coolidge and told her he wanted to quit too. These calls would continue through the entire shoot, but she always talked him out of it.

Several years before, Stoltz had been the original choice to play Marty McFly in *Back to the Future* and had shot five weeks' worth of footage before being replaced by Michael J. Fox. A second such episode, she told him, would devastate his career.

Deutch did make Stoltz cut his hair and go back to a clean-cut look, though. The two barely spoke to each other on the set.

"There was no communication between us," admitted Deutch. "It was not a good time."

Things got so bad that Vance had to act as intermediary. Leaving on a red-eye from Chicago, where she was working on *The Untouchables*, Vance arrived at the airport and was immediately driven to the Long Beach high school where the film was shooting.

She went into Stoltz's trailer to discover a defiant actor paying no attention to anything his director told him. He complained to Vance about everything, including the costumes he was to wear.

"He knew he was going to wear them but was doing this to torture Howie. That's all it was—bad chemistry," said Vance. "I straightened out everything, he wound up wearing the costumes as prepared in the first place, then I took the car back to the airport."

John never called Coolidge to explain why he let her go. They spoke again only one other time, when they found themselves in first class on a flight to Japan for the Tokyo International Film Festival.

"We talked as if it never happened," recalled Coolidge. "It was never mentioned. Bizarre."

"John was like that with everybody," said Vance. "He put up a wall of some kind. He got really short with people after a while. He was tough personality."

"John loved you, loved you, loved you, until he didn't love you anymore," said Vance. "He fell out with almost everybody he started with."

Principle photography began August 11, 1986. The screenplay that had begun as a Spy Kid story then morphed into an Ultimate Date epic comedy had now morphed into *Pretty in Pink Redux*.

"I was surprised how much more dramatic the script was," said Deutch. "It was not a comedy anymore."

implausible twists, the chief virtues of *Some Kind of Wonderful* are the rich details and conflicted impulses John carefully layers into his three main characters.

Stoltz's Keith Nelson fits the pattern of all Hughes outsiders, yet is unique—he isn't much bothered by this status. His passion is to paint. His only motive in making a move on Amanda is sheer attraction; he in no way sees this as a means to climb any social ladders.

He's a doer, a guy willing to get his hands dirty, either working on a vehicle in the service station or coming to school early to paint alone in the art classroom. He has a mechanical mind, not a cerebral one: a car that needs fixing or an image on canvas.

He has a father (John Ashton) who doesn't understand him. His dad is so determined that Keith be the first in his family to go to college that he fails to appreciate his son's single-minded obsession with art.

"When does my life belong to me?" Keith demands in a key showdown. In one way or another, this gets asked by youngsters in nearly all Hughes teen movies. Yet with graduation—and adulthood—looming, Keith's question takes on urgency. He is the first high-school character in a Hughes movie that actually has a future ambition.

The one who truly loves Keith, though, is Watts (Masterson), a tomboy with a passion for drums that equals Keith's for art. In the original script, in fact, her character is simply called Drummer Girl. Drumsticks accompany her everywhere.

Similar to Duckie in *Pink*, she manages to be

The trouble was, everyone thought it *was* a comedy.

In later drafts John changed Amanda Jones (Thompson) so that she became much more sympathetic, but there's never a doubt that his sympathies lie with Blue-Collar and Drummer Girl. He simply invests the Popular Girl with enough intelligence, vulnerability, and sass for the Blue-Collar/Popular Girl relationship to spark.

Thus, an audience empathizes with all three sides of this triangle, reserving its disdain for a cartoon baddie, Amanda's ex-boyfriend: brazenly arrogant, egotistical, and cowardly rich kid Hardy Jenns (Sheffer). With a name like Hardy Jenns, you don't stand a chance in a John Hughes movie. While there are overly broad moments and a few around every corner or right outside school whenever Keith wanders by. Of course, it's understood he has no clue that he loves her.

For his fatal attraction is Amanda, who has compromised herself to make the leap into the Richies' world. If Hardy snidely refers to her as "my property," she doesn't bat a carefully attached eyelash.

Without too much substantial lengthening of the film's ninety-four-minute running time, John might have portrayed her in the same depth as Keith and Watts. Although the challenge in doing so would be that the more an audience got to like her, the harder it would be for John to pull off his ending. For this time he wants the two outsiders to hook up.

To make certain that Watts is never far from Keith's mind, John fabricates a highly implausible situation in which she is, literally, in sight at all times during his date with Amanda. Keith has withdrawn his entire college savings to ensure that this date will be memorable. Much of this goes to the purchase of a pair of diamond stud earrings, but also includes a rental Jaguar with Watts as his appropriately attired chauffeur.

Watts has already overheard a conversation that tips her off that Hardy's invitation to Keith to bring Amanda to a party at his mansion is actually a trap. He intends to let a couple of his beefy buddies jump Keith and kick his ass. Only she misunderstands parts of it and wrongly informs Keith that Amanda is in on the scheme too, and that the whole date is a "joke."

While Keith insists on going through with the date, his mistaken idea about Amanda's participation in the trap adds a curious subtext to the evening's events, especially during a tense dinner at a swank restaurant. It's almost as if the date has turned into a rite of passage that he must endure, instead of a romantic evening out.

Sticking up for her man, Watts at one point attempts to smear Amanda's lipstick by applying the Jaguar's brakes. Later she growls to Amanda: "Break his heart, I break your face."

Earlier in the film, Keith befriends a most unlikely fellow student known as Skinhead (Elias Koteas), a tattooed and leathered punk. So at the concluding party sequence, Skinhead and his gang crash the party to save Keith from a beating. In so doing, they show up Hardy as a coward in front of his own social set.

And Keith's final lines to Hardy—"You want the truth? The plain truth? You're over"—have a real sting.

"With a name like Hardy Jenns, you don't stand a chance in a John Hughes movie."

An earlier draft, however, contains a different and more interesting scene. No cavalry comes to Keith's rescue. Rather, Hardy's own crude sexual insinuations revolt even his own friends who then turn on him.

Amanda delivers the final blow by slapping Hardy across the face. She does this in both versions.

Outside Hardy's mansion, Keith has poignant scenes with both girls. Watts is determined to get away before bursting into tears over the prospect of losing Keith to Amanda. Before she does, she has something to say to her triumphant rival: "Sorry if I misjudged you."

Then she's gone, headed down the street. Amanda sizes up the situation in an instant. She

> **"It was an attempt to see if the geek could get the girl and work. One of my best characters is Mary Stuart Masterson's Watts."** —John Hughes

removes the diamond studs, puts them in Keith's hands, and tells him, "I think you want to give these to someone else."

It's as if that thought has only now dawned on Keith. Suddenly, he can't wait to rush after Watts for a final tearful kiss at the fade out.

While Keith is the protagonist, the film belongs to Masterson's Drummer Girl. This is all part of John's in-joke, connecting the names of all three characters to the Rolling Stones —Watts (after drummer Charlie Watts), Keith (Richards, of course), and Amanda Jones after the name of the Stones' song (which plays in the film).

No one else in the movie has such a range and

Above (top): Keith (Eric Stoltz) and Skinhead (Elias Koteas) form an unlikely friendship in *Some Kind of Wonderful*. Above (bottom): The tender moment where Watts (Mary Stuart Masterson) lets Keith (Eric Stoltz) practice kissing on her is one of John Hughes' best love scenes.

mix of conflicting emotions as Drummer Girl. She has loved Keith forever, but is so protective of him she's willing to escort him on his date. She is often saying one thing and meaning another.

At one point John saw a need for a new scene in the movie. He asked Deutch to come over to the house.

"He's laughing and crying as he types while he's in [the scene] as a character," said Deutch. "He hands me the pages. It's the scene where Masterson teaches Eric how to kiss. It's the best scene in the movie."

Drummer Girl insists Keith needs to practice his kissing for the date and he might as well practice on her. The scene is filled with tenderness and yearning on each kisser's part.

"Pretend I'm a girl, okay?" she instructs him then catches herself. "I mean, pretend I'm her."

It's John's best love scene.

An earlier draft has Drummer Girl offer herself sexually to Keith, just in case his obsession with Amanda is a matter of sexual need. Shocked and flattered, he turns her down. Fortunately, John cut that scene in subsequent drafts.

Keith's dad, in a final fight with his son, finally sees things from his son's perspective. He doesn't want his son to be "selling tires six days a week," like himself, but he wants what's best for his son.

In what is John's final teen movie, he at last got an argument up on screen where both sides reach a rapprochement rather than the parent coming out a well-meaning dolt.

In *The Hollywood Reporter*, John would later comment about the movie: "It was an attempt to see if the geek could get the girl and work. One of my best characters is Mary Stuart Masterson's Watts."

SHE'S HAVING
A BABY

"You want to be a writer, you move to New York. You live here, there's nothing to write about. Nothing happens."

The characters in *The Breakfast Club* are clearly avatars for the young John Hughes. And all the comic and sometimes dramatic manifestations of his family stories, from "Vacation '58" and *Mr. Mom* to his traveling salesmen in *Planes, Trains and Automobiles* and the class-consciousness of *Pretty in Pink* and *Some Kind of Wonderful*, reflect his life and times.

Above: Promotional poster for *She's Having a Baby* (1988).

That all came to an end with the failure of *She's Having a Baby.*

"I think it's the best thing I've ever done," John said. "The most honest and truthful. It was a story that I could tell over a number of years and narrate it."

In the 1980s, the box office for John's pictures, made on fairly modest budgets, would range, on the low end, from $40.5 million domestic gross for *Pretty in Pink* and $41.5 million on *The Great Outdoors* to, on the high end, $66.8 million for *Uncle Buck* and $70.1 million for *Ferris Bueller. She's Having a Baby* made only $16 million.

Above: John Hughes chatting with Kevin Bacon and Elizabeth McGovern on the set for *She's Having a Baby* in 1988.

She's Having a Baby is clearly a loving tribute from the filmmaker to his wife. One doesn't need his note, "Inspiration: Nancy Hughes," at the end credits to realize this is a love letter from John to Nancy.

In the voiceover narration John gives to his alter ego, Jake, he declares: "I love her more than anything on the face of the earth. I fell like a stone the first time I saw her. She fell just as hard. The only difference is—she knew why."

From their wedding at a very early age, before either one is established with a decent job or even the prospects for one, to the birth of their first child, the movie's couple, played with shy warmth by Kevin Bacon and Elizabeth McGovern, capture all the dreams, fears, hesitancies, and joys of the early days in the Hughes marriage.

The film starts off highly comic, then gradually turns a shade more serious. The wedding ceremony at the beginning fits firmly into John's contention that "a wedding is essentially like a funeral, except you have to look like you're having a good time."

All prospective in-laws wear dour expressions, each fretting over the sheer youth of the bride and groom. Pessimism reigns inside the chapel, while outside, Bacon's Jake Briggs is sharing his deep misgivings with best man Davis McDonald (Alec Baldwin). Davis is trying to gently coax Jake into taking a powder. Jake, meanwhile, is trying to get reassurance from Davis that he will be happy in married life to Kristy.

When it becomes clear that Jake won't be dissuaded from his chosen path, Davis sighs and gives Jake his reluctant assurance: "Yeah, you'll be happy. You just won't know it, that's all."

The film then charts Jake/John's journey into a job as a creative advertising director for a downtown Chicago agency and the purchase of a suburban two-story home. Here, the walls literally close in on the husband as he contemplates a life not as a writer as he had hoped, but instead as a superannuated yuppie deeply entrenched in the corporate business life, country club membership, and debates with neighbors over the relative merits of lawn mowers.

Left: Jake and Kristy Briggs (played by Kevin Bacon and Elizabeth McGovern) in *She's Having a Baby* were characters inspired by Hughes' own life with wife Nancy.

Above: Kevin Bacon and Alec Baldwin play best friends and polar opposites in *She's Having a Baby.*

In one sequence, Jake searches for the mother of a baby hired for a client's photo session through the agency's corridors and dressing room—jammed with barely clad models—a perfect symbol of Jake's dilemma as he gingerly holds the very essence of married life, even as he bobs and weaves through a sea of female pulchritude.

Davis drops by from New York with his latest slutty girlfriend to taunt his old pal, not only with his playboy lifestyle, but also with the fact that Jake dwells in no-man's-land.

Davis's motives are about as impure as they get: He actually envies his pal, not only for his life, but his life partner. He even puts the make on Kristy in his pathetic despair. She turns him down with appropriate disgust.

Pregnancy and birth receive similar comic treatment. Infertility caused by Jake's poor choice in underpants gets overcome by diligent mating sessions when body temperature and ovulation are just right—all this to the tune of "Workin' on the Chain Gang." This ultimately produces the desired results.

All of this leads to a rather conventional comic finale of male panic in the face of imminent birth: Jake races off to the hospital forgetting his wife at the door step, engages in more slapstick in the maternity ward, then suffers through a dramatic complication involving Kristy having a C-section.

Bacon is winsome as Jake, an agreeably buffoonish self-caricature that allows John ample

What gives the film its comic zest is the fact that much of it happens inside Jake's head. His wandering mind often takes over in dreams and in waking life. So the film is filled with flashbacks, flash-forwards, hallucinations, and odd fantasies.

A luscious fictional female with a foreign accent (Isabel Garcia Lorca) materializes from time to time (like Christie Brinkley's Ferrari girl in *Vacation*). She beckons to Jake to join her in a carefree existence of artistic and sexual expression.

More surreal moments: Neighbors and lawn mowers break into a musical number of suburban precision and conformity. Jake imagines nightmare scenarios such as his in-laws coaching him during sex. A disco sequence throws any number of enticing hot women at poor Jake, offering him a taste of the single life he never actually enjoyed since he got married so young.

opportunity to poke fun at himself, his former occupation, and anxieties over suburban life.

"How do you feel about slave wages?" Jake is asked at an ad agency interview. Another is: "How do you feel about alcoholics?"

Jake's sexual fantasies, unlike those in, say, early Woody Allen films, don't so much taunt the hero as torment him. We suspect he wouldn't know what to do with his Mysterious Foreign Beauty if she became flesh and blood through weird science. He probably would have to ask Kristy what to do.

McGovern's Kristy, like Sara's Sloane, is another idealized portrait of Nancy, and she barely becomes flesh and blood either. By making her radiant yet somewhat bland, McGovern gets to the heart of the matter about matrimony and motherhood. It's all in the day-to-day. It takes work not glamour, patience not titillation to help your husband grow up into the man he wants to be.

The film was not well received either by critics or fans. The *Washington Post*'s Hal Hinton summed up much of the critical response when he wrote that the film's issues felt too mundane, such as whether or not the sofa will fit along the far wall, and that John was "essentially … an ad man, not a filmmaker, and the dilemmas faced by the characters on screen have no greater urgency than those faced by the actors in television commercials."

John would never again expose so much of what went on inside his head.

By the time of its release, John was thoroughly exhausted. Tarquin Gotch, then in charge of John's Chicago operations, had the temerity to bring up

the subject. John's reply sheds light on his mindset in the late 80s.

When Gotch wondered why John drove himself and his crew at such a hectic pace, John replied: "Blake Edwards."

"What?" asked Gotch, truly not understanding.

"Mel Brooks."

Gotch shook his head: "Your point, John?"

"You're funny and then you're not funny," said John.

John had named two top-grossing, hugely successful comedy directors who were no longer in favor with audiences. When you are hot, even the lame *The Great Outdoors* can make $41.5 million. When you're not, your most personal film goes down the toilet.

Below: *She's Having a Baby* would be the last time that Hughes would put so much of himself and his life in a script.

CHRISTMAS VACATION

In the interim, John rediscovered his interest in the *Vacation* series and got much more heavily involved in *Christmas Vacation*. Even though he produced the movie with Jacobson, what he didn't do, according to Matty Simmons—afforded only executive producer status—was show up on the set.

"He had turned himself into a mini-studio, grinding out three–four pictures a year, all of which he wrote but no longer directed," said Simmons. "He was working six pictures ahead

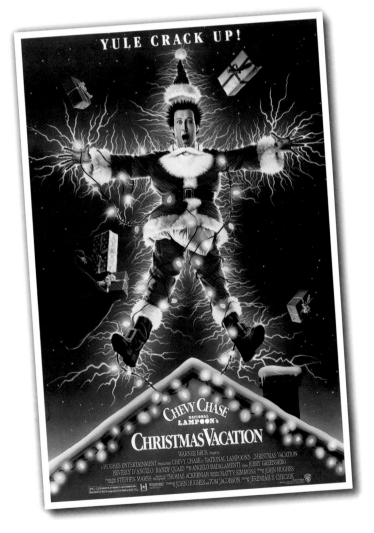

YULE CRACK UP!

CHEVY CHASE
NATIONAL LAMPOON'S
CHRISTMAS VACATION

while one or two were being shot. So there was a sameness of plot—many films were revisions of earlier ones."

Christmas Vacation (1989) is a tepid affair, a film about a dysfunctional family holiday that searches for laughs amid quarreling in-laws, collapsing ladders, road rage, exploding sewers, one accidently electrocuted pet, and several sequences of Christmas light failures featuring tens of thousands of bulbs but no electrical current.

Chase gamely takes one pratfall after another, but even the slapstick falls short—no joke intended. The problem is not simply that the pratfalls are wholly predictable and contrived; they seem more prehistoric than the family's ancient aunt. As with the original *Vacation* film, John looked for inspiration in a *National Lampoon* piece he once penned—this time "Christmas '59." This one, though, again related by the young son, has little narrative. It's mostly a series of discordant notes among a large, bickering family.

About the only mildly amusing new angle is a next-door couple, played by a pre-*Seinfeld* Julia Louis-Dreyfus and Nicholas Guest. They inadvertently take the brunt of all the mishaps happening in the Griswold household, which pretty much destroy their house and quite possibly their marriage.

John's handpicked director, another first-timer, Jeremiah Chechik, assembled an outstanding cast that includes such veterans as E. G. Marshall, John Randolph, Diane Ladd, Doris Roberts, and William Hickey. They had little to do.

As Roger Ebert noted in his review, "The in-laws are handled almost as a tour group, to be shunted around in the backgrounds of shot

Left: The promotional poster for *Christmas Vacation* starring Chevy Chase (1989).

Left: In a classic *Christmas Vacation* moment, Clark Griswold (Chevy Chase) clearly has no idea he's about to cut into a dry and deflated turkey.

after shot or lined up as a quartet to react to Clark's dilemmas."

While making the second and third films of the franchise, D'Angelo admitted, "In terms of the quality and the [*Vacation*] legacy, we were dogged by the feeling we were letting everybody down, that we were not fulfilling what we started out with."

During this same period, John's lawyers were negotiating an exit from Paramount. Tom Pollack, one of John's former attorneys, had taken over as head of Universal and was wooing John to move back to its lot.

The deal wasn't concluded until April 1988. John moved his production office to Universal's East Penthouse and installed his *Ferris Bueller* producer, Jacobson, as production chief.

The previous year, in the last week of filming *Planes*, he had dumped Chinich. As usual with John, Chinich had no idea why. What was unusual, though, was that John did it personally.

"Well, at least you had the balls to do it face to face this time," Chinich told him.

Jacobson would resign the following year to go to Twentieth Century Fox as executive vice president. John followed him there. While keeping his Universal deal, John moved his office to Fox. It was an office he rarely visited since by then he had moved his family back to Chicago. He came to L.A. usually in the summer.

He was now burning through production executives at a rapid pace. Peter Heller replaced Jacobson as the head of John's company, but resigned a few months later when he refused to move to Chicago. This was when John patched things up with Gotch and brought him to Chicago as senior vice president of creative affairs.

Meanwhile, John continued his auspicious teaming with one of the most talented comedy actors of that era.

JOHN CANDY

The films Hughes made with John Candy found him working with an actor who excelled in childlike personalities and grown-ups resistant to adulthood. You could even argue that Candy's roles encompass more adolescent behavior than John's teenage protagonists. The teens *want* to be grown-ups. Candy's characters see adulthood as a fraud. Sure, you get all sorts of responsibilities, worries, and woes, but what happened to the fun you had as a kid? Candy's characters choose to ignore these concerns as much as possible. While they understand they won't always get away with this, it's damn well worth the effort to try.

His man-child characters in *Planes, Trains and Automobiles* and *Uncle Buck* are fully aware of the con they play. They are neither slapstick stooges in the mode of Jerry Lewis, nor innocents adrift like Laurel and Hardy. These grown men are self-aware and defiant in their bad habits and "youthful" behavior. They misunderstand nothing about the sad, unreliable world they find themselves stranded in; more crucially, they understand everything about the clown's existential nature.

The clown sees reality for what it's worth— and it isn't worth much. So he has fun with it.

Candy, a shy and self-conscious man, was part of the Canadian invasion that hit the United

Opposite: John Candy clowning around in Toronto, Canada, on August 19, 1992. Right: John Hughes on the set of *Planes, Trains and Automobiles* in 1987.

Above: John Candy (back) was part of the Canadian Second City comedy troupe that included fellow comedians (from left) Eugene Levy, Dave Thomas, Catherine O'Hara, and Joe Flaherty.

States about the time John was forging his career in comedy—an invasion that included Catherine O'Hara, Harold Ramis, Eugene Levy, Rick Moranis, and Dan Aykroyd.

He honed his craft in Toronto theater before heading for Chicago to work with the Second City comedy troupe. He returned to Toronto at twenty-seven to join that city's Second City troupe, from which evolved the television series *SCTV*. Movie parts beckoned—*1941*, *The Blues Brothers*, and *Stripes*—before his breakout role as Tom Hanks's womanizing brother in 1984's *Splash*.

Like Hughes, John Candy married his high-school sweetheart, Rosemary. He later bought a farm in Queensville, about fifty miles north of Toronto, where they raised their children, along with horses and cows.

While he did appear in the Hughes-scripted *Vacation* in 1983, the intense friendship between

the two men began when they worked on a trio of pictures in the late 1980s. They probably spent more time in each other's company off movie sets than on. The Midwesterner and Canadian found a kinship in comedy, family, strong marriages, and a love of music. Together they frequented small South Side blues and jazz clubs, and took in hockey games.

Their families developed a close friendship that has remained since the passing of both men. Indeed, the Hugheses' visits to the Candys' farm eventually inspired John to develop his own farm.

Bob Crane, who ran Candy's production company, Frostbacks—its name being the playful Canadian equivalent of "wetbacks"—saw this relationship up close.

"They were like brothers," noted Crane. "I know it's an overused term, but they were. They had that quick communication going. The two Johns had a shorthand.

"I saw things on the set in *Uncle Buck* where John Hughes throws out a word while shooting and it steers the scene. It was like John Hughes calls an 'audible' and John Candy is the quarterback and runs a new play while the camera is rolling."

"They were extremely close and would talk every night on the phone for hours," said Deutch. "They loved each other deeply. They were two peas in a pod."

"I never saw John connect with anyone like that," remarked Vance.

Steve Martin, who watched this collaboration up close in *Planes*, saw this in Shakespearian terms: "John Candy was John Hughes's Toby

Belch, he was his Falstaff," referring to two of the Bard's finest comic characters, both mixtures of high spirits, low cunning, and large appetites.

Candy's persona let John work both sides of the generation gap. In *Uncle Buck*, the niece Tia is a standard-issue Hughes misunderstood teen. But her uncle, the guy who never grew up, can see what her parents don't—that she's getting away with murder because of parental neglect.

With Candy as his muse, John began to move into more adult material. He was growing older and knew it. He no longer felt comfortable hanging out with youngsters. Whereas in *The Breakfast Club* era he brought his young actors to those South Side clubs and gave them mix tapes of music, he now found that easy camaraderie with Candy.

The two Johns haunted clubs, each lighting one cigarette with the last. Hughes sipped his diet Cokes while the other gulped down rum-and-Cokes. Neither paid the least bit of attention to his health.

In person or on the phone, they spent hours plotting stories to tell and projects to create. "I always heard that story about Keith Richards being up for nine days once," said Crane. "I don't know if it's true, but the only two people I knew that could do that would be Candy and Hughes. I can see them go nine days without sleeping, just because they were so charged and creative and have more energy than anybody else. It was really exciting to be around."

What Candy loved about working with John is that, unlike other directors, John was a true collaborator. Jeffrey Jones, who had a small role in *Planes* later cut from the film, observed this.

Right: John Candy, John Hughes, and Steve Martin at a press conference for *Planes, Trains and Automobiles*.

"John [Hughes] gave him feedback," said Jones. "When I worked with Candy on another film, John [Candy] was left to his own devices. Everybody thought you could just turn on the camera and leave John alone and he would be funny. John expressed to me his frustration: 'I don't know what I'm doing. Nobody gives me any feedback.' To a certain degree, you don't need to tell John Candy what to do. But he did want to get feedback."

"They were kindred spirits, especially with language and dialogue, in creating character," said Jacobson. "Candy came from that background in sketch comedy and loved detail—a lot of details of dress and the car (he drove)—and John Hughes would include John Candy in those conversations, in the creation of that character."

"They were like brothers . . . They had that quick communication going. The two Johns had a shorthand." —Bob Crane on John Candy and John Hughes

PLANES, TRAINS
AND AUTOMOBILES
"Those aren't pillows."

The original plan was for Deutch to direct *Planes*, since John had just come off directing *She's Having a Baby*. But when Martin agreed to play opposite Candy, John asked Deutch to switch films.

"He loved Steve Martin," said Deutch, "so he said, 'Let me do this. I got another for you—*Big Country*,'" the film that eventually became *The Great Outdoors*.

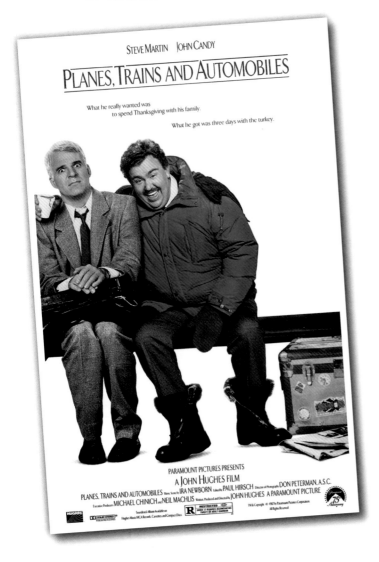

When Martin got the script through his agent, he immediately liked it. Yet he couldn't help noticing the screenplay weighed in at 145 pages. Most comedies aim for about 90.

One of the first times Martin talked to John, he asked him when he was planning to cut it.

"He looked at me strangely and said, 'Cutting?' I realized he had no intention of cutting anything!" said Martin.

So Martin came face-to-face with a dauntingly long script and one of the most arduous shoots he was ever to experience. Yet he understood what an opportunity the film presented.

"At that point in my career, this was the direction I was headed for—more emotional roles," said Martin. "So this was a real breakthrough for me.

"John Candy was one of the best acting partners I've ever worked with. We had a really good connection. When the camera was rolling, we'd look into each other's eyes and it felt good together. We had great timing with each other."

Cold weather, but not the kind that brought the snow so necessary for the story, hampered production from the outset. Weeks were spent waiting for the weather, with the crew eventually giving up in Illinois and moving to Buffalo, New York.

"We actually lived the plot of the movie," said Martin. "As we would shoot, we were hopping trains, planes, and automobiles, trying to find snow."

One actor, a truck driver, had a single line. Rather than hiring him for a day, John kept him on standby. He wound up working for so many days because of weather delays that he was able to make a down payment on a house.

Left: Promotional poster for *Planes, Trains and Automobiles* (1987).

As always, John encouraged his actors to ad-lib while he kept the camera rolling. During one interior motel scene, he shot twelve minutes without cutting. Which was fine indoors, but outside, where it was freezing, the actors suffered.

If an actor ad-libs in a two-shot, then the director can cover this when he goes into single shots. But if he moves into single shots and the actor ad-libs, this will cause the other actor to add something new too. With each new ad-lib, the entire camera crew must turn around to catch the new material all over again from single shots; thus, each new ad-lib forces the crew essentially to start all over.

"It was getting ridiculous, covering everything fifty times if we ad-libbed," said Martin. "This

> **"John Candy was one of the best acting partners I've ever worked with. We had great timing with each other."** —Steve Martin

would go on and on and was happening in very different circumstances—like in an outdoor car with the roof burned off. It was literally freezing. I was in a topcoat and John [Candy] a parka.

"All this ad-libbing was making the camera crew swing around us in the camera car again and again [to cover the shots]. Candy and I finally agreed not to ad-lib anymore."

Soon the production was two weeks over schedule, with many days stretching into

"We actually lived the plot of the movie. As we would shoot, we were hopping trains, planes, and automobiles, trying to find snow." —Steve Martin

Above: John Candy, Steve Martin, and John Hughes on the set of *Planes, Trains and Automobiles* in 1987.

fourteen-hours. It was intense and John was generally grumpy. But he knew he was getting gold.

Indeed, while only a modest hit at the time, *Planes* became one of John's most treasured films. It also became an influential riff on buddy movies. Many fans and critics hoped that John Hughes had turned a corner, that he would now be making adult comedies.

On the surface, the two Johns' first proper collaboration, *Planes, Trains and Automobiles* (1987),

fits neatly into a cinematic subgenre one might call the comedy of aggravated frustration. Among these are Neil Simon's *The Out-of-Towners* (1970), where a simple flight from the Midwest to New York for a job interview turns into a nightmare or Martin Scorsese's *After Hours* (1985), where a young man's impulsive journey to New York's SoHo district to date an erratic woman turns into a series of surreal circumstances.

That's the surface, anyway. In fact, the nightmare John visits on advertising exec Neal Page (Martin) is a regressive journey into adolescence, a comedy of frustration meant to test how thin the veneer of civilization truly is for a man of seeming substance and sophistication.

One could even quote Shakespeare's *Lear*:

As flies to wanton boys are we to the gods.
They kill us for their sport.

John Hughes plays the wanton boy-god, visiting on Neal catastrophes both real and impossible. Taxicabs missed? Yes, of course. Flights cancelled due to bad weather? Happens all the time. But a traveling companion like Del Griffin? And a car that blows up yet still drives as smoke wafts from melted seats? Hmm … never seen that before.

John steers people and vehicles into a mischievous and increasingly surreal landscape that strips his two characters down into nothing but their existential angst. There is a point and a purpose to this odyssey, though, one that John truly treasures—family. Neal wants desperately to get home from New York to spend Thanksgiving in Chicago with his wife and family.

A less worthy goal would reduce the episodic tale to absurdity. So John cherishes the goal but asks at what price: what good is this quest if Neal loses all sense of humanity?

A funny gag, which finds Neal driven to a parking lot miles from the St. Louis airport only to discover his rental car vanished, propels him into a dangerous trek across highways and runways to arrive back at the rental counter, where he subjects its blameless clerk (our old friend Edie McClurg in flame-red hair) to an abusive tirade of "F-bombs." At this point he has lost all sense of himself and others. What would his family think of this Neal Page?

The film undergoes a subtle tonal change

during the famous argument scene in the Braidwood Inn. It is here, in the middle of the night, that Neal reaches his breaking point.

Suffering a meltdown in sheer exasperation with the disgusting hygiene and endless chatter from Candy's blabbermouth character, Neal scathingly derides everything about the man.

Candy's face breaks out in the best expression of hurt from his amazing repertoire of rubbery facial contortions. He then offers up a pitch-perfect defense of his aggressive bonhomie:

"You want to hurt me? Go right ahead if it makes you feel any better. I'm an easy target. Yeah, you're right: I talk too much. I also listen

Above: *Planes, Trains and Automobiles* became the buddy-comedy model for many future films and directors.

Above: Steve Martin gets a rather big surprise in *Planes, Trains and Automobiles*.

Ring division, is a piece of work.

What might go unnoticed is that Del is also a facilitator. Thanks to his connections as a traveling salesman, the two travelers get an impossible-to-find motel room, a ride to a train station (albeit in a pick-up's freezing flatbed), and a rental car when Neal strikes out.

He even finds ingenious ways to sell shower curtain rings to raise cash when needed. Neal would not make it home for Thanksgiving, were it not for Del.

Del's childlike approach to life allows him to recast all misfortune as opportunities or events requiring alternative explanations. When a cabbie takes the men on a fare-boosting ride rather than directly to their motel, Del sees this as a local man's pride in his town and its sights. "That's rare these days," he insists.

Planes became the buddy-comedy model for many future directors. The insider/outsider characters played so well by Martin and Candy have come to dominate many of the buddy or "bromance" films of today.

In one sense, the lineage can be traced back to Neil Simon's *The Odd Couple*, where two men off-set one another with deliberately calibrated differences in attitudes, behavior, and personalities. But Simon's men dwell within the same circle of status, class, and outlook. Their superficial differences—one is neurotically neat and the other a filthy slob—are exaggerated to comic effect.

In *Planes*, John sees the disparities as a carry-over from high-school cliques and social order. Their very partnership, however brief and

too much. I could be a cold-hearted cynic like you. But I don't want to hurt people's feelings. You can think what you like about me. I'm not changing. I like me. My wife likes me. My customers like me. 'Cause I'm the real article—what you see is what you get."

John wisely has Neal saying nothing in response. His face, crushed by the awful truth in Del's comments, says all that needs saying. And Hughes has given a serious context to Candy's clowning.

Del is sentimentalized, to be sure, but not before loading on his shoulders about as many unredeeming characteristics as Hughes can dream up. From his bizarre manner of clearing his nasal passages and chain-smoking to his atrocious personal habits in motel rooms and layers of mismatched clothes, Del Griffith, Director of Sales, American Light and Fixture, Shower Curtain

circumstantial, is an affront to the insider's sense of himself. For the anal and arrogant Neal sees himself as the natural enemy of the obese and uninhibited Del.

To apologize for the first of the many wrongs committed by Del (in Neal's mind), Del offers to buy Neal a beer and hot dog. Refused, he tries again for simply a hot dog. Neal's retort—that he cares about what he puts in his body—is meant to rebut Del's entire lower-middle-class, slovenly, careless existence.

What makes *Planes* dramatically different—and in many ways dramatically better—than *The Odd Couple* is the emphasis John places on empathy. These two are forced to put themselves in the other's shoes time and again. Del's upbraiding of Neal in that cramped motel room brings out the humanity in both men: one is genuinely hurt and chastised—but unwilling to change his sunny behavior—while the other is acutely embarrassed and remorseful.

The travails hurled at these travelers are skillfully engineered comedy. In probably its most famous piece of slapstick, Del and Neal awaken in that same motel room, snuggled in sleep much too closely for two heterosexuals. Bad enough that an awakening Neal has to ask why Del just kissed him. But then Del has to ask Neal why he's holding one of his hands. Then Neal asks where his other hand is. Between two pillows, comes the reply.

"Those aren't pillows," Neal explains.

The men leap from the bed, shrieking in terror. They continue to shout and jump about, waving now unclean hands, and turning the conversation to last week's Bears game, the most masculine subject that comes to mind.

There is even a great gag John doesn't even bother showing us; instead, he lets us see it in our minds. Del sets their shared mattress to vibrate while Neal is in the bathroom. A while later, Neal, clearly uncomfortable in beer-soaked bedclothes, grumbles to Del, "You should have known what would happen when you left a six-pack on a vibrating mattress."

Beyond the superior comedy, though, John is looking at a harder truth. These men, the slob and the snob, are troubled souls. The outsider lives a life of despair. The ending reveals what many will have already guessed: Del's wife has been dead for some time and his casual remark that he hasn't been home in years means exactly that—he has no home.

So the garrulousness and sunny optimism take on a tragic aspect. This is not a bumpkin seriously misunderstanding the chaos he moves through, but rather a man who chooses to ignore these slings and arrows while laughing at outrageous fortune.

Meanwhile, Neal's smug self-satisfaction has a nastiness that a lesser comic actor than Steve Martin might have made unbearable. His reactions, not only to Candy but to all the misfortune he suffers, is the stuff of classic comedy, an extension of every wince, look of horror, and double-take performed in filmed comedy from the silent era onward.

At a deeper level, Neal's frustrations are with himself. The occasional cuts to his Chicago-area home, when Neal calls to relay his latest travel disaster, see a family essentially growing up without a father. His wife finds the travel delays slightly suspicious, and the kids' Thanksgiving pageant must go on without dad present. Neal realizes something is wrong but can't quite figure out what it is. In many ways, Neal is a lonelier person than Del.

THE GREAT OUTDOORS

"Isn't it illegal to drive with a bear on your hood?"

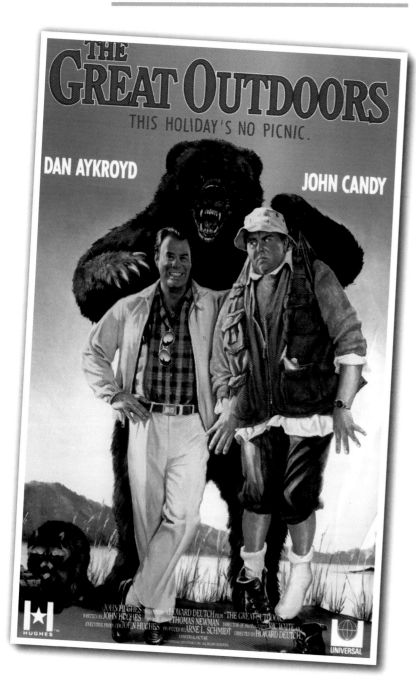

Above: Promotional poster for *The Great Outdoors* (1988).

Filming for *The Great Outdoors* began in the fall of 1987 in Bass Lake, California, doubling for Pechoggin, Wisconsin. The remainder of the shoot, mostly interiors, happened back at the Universal lot, where a 1,400-pound Kodiak grizzly bear named Bart awaited cast and crew. Things got off on the wrong foot and, truthfully, the production never found its right foot. For one thing, director Howie Deutch felt himself miscast.

"It was a broad comedy and that's not me," said Deutch. "But I did it. I didn't feel I was the right guy and don't think I did a good job."

Also, in a repeat of *Some Kind of Wonderful*, Deutch immediately had a falling out with his lead actor. Candy arrived on the set in a big beard that completely covered up his face. As usual, Hughes avoided any confrontation—especially with his favorite actor—and Deutch had to insist on a shave.

"So Candy was very upset," recalled Deutch. " 'This is my character, an outdoor guy,' he kept saying, and I kept saying, 'I can't see your face.' He shaved but it was a black spot on my soul, and that's how we started the movie."

In *The Great Outdoors* (1988), John tries to repeat the *Planes* formula of pairing two seemingly incompatible males in a nightmare adventure. Then he throws in some elements from the *Vacation* series, where all family holidays wind up in disaster.

Unlike with Steve Martin, whose cerebral and physical slapstick meshed so beautifully with Candy's improvisational techniques, Candy never finds a rhythm with his new mate. What makes this strange is that both he and Dan Aykroyd shared a mutual background with Toronto's Second City. Yet their comic teaming in *The Great Outdoors* is oil-and-water right from the start.

Unlike *Planes*, the characters are poorly

Above: Tensions rising between Chet Ripley (John Candy) and Roman Craig (Dan Aykroyd) in *The Great Outdoors*.

defined and John never achieves the mutual empathy that made the earlier film such a triumph. What's at stake is never clear, and the comedy is routine to the point of utter predictability.

Candy plays a Chicago husband and father, Chet Ripley, who wants to get away with his wife (Stephanie Faracy) and two boys for a relaxing week in the north woods of Wisconsin.

The plan is abruptly interrupted by the surprise appearance of his annoying brother-in-law, Roman Craig (Ayrkoyd), along with his wife (Annette Bening in her first movie role) and twin daughters. Why they crash the Ripleys' vacation retreat remains ambiguous until the very end—why does no one at least ask?—nor is the reason why Chet and Roman are at loggerheads the entire time explained.

Without invitation, Roman and the family move into the Ripleys' large log cabin by the lake, where everyone tries to coexist with the wildlife—only the wildlife fails to cooperate. So the episodic script breaks down into human entanglements with leeches, a bat, bears, and a colony of raccoons. Only the latter achieves solid comedy, as John supplies them with subtitles so they might discuss ways to bedevil the tenderfoot tourists.

There's choppiness, too, in the movie that may reflect changes on the set and panic in the editing room. (John wanted to recut the entire movie when the preview tested so poorly, but Universal ran out of time for the summer release.)

Above: John Candy in New York City on March 10, 1990. Candy's father had died at age thirty-five from heart disease.

Vinegar, then in early pre-production. Deutch's fiancée—he and Lea Thompson had fallen in love after *Some Kind of Wonderful*—rebelled against his doing back-to-back productions, fearing he might have a heart attack.

"I said okay and didn't do it," said Deutch. "I also wanted to establish myself, my own person, instead of being his [Hughes's] director. The film never got made and John and I didn't talk again for several years."

If *The Great Outdoors* lacked for good gags and dialogue, John more than made up for it in his next collaboration with Candy, *Uncle Buck*. With John returning to the director's chair, gags not only were built with craft, but one gag led to another and another. His dialogue was never sharper, and age was no handicap as Macaulay Culkin, then eight years old and making his first film with John, got in great zingers.

The production was the one time John Hughes became upset with his fellow John. Candy arrived on the set one morning much the worse for wear after a night of heavy partying. This movie was entirely on Candy's shoulders, so John was extremely irritated that his star clearly had had little or no sleep.

"On the flip side," noted Crane, "I never saw John Candy miss a day of work. He could go all night with his buddies, party away, but report on set next morning, 6:30 for makeup, knowing all his lines for the day. No delays, not a minute missed because of his activities. John Hughes could tell John Candy had been up all night. Yet he went through the whole day and did all the scenes."

By now Candy did not look healthy. Carrying some 330 pounds on his 6-foot-3 frame—and often smoking a pack of cigarettes a day—Candy was tempting fate. His father, Sidney, a Toronto

The film ends with Candy being chased by a Kodiak grizzly. Bears have been menacing humans in outdoors movies at least since Chaplin's *The Gold Rush* (1925). For that matter, leeches and bats have made their cameos down through the years. But John finds no new angle or gag for any of this. For someone as meticulous in his constructions of gags and funny dialogue, *The Great Outdoors* is shockingly banal, perhaps a precursor of his lazy comedies to come in the 1990s.

Hughes and Deutch fell out after *The Great Outdoors*. Not only was John unhappy with the final film, but Deutch pulled out of *Oil and*

car salesman, had died of heart disease at the age of thirty-five.

He feigned concern with his weight but it was mostly for show. Steve Martin remembered when, on the first week in a hotel on *Planes*, considerable exercise equipment was moved into Candy's suite.

"I don't think he ever touched it—that was a dream," said Martin.

About his weight, "no one could tell him anything or offer advice," said Crane. "That was not his path. He wasn't going to listen to anybody."

The only time Candy lost weight was for a role. When he was cast in *Brewster's Millions* (1985), he was to play a baseball catcher, so he had to lose weight and he did. He checked into the Pritikin Center in Santa Monica for a month in April 1984.

"He was serious about it for a movie," Crane remarked. "But that was the last time I ever saw him be serious about it."

Uncle Buck started filming January 4, 1989, in a vacated high school in Northfield that became a production facility.

UNCLE BUCK

"If my whole family moved away from me, I'd have a heart attack too."

John designs two of his very best comic characters for this film and throws them into the ring as ardent foes.

In this corner, at age forty and with more distressing personal habits than a grown man should be allowed, is Candy's Buck Russell. He loves to gamble, hates to work, and has successfully avoided marriage to long-suffering girlfriend Chanice Kobolowski (a pert Amy Madigan) for eight years.

In the other corner, at age fifteen and with a darker world view than any teen should be allowed, is his niece Tia Russell (Jean Louisa Kelly). She hates her life and takes a dim view of men in general—her uncle in particular.

"I'm stunned I'm related to you," she tells him.

Witnessing this bout with more than a casual interest are Tia's much younger siblings, Maizy and Miles (Gaby Hoffman and Culkin). They show affection and even admiration for both parties, but probably lean toward Uncle Buck's corner.

Above: Promotional poster for everyone's favorite uncle in 1989.

Right: Some domestic problems can be solved with the right tool, as demonstrated by Uncle Buck (John Candy)

John gets the two combatants into the ring through an emergency-babysitting chore. Buck's estranged brother must accompany his wife out of town after her father suffers a heart attack. Not that either parent trusts Buck with the kids. There is simply no other choice as they hurriedly board a plane for Indianapolis.

Uncle Buck is nobody's fool. He may play it that way—it never hurts if an adversary underestimates a gambler—but he is shrewd and self-aware. What makes him a worthy adversary for Tia is that, after only a brief exposure to her fifteen-year-old pouts, sarcasm, and life issues, he's on to her. He knows exactly how to play her: threats work best.

Taking the responsibility of looking after his brother's kids seriously, he insists on picking Tia up from school in the afternoon. When she refuses, he casually mentions that he might then escort

her to class the following morning in his bathrobe and pajamas. She decides to cooperate.

Buck does fail to anticipate Tia's dirty tactics in fighting back. Learning of the unstable Buck/Chanice relationship, Tia sees to it that Chanice gets the wrong impression about Buck's friendship with a divorcée across the street, one Marcie Dahlgren-Frost (Laurie Metcalf), who in one of the script's wittier lines says, "I never bothered to lose the Frost."

Buck has no problem charming his much younger charges. Maizy and Miles instantly see him as one of their own. He gets the younger point of view. Which can mean inventing unique ways to make huge pancakes for Miles's birthday—a snow shovel does the trick—or, when the drying machine malfunctions, flinging clothes into microwaves or onto ceiling fans.

This can also involve explaining to Tia why he understands all too well the objectives of her scruffy, predatory boyfriend Bug (Jay Underwood): the objectives were the same when Buck was Bug's age and he was "zooming the girls like you."

Yes, he remembers.

Only her parents don't. Like nearly all parents in Hughes World, they long ago lost touch with their younger selves. Buck, with his inner child forever linked to adult vices, never has. So for once, John gives audiences a savvy adult: he's one, if not three, steps ahead of the kids.

This includes suggesting to the younger ones that his connections at a local crime lab can determine whether or not they actually used their toothbrushes for the purpose intended. At this exact moment we hear a distant police siren. Maizy and Miles eye one another in alarm. (Yep, they're just young enough to buy that.) Later, Buck asks Bug if he is aware of what's involved in "a ritual killing."

That crazy uncle stuff works magic.

The film is chock-a-block with great gags. When he wanted to, John could build gags carefully, piece by piece, so each step gets funnier. Early in the movie, he introduces the concept that some words uttered by the Russell offspring are acceptable, while others are not. This begins with a conversation between Maizy and her very crabby older sister over whether "crap" is acceptable.

Tia insists she has confused this word with "shit." Maizy agrees she has indeed made that mistake. Moments later, Tia says, "Shit!"

"I'm telling on that one," responds Maizy.

"Shit your face," retorts her exasperated older sister. Cue Miles's entrance. In his interaction with Tia he utters a "God damn it" that no one even notices.

The very idea that the Russell children must deliberate over the correct vernacular, out of earshot of the parents, of course, while using the very words that are forbidden is in itself amusing enough. Not enough for John, however.

Later, another word comes up for debate. Miles says "balls" in his mother's presence. She rules this unacceptable. Miles reasons there must be an alternative word to convey his meaning. Now, a less sagacious comedy writer would insist upon finding that alternative word immediately, while the question hangs in the air. Not John. He waits for a few beats as Miles exits his parents' bedroom. It comes to him. "Nuts!" he exclaims, and snaps his fingers in triumph.

Like all good comedy writers, John rewards his audiences for paying close attention.

Uncle Buck is John's first outing with the amazing child star Culkin, prior to their mutual gold strike of *Home Alone*. John had enough confidence in his young actor to let him go toe-to-toe with Candy in Miles's straight-faced interrogation of his babysitter. This was known on the set as "the *Dragnet* scene."

"I don't know how many feet of film was shot on that scene, but John Hughes would throw out a tweak and keep the camera running, redo lines, or add new ones," recalled Crane.

The end result goes like this:

"Where do you live?" demands Miles.

"In the city," replies Buck.

"Do you have a house?"

"Apartment."

"Own or rent?"

"Rent."

"What do you do for a living?"

"Lots of things."

"Where's your office?"

"I don't have one."

"How come?"

"I don't need one."

"Where's your wife?"

"Don't have one."

"How come?"

"It's a long story."

"Have kids?"

"No, I don't."

"How come?"

"It's an even longer story."

"Are you my dad's brother?"

"What's your record for consecutive questions asked?"

"Thirty-eight."

"I'm your dad's brother, all right."

"You have much more hair in your nose than my dad."

"How nice of you to notice."

"I'm a kid. That's my job."

During his first night in the Russell home, Buck knocks an heirloom plate from the mantle that fails to break. Candy picks it up, muses that it must be unbreakable, hits it against a piano and it shatters into pieces—a perfect delayed joke.

Tia's real issue, of course, is not with her Uncle Buck, but rather her parents. In an unintended moment of candor, she admits, "They don't know my personal life." The family has recently moved from Indianapolis, "where we were perfectly happy," to Chicago, where she has no friends.

Like Sheedy's Allison, she is mostly ignored; her parents' careerism and detachment from their youngsters' lives take a much greater toll on their eldest offspring. This may not have been obvious in Indianapolis, where she did have friends. Now, in the North Shore suburbs, life feels wretched.

The kicker, of course, is that Buck does play close attention. He begins sizing her up the minute she enters the kitchen, the first morning of his stay, and deliberately ignores the breakfast feast he's preparing to go to the coffeemaker and pour a hot *adult* beverage for herself. Soon enough, Buck knows more about Tia than her parents ever will.

Candy, operating solo without a Martin or Aykroyd as side-kick—although Culkin nearly becomes one—takes the film by the scruff of the neck and shakes all the comedy out of it there is to be had. He's a force of nature but plays each scene differently.

Left: In one of the few comic mis-fires in the film, Buck punches out a clown who shows up drunk to a children's party.

With Chanice, he's sweet yet honest. In a classic bit of verbal slapstick, he literally can't get in a word edgewise: trying to explain over the phone about the family emergency, he rarely gets in more than a word or two, maybe only a syllable, before being angrily cut off.

With the two youngest kids he is closest to his real self, always seeing a sunny side to things. He plays off these two extremely talented child actors with smooth aplomb, honoring Miles's brainy decisiveness and opening his heart to Maizy's unvarnished manipulation.

With Tia, the hard-ass approach works best. With Bug, he finds that a hatchet, a large power drill, and duct tape are the best props.

When Tia runs out on him and her promise to look after the kids so he can go to the track to earn enough on a sure-thing bet for next year's rent, he sits in his aging car, forced to make a key decision. Torn in every direction, we can read every thought going through his character's mind—the best thing to do, the right thing to do, the wrong thing, and the sheer desperation of his predicament.

In *Uncle Buck*, John improves on *Mr. Mom*—which was a sort of dress rehearsal for this movie—with many of the same elements, such as an uncooperative washing machine and oversexed female neighbor.

The film has a few sequences that misfire. One comes when Buck punches out a children's clown who shows up drunk. Another has Buck telling off one of John's caricatured academics, an assistant

Right: John Candy exploring his dramatic side as Danny Muldoon in *Only the Lonely* (1991).

principal with a hideous facial wart who rails against Maizy for being a "dreamer" and "silly heart" that doesn't take school seriously enough at age six. The targets are just too big to be funny. This film also acts as a transitional one for John. It's the last one to contain teen angst but, along with *The Great Outdoors*, the first geared toward the family comedies to come with Culkin and other child actors.

The two Johns didn't work together immediately following *Uncle Buck*. But that's not to say they didn't plot more projects during late-night phone conversations and visits to the Hughes house in Lake Forest.

One of the more intriguing ones was *Bartholomew v. Neff*, a comedy about feuding neighbors that John hoped to direct, with Sylvester

Stallone and Candy in the lead roles, in Chicago in the summer of 1991.

The problem was always that of translating those late-night conversations in John's upstairs office in the Lake Forest home, with its great stereo equipment, thousands of music cassettes, bowls of pistachios, and bottomless diet Cokes, into concrete reality.

"Candy once said to me, 'The suits in the high towers will just sap every bit of energy and fun out of a project,' " said Crane. "John Hughes with all his success was going through similar struggles. You get those raw ideas. Then in come the deal-makers, attorneys, studio heads, publicity department, and it all changes from that raw, fun meeting or phone call as it starts to be 'developed.' "

Candy did do a couple of cameos as a favor for John. In *Home Alone*, Candy appears to have an extensive role. It was, in fact, shot over a twenty-two-hour stretch. John was on the set for the entire shoot, even though Chris Columbus was the actual director. Candy also flew to Atlanta to shoot for a day at a Target store for *Career Opportunities*.

Each cameo was a "thank you" from John Candy to John Hughes, who had meant so much to his career. In gratitude, Hughes offered Candy one percent of the profits on *Home Alone*.

"No, I did it for you," Candy told John. He performed the role for union scale, thus passing up probably his biggest payday. *Home Alone* became the largest-grossing comedy of all time.

In the 1990s, Candy took mostly supporting work, frequently looking for roles that leaned on the serious side (*JFK*). Yet he said yes to too many comedy scripts of dubious merit.

His career hit a slump due to pictures frequently flopping. *Only the Lonely* (1991) was no different in terms of box-office success, but it did prove how skilled Candy could be as a dramatic actor.

Had it not been for a major scene cut from the final release print of *Planes*, the serious side of Candy may have been on display much earlier. His co-star recalled shooting a scene late in the story where Neal comes back to fetch Del from the train station and bring him to his house for Thanksgiving.

"I was three feet away from him when he went through this scene for three or four different takes," said Martin. "He confesses that since his wife died, every year around the holidays he would latch onto someone, but this time he just couldn't let go. I thought it was a killer scene and he was so brilliant. It's so unfortunate that it got cut."

ONLY THE LONELY

Between directing the first two Home Alone films, Chris Columbus penned a romantic comedy about an Italian-American family where, as often happens, a son lives with the mother, and thus, has a difficult time transitioning to a single life and dating. When Columbus showed it to Hughes, he suggested Candy would be great in the lead.

Columbus agreed and readjusted the screenplay for an Irish-American family. Although

Above: Promotional poster for the Chris Columbus film *Only the Lonely* starring John Candy (1991).

Candy was "concerned how he would be perceived" in a romantic lead, Columbus said the actor agreed to make the leap.

Columbus, who wrote and directed the film for Hughes Entertainment, persuaded screen legend Maureen O'Hara to take on her first movie role in twenty years as Danny's mother, Rose. And for Theresa, a funeral home cosmetologist and Candy's love interest, Columbus cast *The Breakfast Club* alumnus Ally Sheedy.

During filming, O'Hara told Candy more than once that he reminded her of Charles Laughton, and that underneath his clown character was a powerful, complicated actor. He needed to trust in his talent as an actor, she told him, and not always play the clown.

This, of course, was easier said than done. Candy made good money being a clown, and this supported his lifestyle and family. In *Only the Lonely* he was beginning to look for a way to balance his success as a comic while moving into a more dramatic direction, a career trajectory that Bill Murray was ultimately able to do.

"I think he would have figured it out," said Sheedy. "But he ran out of time."

MARCH 4, 1994

It was a Friday, often a slow news day at *The Hollywood Reporter*, since the trade publication didn't publish again until the following Monday. That morning, I fielded my first call of the day from a publicist who gave me startling news.

"I think John Candy died today in Mexico," he said. But he wasn't sure.

Candy was shooting a western comedy called *Wagons East* near Durango. I checked the Associated Press wire and saw nothing.

In fact, Candy's body had been discovered that morning at his residence. Eventually, I did get confirmation and put in a call to John Hughes in Chicago. He returned the call a few hours later. He was, of course, mightily shaken and spoke in an even softer voice than usual when we talked.

"There's a lot of guys driving cement trucks who will be feeling bad tonight," he told me. "He was everybody's Uncle Buck. He played all those little guys that no one gives a damn about. It takes a certain amount of guts to go out in every role and play the fool and bring the kind of voice he did to those seemingly insignificant characters. I don't know who's going to speak for those kind of characters now."

He then said something very interesting: "My dream was to make a movie with him with no script, just a cameraman, a box of film, coffee, and Teamsters. He is the only guy who could ever do that."

Those who knew John understood how much Candy's death hit home. Not only had he lost his muse, but he had lost his best friend in whom he saw a mirror image of himself.

John Hughes never took very good care of himself. Even when he first came to Hollywood, an associate (who asked not to be identified) noted he was "heavy, smoked way too much, and was not a healthy guy. He had a kind of pallor to him. He was always anxious, a pretty tightly wound guy."

So John gleaned a sense of his own mortality from Candy's death. He eventually even gave up smoking.

"Candy was his creative muse and really good friend, so after Candy died that affected him in a very, very profound way," said Rapke. "It was so

easy—John called John Candy and would say, 'I want to do this movie,' and John Candy would say, 'Where do I report?'

"John Candy had absolute faith John would deliver a great script, and John didn't have to go into the world of chasing various different actors [for his lead roles]."

There was one place the two differed, though. Unlike John, who wanted to spend less time on movie sets, Candy loved it.

"He loved the people, loved being on sets, loved being around microphones, cameras, makeup, hair people—he loved it," said Crane.

The refusal to mend his unhealthy ways was deeply ingrained, Crane figured.

"Unfortunately for John Candy, his dad died of a heart attack at thirty-five," said Crane. "I think he always had that over his head. He felt like he wasn't going to be around here long and he was going to pack as much in that time that he could. I thought he did. He packed five lifetimes into forty-three years."

ANTIC COMEDY

Although they had never met, John sent his screenplay for *Christmas Vacation* to Chris Columbus in 1988 through their mutual agent, Jack Rapke, and asked if he wanted to direct the comedy. Columbus, who had helmed the Hughes-like comedy *Adventures in Babysitting* three years earlier, was enthusiastic. "It was funny and I have an affinity for Christmas movies," said Columbus. Columbus had a couple of meetings with Chevy Chase, but he did not get along with the actor. "I was in the awful position of having to back out," he said. "I told John, 'I can't work with this guy.'"

John understood and, three months later, sent two more scripts to Columbus to look at: *Reach the Rock* and *Home Alone*.

John also gave these scripts to another young director, Patrick Read Johnson, but he turned both down (see pages 172–173). Columbus, on the other hand, with his affinity for Christmas movies, immediately accepted John's offer to direct *Home Alone*.

Few in Hollywood thought it was wise to build an entire comedy around a small child. But John felt otherwise, so Warner Bros. agreed to make *Home Alone*.

Then the studio ran the numbers. This is what every studio does: compare a project to similar movies and the box office achieved. The highest

Opposite: John Hughes attending the premiere of *Home Alone 2: Lost in New York* on November 15, 1992. Above: Director Chris Columbus with Macaulay Culkin on the set of *Home Alone* in 1990.

"Few in Hollywood thought it was wise to build an entire comedy around a small child. But John felt otherwise."

total Warners came up with for *Home Alone* was $40 million domestically and overseas.

Since the budget for John's screenplay was $19 million, Warner Bros. insisted John cut his budget by $1 million. John refused. So Warner Bros. promptly put the film into "turnaround," essentially making the film an orphaned project.

Twentieth Century Fox chairman Joe Roth picked the film up quickly enough, and at $19 million. But the decision by Warners to put *Home Alone* into turnaround would have lasting repercussions at that lot.

Home Alone became the highest grossing comedy of all time, at $285.8 million domestic. It is also among the few Hughes films to score with an international audience and, of course, it launched a franchise.

As a consequence of its decision to pass on the top-grossing comedy of all time over an embarrassing $1 million, Warner Bros. refused to allow any project to go into turnaround. Until very recently the studio held on to all projects it owned, even if many never got made. This disastrous decision also made the studio reluctant to confront John on his next Warner Bros. project, *Dennis the Menace*, when perhaps it should have. Now working at Fox, John and Columbus set out to gear a comedy starring a child not only toward children, but adults as well.

"I treated it very seriously," said Columbus. "There's a tendency with those types of films to dumb down the film for audiences. We didn't do that. We hired John Williams to do the score."

John wrote the role of Kevin for Macaulay Culkin. However, Columbus auditioned hundreds of boys before agreeing on Culkin. "I realized he was perfect. The camera loved him," said Columbus.

Three weeks before production, Columbus asked if he might take a crack at a rewrite.

"There's a line in *The Godfather II*—'Can a man really lose his family?'—that has stuck with me as a through-line of all the pictures I want to do," said Columbus. "It's applicable to *Harry Potter* or *Mrs. Doubtfire* or *Home Alone*."

So Columbus's rewrite added dialogue and action for the character of Old Man Marley, to emotionally tie up the end of the film, where Kevin sees Marley reunite with his family. Columbus made sure that Marley's level of loneliness was complementary to Kevin's loneliness with his family gone. This gave a slapstick comedy its emotional underpinnings.

HOME ALONE
"I made my family disappear!"

Mack Sennett would have loved the *Home Alone* movies. Charlie Chaplin would have loved them even more.

They harken back to the original American silent comedies, whose primeval principles were formulated by Mack Sennett in his Keystone films, beginning in 1912.

WHEN KEVIN'S FAMILY LEFT FOR VACATION THEY FORGOT ONE MINOR DETAIL: KEVIN.

BUT DON'T WORRY...

HE COOKS. HE CLEANS.

HE KICKS SOME BUTT.

FROM JOHN HUGHES

HOME ALONe

A FAMILY COMEDY WITHOUT THE FAMILY.

Above: The promotional poster for the highest-grossing comedy at the time, *Home Alone* (1990).

As Walter Kerr pointed out in his classic work *The Silent Clowns*, film comedy began as though comedy had never existed, as though Aristophanes had never written his sophisticated comedies nor Shakespeare and Oscar Wilde found means to evoke emotions with laughs. "The world had become new through the medium of the camera," Kerr remarked.

Amoral characters were at the level of chimpanzees, he observed. Thus, a Sennett comedy would feature "Chaplin, actually in a bearskin, swinging a spiked club and swatting Mack Swain on the head for no other reason than to see what

response the exercise will bring or Chaplin and Marie Dressler conducting their wooing by throwing bricks at each other."

This chimpanzee play took place "before *mores* were heard of, play without cause or consequence or social feeling," Kerr noted.

John, on the other hand, understood the force of a comic-fantasy conscience. As the great silent clowns—Chaplin, Keaton, and Lloyd—discovered, sheer vulgarity was wearisome. Individual personalities had to come into play; mores needed to underline even the crudest violence. A knock on the head or fall down the stairs needed to be rooted in sanity.

In *Home Alone*, Kevin is defending his home and, after all, a man's … er, a boy's home is his castle. Kevin's world is post-Sennett. Not a chimpanzee but a boy no one will listen to, not his parents, not his horrible older brother Buzz, and not the villains.

Kevin's world is Chaplinesque, meaning it belongs to the character Chaplin invented after leaving Keystone. From his very first films, Kerr noted, Chaplin "adjusted the rest of the universe to his merely reflexive needs … Chaplin made it malleable, made it suit his conveniences even when that convenience was most temporary and inconsequential. A man must be comfortable."

Kerr went on to point out that Chaplin appealed directly to his audience, that he wished to communicate with his audience in the first person and to belong to its world, not that of the other characters.

Thus, Kevin, hiding in fright under his bed, abruptly asserts: "Only a wimp would be hiding under the bed. I can't be a wimp. I'm the man of the house!" And just like that, he scrambles out from under the bed.

"*Home Alone* became the highest grossing comedy of all time, at $285.8 million domestic."

Although Kevin's actions are entirely implausible, he asks us to embrace the emotional truth that this is how things should happen, even if they never do.

Even the sound in the *Home Alone* movies harkens back to the off-stage effects created live for silent comedies. We remember Culkin's shrieks with his hands slapped to his cheeks in that iconic, wide-eyed pose (which he tried out a few times in *Uncle Buck*). We remember Joe Pesci's mumbled curses that never quite make it into actual words. The sounds of smacks and thuds echo still in the mind. Who remembers any dialogue in these pitched battles?

At a very basic level, *Home Alone* is a comic version of Sam Peckinpah's bloody action-melodrama of revenge and self-defense, *Straw Dogs* (a film that John actually loathed). In each, a homeowner must defend his domain from criminal invasion using only his brains and household appliances. In *Home Alone*, however, the homeowner is eight years old and we're meant to laugh, not gasp.

It was an impressive leap of faith to write a screenplay for an actor who would not turn ten until after production. John's faith was rewarded with one of the best adolescent performances in film history, one that would establish Culkin as a major star, earning him $8 million on his last two films as an adolescent, the highest ever paid to a child actor.

The story was simple enough: A child is left behind by a family frantic to catch a plane to Paris

Right: Macaulay Culkin (Kevin) and Daniel Stern (Marv Merchants) finally meet eye to eye in *Home Alone*.

Above: Joe Pesci and Daniel Stern as the Wet Bandits in *Home Alone*.

for a Christmas holiday. He must then defend the family house against a pair of burglars, albeit comically hapless ones.

From the opening bell, John begins planting set-ups, story points, and weapons he will pay off later in the climactic battle between young Kevin and his adult nemeses. Even as he does so, John just as carefully starts planting the film's subtext—which is the real meaning of family. This is a familiar driving force in the Hughes World.

The movie begins in uproar as the McCallister family chaotically prepares for an invasion of France unequaled since the Normandy landing. As all the frantic dialogue from a dozen or so characters flies, two characters are largely ignored. One is an apparent policeman standing in the foyer. He is, in fact, one of the two burglars casing the joint in disguise, gleaning intelligence about the departure date and alarm system.

John mischievously calls him Harry Lime, the name of Orson Welles's evil black-market operator in *The Third Man*. He is played by an Oscar winner, Joe Pesci, more normally associated with brutal characters in Martin Scorsese gangster movies.

"Joe in *GoodFellas* always makes me laugh," said Columbus. "He has that sense of comedy in dark places. He really wanted to do the film."

The other ignored figure is Kevin McCallister (Culkin), the youngest child, snubbed by his parents and denigrated by family members.

It's bad enough that his parents (Catherine O'Hara and John Heard) ignore him. But listen to what's said to our Kevin by other family members: "You're completely helpless." "You are what the French call *les incompetents*." "Kevin, you're a disease."

And this from Uncle Frank: "Look what you did, you little jerk!"

"Why do I always get treated like scum?" Kevin asks.

His mom replies: "Maybe you should ask Santa for a new family." Then, in a strong foreshadowing, she remarks moments later: "You'd feel pretty sad if you woke up tomorrow and you didn't have a family."

Which is exactly what happens.

Consigned to a third-floor attic for fighting with older brother Buzz (Devin Ratray)—the worst older brother on film since Chet in *Weird*

Above and below: Kevin (Macaulay Culkin) finding adult behavior a bit ridiculous in *Home Alone*.

easily agitated Harry and the thoroughly stupid Marv (a marvelous bit of clowning by Daniel Stern). The latter hopes the media will dub them "the Wet Bandits" due to his criminal signature: he leaves on water taps in burgled houses.

Kevin initially rebuffs the Wet Bandits through sly subterfuge: using music, mannequins, a Michael Jordan cutout, and puppetry, Kevin "throws" a nighttime party that makes the house, from outside, look occupied by dozens of revelers. But the burglars won't be deterred.

"When those guys come again, I'll be ready," Kevin tells himself.

The film climaxes with an orgy of tricks and booby traps that leave the robbers praying the police will soon arrive. Each gag tops the preceding one as John carefully escalates the "violence," using all the props planted earlier—from the VCR's playback of the gangster movie and Buzz's tarantula spider to a rifle spotted in the first act and, yes, those firecrackers.

Science—Kevin awakens the next day to discover that, in their haste to make the plane at O'Hare, children's heads were miscounted and his family left without him. His mother only remembers after the plane reaches cruising altitude.

Kevin assesses his situation, and then decides he feels entirely comfortable with it. He eats ice cream in the morning, orders pizza, finds nifty firecrackers (more weapons, of course), watches a forbidden gangster movie, and generally enjoys that home-alone feeling. He even pages through his brother's *Playboy* but isn't charmed. ("No clothes on anybody—sickening!")

No parents or siblings are yelling at him and he has the house to himself. Then he grows aware of the burglars' plans.

We, of course, have been made aware of this pair much earlier—the prickly,

None of this is done with anything approaching realism. Pesci's head catches fire at one point, and at another, Stern puts his bare feet down on a nasty spike. BB gun shots hit the crotch and forehead. The burglars do not just slip on ice or toys, they somersault over them. Everyone screams, but there's never a drop of blood.

Critics at the time fussed and fumed over the film's plausibility, failing to recognize that, unlike previous Hughes comedies that pushed the boundaries of reality without completely violating them, *Home Alone* conjured an unreal, Chaplinesque world.

The things Kevin does to save the family home turn out to be, in fact, the very things every parent tells his kid not to do: leave toys on the floor, insult grown-ups, play with guns or firecrackers.

Meanwhile, John stays busy on the sub-textual level. Our little Kevin walks down a cold, dark residential street and stares through windows at families celebrating Christmas together. He then visits a church and encounters Old Man Marley (Roberts Blossom) who, he has been assured by Buzz, is a mass murderer.

Instead, the man turns out to be a father estranged from his only son. Kevin suggests he call his son. The son may refuse to talk, but the old man will at least have overcome his fear of calling him and can stop worrying about the estrangement.

Can a man really lose his family?

The movie opened before Thanksgiving and stayed in cinemas past Easter. The film that no one other than John thought should be made was the number-one domestic-box-office film of 1990. Worldwide gross was a staggering $478 million.

Right: The face that launched adolescent comedies— Macaulay Culkin as Kevin in *Home Alone 2* (1992).

HOME ALONE 2
AND 3
"We did it again!"

In Hollywood, the understood concept behind sequels—a fact of moviemaking much more prevalent now than in John's heyday—is that few are true sequels. Sequels are remakes in disguise, meaning the audience expects essentially the same hit film everyone thrilled to earlier. Any deviation goes unrewarded.

John not only understood this, he made a joke of it when he sat down to write *Home Alone 2: Lost in New York*. He delivered exactly the same movie, other than a change in location and bigger budget. He playfully copied everything but added knowing winks.

"I prefer the sequel to *Home Alone* in some ways. I honestly think it's the better film." —Chris Columbus

The opening is nearly identical: The same characters are chaotically preparing for yet another family Christmas excursion, this time to sunny Florida. Buzz is still being mean to kid brother Kevin, Uncle Frank is still unapologetically foul-mouthed toward his nephew, Kevin's angry reaction to his brother's bullying consigns him to that third floor attic, his dad's habitual lack of preparation regarding electrical travel equipment will cause the family to oversleep their wake-up, and the family will again lose Kevin.

No, not at home, but at O'Hare this time. The twist is that in the airport confusion, Kevin boards a plane bound for New York instead of Florida.

John amuses himself by seeing just how close he can stick to the original, even allowing the Wet Bandits to escape from prison and flee to New York, where Kevin foils their toy-store robbery.

John creates a seemingly scary street elder similar to Old Man Marley to frighten Kevin, only for the kid to realize he shares a kinship with this lonely soul. That would be the homeless Pigeon Lady (played by Oscar-winner Brenda Fricker). And Kevin again makes strategic use of the soundtrack from the same old gangster film.

Of course, the *raison d'être* is once more the painful, slapstick battle of wits between our half-witted burglars and a fully armed Kevin backed by a team of studio prop-and-special-effects masters.

From the simple expedient of throwing bricks off the roof of a building under renovation, he lures the Wet Bandits into his lair to inflict on them with enormous glee such indignities as electrocutions, a staple gun, more slippery surfaces, falling hardware, another head fire for Harry, bags of cement, paint, and glue, an exploding toilet, tumbles through floor holes, and a rolling tool chest that collides with battered bodies.

Columbus admitted seeing stuntmen perform these stunts "was very difficult for me to watch, they're so violent. In *Home Alone 1* and *2* stuntmen were flipping on ice or stairs or falling on a car from three stories up and walking away. There was no CGI then. Those stunts were real."

The climax follows the original, with Kevin's advice forever changing the street person's life, followed by a reunion with his family that finds

everyone contrite and realizing they all belong together. Cue the Christmas carols.

So the critics gnashed their teeth, box office went through the roof, and Fox ordered up *Home Alone 3*.

Opening November 20, 1992, the film took in $173.6 million against a $25-million budget. Again, the film proved popular overseas, making $359 million worldwide.

"I prefer the sequel to *Home Alone* in some ways," said Columbus. "I honestly think it's the better film. The purity of the first film is great but when I see the sequel on TV the stunt sequences make me laugh. The scope of film is just bigger visually."

After writing the screenplay for *Home Alone 3*, John turned the direction over to the series' editor, Raja Gosnell. No actors from the first two films remained. A new precocious ninja fighter named Alex Pruitt (Alex D. Linz) was recruited to face off against a group of villains more out of a James Bond movie than the domestic criminals of the earlier movies.

The film may be most memorable for an early appearance by a young Scarlett Johansson, playing Alex's sister Molly, shaking her head in the background while her brother tries to explain his latest-seeming misdeed.

With the series budget creeping up to an estimated $32 million, a national gross under that figure was a clear sign the franchise had run its course. Fans didn't like it and most critics never liked the series.

The National Association of Theater Owners holds an annual convention in Las Vegas early every year. In 1991, in a genuflect to the astonishing box-office performance of *Home Alone*, NATO's ShoWest, as it was then called, honored John as its Producer of the Year.

Opposite page: The promotional poster for *Home Alone 3* featuring an all-new cast. Above: John Hughes with his award for Producer of the Year at NATO's ShoWest convention in 1991.

In retrospect, the award can be seen as a curse. Over the next few years, his management style grew increasingly erratic as he hired and fired directors, quarreled with the suits, and became isolated in the Windy City, keeping his productions as much as he could in the Chicago-area while trying to manage his business interests from two thousand miles away.

The 90s saw a significant change in the subject matter in a John Hughes film or, to put it another way, changes in the ages and even species of John's protagonists. From Macaulay Culkin, nine years old when he shot *Home Alone*, and Alisan Porter, about the same age at the time of *Curly Sue*, John moved on to *Dennis the Menace*, a first grader, and then to an infant for *Baby's Day Out*.

John began telling journalists, "I've got an embryo thing I'm working on."

Then came the critters: He wrote two dog movies involving a slobbering St. Bernard named *Beethoven*, and a live-action version of Disney's *101 Dalmatians*. His pet project, though, which he was never able to realize, was *The Bee*—a comedy about a battle between a developer and a bee, all told from the bee's point of view.

Many of these made money and, in some cases, especially for John, lots of money. By the middle of April 1991, Rapke and John's lawyer, Jake Bloom, wrapped up a seven-picture, non-exclusive deal at Fox that gave him total creative control after concept approval on pictures with below-the-line budgets of $15 million.

It was, of course, unrealistic to believe all seven films would ever get made. Indeed, by July, Warner Bros.—the studio that would never live down putting the biggest film comedy ever into turnaround—cut a deal for John to write and produce *Dennis the Menace*.

CAREER OPPORTUNITIES AND DUTCH

Career Opportunities (1991) represented no such thing for anyone involved with the ill-conceived project, with the possible exception of Jennifer Connelly.

Only twenty-one, but having made an impressive movie debut as the young dancer in Sergio Leone's *Once Upon a Time in America* (1984), Connelly makes a solid impression in this otherwise desultory comedy, featuring a seriously miscast Frank Whaley and a botched third act.

1991 also saw the release of *Dutch*, released July 19, and *Curly Sue*, John's last directorial effort, released October 25. Neither of these films was likely to lift the cloud of anger and gloom that enveloped him following his Producer of the Year honors.

Dutch, poorly cast and indifferently directed by Australian Peter Faiman (*"Crocodile" Dundee*), is a spiritless affair, sporadically funny yet potentially much funnier had the film not resorted to cartoonish behavior and a surprising amount of crudity.

Ed O'Neill—star of Fox TV's comedy series *Married … with Children*—plays working-class slob Dutch Dooley, who agrees to pick up the snot-nosed brat son of his fiancée from his Southern prep school to bring him home for

Opposite page: Promotional poster for *Career Opportunities* (1991) starring Jennifer Connelly and Frank Whaley. Above: Promotional poster for *Dutch* (1991) starring Ed O'Neill and Ethan Embry.

Thanksgiving. That son (Ethan Embry) wants nothing to do with his divorced mother or her new boyfriend.

O'Neill lacks the slapstick chops to pull off any of the antics John dreams up. He remains a TV actor, mugging and winking at an audience, perfectly acceptable on the small screen but off-putting on the big one.

CURLY SUE

Curly Sue would turn out to be the last film John would ever direct. Yet rather than a valedictory air, the film mostly feels tired, the work of a man who's lost focus.

The movie acts like a comedy but laughs are few. It contains screwball elements from, say, *My*

Man Godfrey (1936). Additionally, in the adult con artist and his little-girl companion in scams, we get hints of Peter Bogdanovich's *Paper Moon* (1973), another Depression-era story that combines the comic with the dramatic. But that film had real bite—and much greater poignancy.

Curly Sue is all too willing to settle for being a tearjerker. A tearjerker with humorous touches, but the center is so mushy-soft, the whole thing falls apart.

James Belushi plays a drifter who travels the roads and rails of America with a little girl, Curly Sue (Alisan Porter)—named not for her hair, but after one of the Three Stooges. They pull cons for

Above: *Curly Sue* (1991) is the last film that John Hughes would direct in his lifetime.

food and shelter, including an "accident" staged so a cynical, high-powered Chicago lawyer (Kelly Lynch) is suckered into thinking she hit Belushi with her car. She takes the two to dinner at a greasy-spoon diner.

Predictably, she falls for the little girl, becomes attracted to the man, and soon changes her whole attitude toward life—and dumps her smarmy, rich boyfriend.

For all her charm and angelic face, Porter feels like a pawn being played rather than a small human involved in a challenging predicament.

The opportunity did exist here for an incisive yet funny look at what it means for a child to go without shelter or even food, though because she is loved, not feel deprived. John backs away from all of this in favor of not only weak gags, but oldies at that.

John himself recoiled from this film. Five years later, he told syndicated columnist Marilyn Beck that he thought the film was "awful. I did a

Above: Two of a kind—Curly Sue (Alisan Porter) and Bill Dancer (Jim Belushi) in *Curly Sue*.

terrible job with it … It didn't even meet my minimum standards, which are pretty darn low."

Little wonder he never directed again. Rapke has this perspective:

"So Chris Columbus does *Home Alone* and it's a giant hit. It eclipses anything John's really done. I don't think if a movie is big you get all accolades, but if it's not you can't hide. You can hide as a writer/producer, but you can't hide as a director [of *Curly Sue*]. I can't say whether he did or did not like the experience [of directing]. But I will say, my own view is that because he didn't get the validation of directing, he just couldn't go back into it and take the criticism."

Then there was the anger, which had reached a molten stage after *Home Alone*.

"You have a guy on tremendous roll. Everything he's doing is golden, certainly in the sweet years I was with him," noted Rapke. "Then everyone says you can't do a movie with a nine-year-old. He does *Home Alone* and it's one of biggest hits ever. He was very angry after *Home Alone* opened and was a phenomenal success. Okay, now he's vindicated. So why is he so angry?

"Years later, I understood that being told 'no' so many times by naysayers and now you're right—sometimes that manifests itself in anger. It's been pent-up this entire time and for the first time you get to show your emotions, and part of those emotions are residual anger."

BEETHOVEN

Beethoven, a Hughes screenplay left behind when he quit Universal, was set up with Nick Castle aboard to direct and Candy to star. But Candy had developed a conflict with another project he

Above: John Candy was the original choice to star in *Beethoven*, but prior commitments prevented him from taking the role.

DENNIS THE MENACE

While John had never adapted someone else's material, comic strips had begun to catch his attention. Even as he came aboard to supervise Warners' live-action version of Hank Ketcham's *Dennis the Menace*, he was mulling over a film version of Johnny Hart's savvy strip *Wizard of Id*. Then, a little over a year later, he signed a deal to write and produce a movie version of Charles Schultz's tremendously popular *Peanuts* strip.

Above: Promotional poster for *Dennis the Menace*, a Hughes film which had a huge budget of $30 million.

couldn't get out of, so production was postponed. Castle moved on and John wound up having little to do with *Beethoven*. Amy Holden Jones (*Mystic Pizza*) rewrote the script and Charles Grodin was cast as the father.

The main comic action centers on the antipathy of the head of the household, Grodin, playing one of his anal-retentive types, for Beethoven. While this huge animal indeed has criminal propensities—any food left out is fair game—he saves the life of the youngest daughter, prevents Grodin from signing away his company to a pair of corporate raiders, and foils a dognapping ring. Clearly, he's the smartest one in this household.

The Ivan Reitman production grossed over $57 million for Universal in 1992 and spawned four sequels, before the steam ran out of the franchise early in the new century.

"It was a love fest. Amazing—John Hughes is taking my notes! When do I wake up?" —Patrick Read Johnson, director *Baby's Day Out*

John's attraction to comics went back to that first writing job, ghostwriting a few strips for *The Berrys*. However, John was initially reluctant to tackle the live-action movie version of *Dennis the Menace*.

John worried about comparisons being made to *Home Alone*. Then, too, he disliked the TV series based on the comic strip in the 1960s, which starred Jay North.

He agreed to meet Ketcham in June 1991 at his Northern California home in Monterey. In their discussions, he came to see the essential differences between his Kevin and Ketcham's Dennis. Kevin was a nine-year-old behaving in what he thinks to be an adult fashion. Dennis is six and takes a childish view of the world.

Then Ketcham let him in on a secret: if Mr. Wilson didn't have Dennis to worry about, he would have nothing to live for.

There remained the TV show, but John saw his way around that. He would cast someone the right age. He needed a real five- or six-year-old. Sifting through forty-two years of the daily comic strips Ketcham wrote and drew, John found no real story to hang his film on. Instead, he encountered incidents and observations about family life from the point of view of a child. So his screenplay focused on an undeclared war between Dennis, completely oblivious to this conflict, and his next-door neighbor.

After penning the screenplay, John's choice for director stunned many.

Patrick Read Johnson, a twenty-eight-year-old filmmaker and visual-effects guy, had in 1989 made *Spaced Invaders*, a goofy little film, for $1.75 million. Disney's Touchstone Pictures bought the movie, fussed with it a bit, and then released it in 1990 to some acclaim as a homemade sci-fi movie.

It made over $15 million so, with such an amazing return on investment, Johnson created the kind of buzz that made him one of the town's flavors of the month.

Filmmakers including Spielberg wanted to work with Johnson. John took notice and called him in. "I've got a script that's perfect for you," he told Johnson. "It's exactly what you should be doing."

John handed him *Reach the Rock*. It was, Johnson admitted, "one of the most intriguing pieces of material I've read to this day. It showed a side of John Hughes no one had ever seen before or since."

The story takes place on a hot summer night in southern Illinois and concerns a layabout and former high school bad boy, who had never left town, and the girl he loved. She left to become a lawyer in L.A. and has returned for a high-school reunion.

"It was this beautiful character study," said Johnson. "They're adults—no lick of hijinks, grand comedy, stunts, or effects. And nothing in my wheelhouse."

Johnson hesitated for another reason. By now, whether deserved or not, John had acquired a reputation for "ghost-directing" his screenplays, which he produced with others in the director's chair. Johnson knew he possessed a rebellious streak and was terrified that, on his first studio film, he would find himself in a creative conflict with a brilliant, powerful person such as John.

So Johnson passed. Which did not sit well with John.

(Many years later John gave *Reach the Rock* to William Ryan to direct. Ryan, a Hughes assistant who went on to run his Chicago company, had never directed a movie. The 1998 release was a failure. Johnson now believes he should have taken the film.)

Two weeks later, John offered Johnson another film. It was *Home Alone*. Again, a big payday loomed, but everyone told Johnson: "Somebody can sit in the director's chair because the DGA [Directors Guild of America] requires it, but John will direct every step."

"So if it fails, the blame is on me, and if it succeeds, everyone knows it's John's movie," reasoned Johnson.

Again, Johnson passed.

Given Columbus's experience on *Home Alone*, where he made his version of John's screenplay in a collaborative atmosphere, this "everyone" who whispered to Johnson was perhaps misinformed.

Against all odds, John reached out to Johnson again in 1992. John asked to meet him at his Lake Forest house to discuss *Dennis*. Johnson flew into Chicago, was put up at a nearby hotel, and proceeded to have a great meeting at the house. The two men played music, ate bowls of pistachios, and drank diet Cokes.

"We agreed on everything; it was a love fest," recalled Johnson. "John had found an angle into human emotions in the midst of goofy comedy. Mr. Wilson, in the old TV show, was so irascible. But there was a tenderness to John's approach to

Above: They interviewed 20,000 boys before selecting Mason Gamble to star as Dennis Mitchell alongside Mr. Wilson, played by legendary actor Walter Matthau.

that relationship. It was beguiling and caught me."

Walter Matthau came aboard to play Mr. Wilson. For their Dennis, John, Johnson, and the head of John's company, Richard Vane, saw twenty thousand boys. It was partially a publicity stunt, but out of a handful of serious auditions, they narrowed the possibilities down to five.

They pretty much knew they had found the right child when Johnson asked Mason Gamble, age six, if he had any special skills. He answered, "Kung-fu. I'll show you."

He then ran over to Vane and delivered a karate chop to the startled man that nearly knocked him over.

"It was terrifying and funny—just the right combination for Dennis," said Johnson. "No moral compass!"

Two weeks before production in Chicago, John phoned Johnson.

"You've been awful quiet about the script," said John.

"What do you mean?" asked his director.

"Do you have some notes or worries?" John asked. "Anything you'd like me to take a look at for rewrites?"

Johnson admitted he had all kinds of ideas but these were things he assumed they could get to as the film got made.

"Come to the house," suggested John. "We'll stay up all night and go through it page by page."

They talked until 6 a.m. Many of his suggestions concerned visual ideas. For instance, Johnston suggested the train bringing to town the character of Switchblade Sam, the film's villain, might appear like a mystical ghost train that had run on these tracks for a hundred years.

John chain-smoked and made notes on a pad of paper, chuckling over his collaborator's ideas.

"It was a lovefest," recalled Johnson. "Amazing—John Hughes is taking my notes! When do I wake up?"

The next day, as it happened. While scouting locations the following morning, Johnson took a phone call from his agent, Jay Maloney.

"Patrick, what the fuck did you do?" asked a pained Maloney.

"What do you mean?" asked Johnson.

"You've been fired. Pack up your office," Maloney replied. "John said you came up to the house last night and trashed the movie. You said John was a terrible hack writer, wanted the script overhauled and to get rid of great stuff!"

Many years later, Johnson can only shake his head: "Those quotes are antithetical to how I would speak. I was blindsided. When I got back, the production office had my stuff boxed up already."

It was Martha Coolidge and *Some Kind of Wonderful* all over again.

"John didn't feel like Patrick had the right take on *Dennis* so he had to make a change," said a diplomatic Vane. Nick Castle, who was originally going to direct *Beethoven*, came on board to direct *Dennis*.

By the time Johnson was driving through Wyoming, he got a phone call from Maloney with awkward news. Even though his contract was "pay or play," meaning he would get his full salary no matter what, CAA head Mike Ovitz didn't think pressing for the money was going to play out well with John, one of their key clients. So Johnson never got paid for any of his prep work.

Otherwise, the money tap was flowing. With a budget around $30 million, Warner Bros. went out of its way to make amends for its mistake on *Home Alone*. An indoor tennis facility in Chicago was converted into a studio for all the interiors. The film would eventually take over one hundred days to shoot, with little expense spared.

Castle said the $30 million budget and one hundred day shooting schedule were "insane as far as I'm concerned for a little *Dennis the Menace* film."

Plus, "It was the longest script I ever shot. It was like *Gone with the Wind*—John kept adding pages. On his first film back at Warner Bros., he did whatever he wanted. Who was going to say no?"

The 135 scripted pages expanded by another twenty-some by Thanksgiving. So the company needed another month to shoot those pages. "It was a crazy atmosphere. It was okay for me to do what I wanted and take as long as I wanted," said Castle.

For all the rewriting and added pages, John never found the ending he wanted. "He wanted a much bigger deal with the Christopher Lloyd character but couldn't find it," recalled Vane.

Above: John Hughes had reportedly wanted to do more with Sam (Christopher Lloyd), but he was never able to figure out the ending he wanted.

deserved and the booby traps deliberate. We aren't quite sure what we're laughing at in *Dennis.*

The other disquieting element to the family comedy is the film's real menace—a scruffy drifter with bad teeth and hair, who hangs around schoolyards far too often for the comfort of adult viewers.

Lloyd plays Switchblade Sam, a moniker never actually used in the film, as an ominous creature more suitable to a suspense or even horror movie. Castle even frames Sam, when first glimpsed, at an angle with an exaggerated spatial relationship worthy of *The Cabinet of Dr. Caligari.*

There is the strong suggestion at the climatic dual between Dennis and Sam—again, a battle to which Dennis is blithely unaware—that Sam would have willingly slayed the tyke if another catastrophe hadn't befallen him.

Preview audiences certainly objected to one scene involving the malevolent Sam. He uses the boys' tree house as a place to stay and find out where the gold is in Mr. Wilson's house. The film-makers were genuinely surprised by the reaction from mothers: they did not want to see that guy unmonitored with six-year-olds in a tree house!

The scene was cut.

John's suburban obsession with burglars and lethal household objects notwithstanding, the film never finds its comic footing. And like *Christmas Vacation,* the film wastes an unusually fine cast.

Dennis is a well-intentioned kid, whose curiosity and resourcefulness get other people into trouble. The misfortunes Dennis visits on the elderly horticulturalist Mr. Wilson range from the destruction of the front of his dentures—for which he substitutes two pieces of Chiclets gum—to unwitting booby traps in the Wilson household that cause the poor man to do pratfalls not unlike the Wet Bandits in *Home Alone.*

Indeed, one of the major drawbacks to *Dennis the Menace* is that so much humor must derive from the misfortunes of an elderly man caused by a poorly supervised child. In *Home Alone,* the stunts were funnier because the misfortunes were

Along with Matthau and Lloyd, John was able to recruit British stage and screen legend Joan Plowright as Martha Wilson, who never seems to encounter the same problems with Dennis as her grumpy husband. Paul Winfield, no less, has a purposeless role as town chief of police and Lea Thompson from *Some Kind of Wonderful* plays Dennis's mom—a mom who, in Hughes tradition, must be virtually absent.

Strangely, young Gamble doesn't live up to his one-in-twenty-thousand billing. He's cute and delivers his lines smartly but lacks the spark of Culkin.

Warners' high hopes for the film were dashed, with a box-office domestic gross of $51 million. Looking for *Home Alone* numbers and a possible franchise, Warner Bros. was keenly disappointed.

John had already moved on. His goal, he told Vane, was to have one movie in post-production, one in prep, and another shooting. If one didn't work, he reasoned, on the next one he would find a way to improve.

John mentioned to Castle that he was tinkering with the idea of getting remake rights to the 50s stage and screen musical *Damn Yankees*. Another musical project John contemplated was *The Pajama Game*.

It made perfect sense for John to consider musicals. Few film directors then had a better musical sense than he did. His soundtracks percolated with brilliant juxtapositions of music cues and action.

John did complete a script for *Damn Yankees* in 1993, but the project was abandoned. He never did a musical.

John visited cartoonist Charles Schultz at his Santa Rosa home in Northern California to discuss a possible adaptation of *Peanuts*. As a kid, John would trace the characters in Schultz's strip, which he absolutely loved.

The project was announced in November 1992.

"It's been a long time since I've jumped up and down and ran around the house with joy," Hughes told me. "It's an honor to work with this material."

He started reading every strip Schultz ever wrote. Twenty years into his body of work, John had not found one that wasn't funny and a carefully observed statement about life in four panels. As a fellow writer, he may have found that intimidating. Or perhaps the challenge of an entire cast of children was even more daunting. Whatever the case, this project too never went anywhere.

THE BEE

Even more demanding technically and creatively was a project that came to obsess John during this time. It was called *The Bee*. It no doubt was inspired by John's passionate involvement in the development of Redwing Farms, where he worked to reforest the land and turn it into a proper English farm.

John's story concerns a developer who plans to turn a farmland into a massive housing development. But a bee on that property intervenes. The flying insect "through plausible circumstances," in John's words, "ends up in this guy's house and, putting two and two together, sets things in motion so that man can bring about his own destruction."

The film was conceived of as live action, though, not a cartoon. In the days before computer-generated imagery, this proved a nearly insurmountable challenge, for much the film was to take place from the bee's point of view.

Industrial Light & Magic worked on creating a mechanical bee. Meanwhile, bee "actors" were being bred under the guidance of a University of California, Davis bee expert. John also experimented with pheromones, a secreted chemical that can entice bees to land wherever a director wants them to.

The screenplay contained a scant ten pages of actual dialogue, so a stellar comic performer with considerable physical gifts was needed. Steve Martin was considered for a while.

The project was originally developed at Fox under John's production deal, but in early 1993, Fox more than willingly let it fly off to Warner Bros.

"He was passionate about *The Bee* but we could never get it financed," said Rapke. "It was a concept. How big was the bee? Do we see the bee? Does it have human qualities? It was a Tex Avery cartoon as a one hundred minute film."

Alan Riche, who had joined Hughes Entertainment as president and COO in October 1992, called it a film "way ahead of its time. It was a very interesting, inventive idea but needed CGI. It couldn't be done then."

Vane recalled "tests with miniature helicopters with tiny cameras to get a sense of the bee's point of view. Danny Stern was thinking of directing it. But it's not an easy movie to make with cuts of the bee flying and then its point of view and all these shots with no dialogue."

When John finally did settle on his next project, it may have been, as several people close to him suspected, under the indirect influence of Joel Silver, his *Weird Science* producer.

Silver had become one of Warner Bros.' star producers, rolling the dice on big, expensive action movies—the *Lethal Weapon* and *Die Hard* series were among his films—while strutting about the Burbank lot as a larger-than-life movie mogul.

Above: John Hughes talking with Joel Silver on the set of *Weird Science* back in 1985.

The massive success of *Home Alone* had inspired John to want to play in a bigger sandbox. Abandoning Booth Tarkington Jr. as his model, John now wanted to be a Midwestern Joel Silver; he wanted to roll the dice at $50 million, even though on his best movies the budgets were modest.

So, as part of his multi-picture deal at Fox, he presented the studios' hierarchy with an epic movie. It was an epic movie starring a baby.

9

ENFANT TERRIBLE

It came close to being an unmakeable film. Its star would be an infant still in the crawling stage. No major stars would be willing to play second fiddle to a baby, so forget about the marquee—John Hughes was the only name to sell. Such a project would challenge studio technology and set design, too, not to mention "baby wranglers" and safety issues on a movie totally reliant on the reactions of an actor who most definitely would not take direction.

John's *Baby's Day Out* pushed the limits of what an audience—especially parents—will accept concerning children in jeopardy, even for a comedy. A kidnapping is every parent's nightmare. But when the toddler escapes the clutches of his abductors and courts disaster at every turn, Fox executives had to wonder if any of this was actually funny, even in a cheerful fiction where clearly no harm would come to this indestructible infant.

But the script came from a man who was making the studio a fortune with another comedy involving a child that all the smart guys thought was ridiculous.

A greater shock was yet to come.

Opposite and above: One of John Hughes' most ambitious projects, *Baby's Day Out*, faced challenge after challenge, from safety issues and casting to audience approval.

BABY'S DAY OUT

"This isn't funny anymore!"

A year after his firing, Johnson was picking up the pieces in his life. Warner Bros. had given him an office and he was hard at work on several projects. Indeed, he had even found a considerable silver lining to his John Hughes experience: he'd married a woman who had interviewed for a crew position on *Dennis*.

One morning, around 3 a.m., as he slept beside his pregnant wife, the phone rang.

NO BIB. NO CRIB. NO PROBLEM.

BABY'S DAY OUT

In those days in the film business, a phone call at that hour could only mean one thing: that John Hughes was on the line.

He picked up the phone and muttered a drowsy hello.

"Patrick?" asked a recognizable voice.

"What?" he answered.

"Hughes."

Patrick couldn't think of any reply to that, so he went with, "Yes?"

"First question," said John. "Do you hate me?"

"What? John, I don't hate anyone. I don't understand you."

"I know I fucked up. I fired all the wrong people. Did you see the movie?"

"Yeah."

"What did you think?"

Three o'clock in the morning is not a time for carefully chosen words so Johnson answered, "Awful."

"You're right," said John. "I just got caught up in thinking you didn't like it. People reporting to me wanted to change and I thought you didn't like me."

"Wait, slow down," said Johnson, now fully awake and not much interested in the direction of the conversation. "I've got a pregnant wife next to me and I don't understand. If you want to confess your sins to me I'm not the guy."

"No, I've got a movie for us," said John.

"Whoa."

"No, this time for real. We're doing it."

At this point, a desperate sadness overcame Johnson. While he hadn't thought about it until this moment, he knew that if John didn't do

Left: Promotional poster for *Baby's Day Out* (1994), starring Adam Robert Morton and Jacob Joseph Worton as Baby Bink. Opposite page: Director Patrick Read Johnson on the set of *Baby's Day Out*.

something amazing right then, he would be devastated. Clearly, he would never speak to John again and never get to work with this guy—a genius, yes, but perhaps a crazy one.

"John," said Johnson, "whatever you say next, I'm pay or play. For real, 100 percent, or I'm hanging up."

"Okay," said John.

Many years later, Johnson would explain what happened next.

"He said three words that terrified me because I knew of the script—*Baby's Day Out*. It was legendary. It was this unmakeable, giant, epic movie starring a baby."

John said Johnson should go to his office at Fox the following day and read the script.

"If you like it, we're done!" John told him.

Dutifully, Johnson went to the Fox studio office John never used, sat in John's chair behind a desk he never used, and read the screenplay. He made sure to put away the pencil and yellow legal pad carefully laid out for him beside the script, lest the female assistant monitoring him in the outer office report back to John that he had made notes about his screenplay.

"Great script. It was so much fun to read," said Johnson as he made his way past the assistant after reading it.

A few days later, Johnson found himself summoned to an urgent meeting in the executive suites at Fox attended by Peter Chernin, Rupert Murdoch's right-hand man, Tom Jacobson, and other suits.

"They looked terrified," said Johnson. "They were on the edge of their sets. 'So you're going to direct *Baby's Day Out*?' 'Apparently,' I said.

"They couldn't believe John Hughes would give this movie to a kid who had done *Spaced Invaders*,

"He [John Hughes] said three words that terrified me because I knew of the script—*Baby's Day Out* . . . It was this unmakeable, giant, epic movie starring a baby." —Patrick Read Johnson

homemade in a warehouse in North Hollywood. They were mortified. 'What tone do you see?' 'How will you cast it?' They were beside themselves with fear. John was making them hire me to do this movie they were already terrified of!"

He might have added: and with a director John had fired the year before.

Johnson found himself boarding a train nearly in full motion. Production designer Doug Kramer was already six weeks into designing and building

Right: Baby Bink finds a new friend in *Baby's Day Out*.

sets in Chicago. John's two guys, Richard Vane and William Ryan, also had pre-production well under way. John told Johnson that he could change things but at least he had many things already at his disposal.

"It's a sandbox full of cool toys," John said.

Identical twins, Adam Robert and Jacob Joseph Worton, nine months old, were cast as Baby Bink and immediately got photographed crawling against green screens (a complex type of matte used to shoot backgrounds and foregrounds separately). The production needed to bank as much footage of the babies as possible because soon enough, the two brothers would stop crawling and start walking.

One morning Johnson came in for more "baby banking," only to find his cinematography crew absent. After a few inquiries, he learned they had been called up to John's farm to film tests for *The Bee*.

"He was using *Baby's Day Out*'s budget and equipment to do camera tests for *The Bee*," said Johnson. "He wanted $15 million to do *The Bee* but Fox said no, it had to be $13 million. Why cheap-skate John Hughes at this point? I was half mortified and half impressed."

John certainly enjoyed spending Fox's money. Refusing to go to a location, he insisted on building Baby Binks's palatial home on a set. And those marble floors in the mansion were not Masonite, but real marble.

For the baby's room, Kramer constructed an oval set costing $200,000 for a mere two scenes in the movie. John approved the design and came to oversee its construction. But the day it was finished, he walked in, looked around, and said, "Naw, bulldoze it. Start over."

The set came down.

On the first day of shooting, John came to observe. Looking to impress his producer, Johnston found a way to combine shots so as to get an entire day ahead of schedule.

John was impressed. "Well, this works," he told Johnson. "I'm going to England."

John had long planned a trip to England and saw no reason to stay in Chicago to oversee his biggest and most-expensive production ever.

John flew to London with Riche. They stayed at Claridge's, where they acquired an addiction to fancy scone trifles. This was an exploratory trip to scout British talent for future projects. John loved all things British, not just music.

He met with comedians Rowan Atkinson, Lenny Henry, and Hugh Laurie, as well as writers Richard Curtis and Stephen Fry. Atkinson became the next actor to get attached to *The Bee*. Meanwhile, Laurie would later work with John on *101 Dalmatians*.

John loved being in England, even taking time to spend three days in the Cotswolds, a beautiful rural area in the south of the country, making mental notes for further development of his farm. He also didn't mind basking in the warm reception given to the man who made *Planes, Trains and Automobiles*, a highly respected film in the U.K.

John began getting reports from his associates that Johnson was making changes to his script. While he was okay with this for a while, he soon sent word to his director to please shoot the movie as written.

Meanwhile, Johnson had mixed reactions to making a $50 million John Hughes movie without the presence of John Hughes.

"There was a lot at stake and I'm terrified," said Johnson. "He's not there beside me. What if it's not funny?"

Tension developed over a stunt that required three stuntmen, subbing for the villains, to jump over a large wall and tumble into a ditch, falling out of frame in comical poses rather than doing a tuck and roll to ensure a safe landing.

Ryan, relaying John's instructions from England, insisted that it be done the way it was storyboarded. The stunt coordinator refused to put his men in danger.

John returned for the final two weeks.

The film wound up two days over schedule on ninety-five day shoot and close to $1 million over budget. "Not terrible for a giant film loaded with special effects and babies," mused Johnson.

Johnson retreated to the editing room to pull together a rough cut with temporary effects. When he showed it to John, he had a hard time reading his reactions, but when the lights came up, John acted delighted.

John told his director to take a month off and relax. "I'll come into the editing room and fuss around, and then we'll look at it together," he said.

John brought in the trusted editor of *Home Alone 1* and *2*, Raja Gosnell, to take everything back to dailies and trims. In other words, John went back to an uncut film.

When a flabbergasted Johnson asked why, John said that while Johnson shot great stuff, he wanted to try new angles and his own attack on scenes with the footage shot.

In early March 1994, Fox executives, along with John's attorney, flew into Chicago for a screening at the Old Orchard Theater in Skokie, where

"The film contained what was always an unfixable problem—mothers hated the kidnapping. It made their blood run cold."

Above: from the left, Joe Mantegna, Adam Robert Worton/ Jacob Joseph Worton, Brian Haley, and Joe Pantoliano in *Baby's Day Out*.

John liked to test his films. The new cut went over poorly. For one thing, the film contained what was always an unfixable problem—mothers hated the kidnapping. It made their blood run cold.

Afterward, in the lobby, John huddled with disheartened Fox executives. Heads where shaking. Jake Bloom, whose law firm handled both the producer and director, could only look over at Johnson and shake his head.

Finally, as the executives melted away into the night, John came over to Johnson. "What do you think?' he asked.

"It's terrible," said Johnson.

The conversation swiftly turned into an argument. Bloom insisted the men take the shouting outside. So it continued in the parking lot.

All their mutual frustrations came out, about John's "abandonment" of Johnson to go to England, his casting of Lara Flynn Boyle instead of a "South Side Irish girl" as Johnson had wanted, about John's insistence that audiences would suspend belief about a baby crawling on sidewalks and across streets with no one noticing.

Utterly exhausted from their mutual yelling, the two men sat on parking curbstones in sullen silence. A thunderclap sounded over the town. Moments later, heavy rain pelted the two men.

With the comic timing of a man who still knew how to get laughs, John murmured, "Well … *this* is perfect."

The two broke out in laughter as loud as their previous shouting. By the time they stopped, each was apologizing and John said, "Look, go home and sleep. Come over tomorrow and we'll go through the movie and figure it out. There's a movie here. I know."

The two men parted company that night friends and colleagues once more. Neither one could possibly have known they would never see each other again.

The next day, on his way to John's house, Johnson received a call from Ryan. He told him not to come. John Candy had died that morning and John was very shaken. He would be in touch.

But he never was.

Ryan would relay John's instructions to Johnson in the editing room. The director went back, more or less, to his original cut. He also asked for, and got, three days of reshoots at Raleigh Studios in Hollywood.

"The end product was more Patrick's than John's," said Vane.

Baby's Day Out was released July 1, 1994. Not all the visual effects were finished, since the movie was rushed into theaters. Fox had secured 3,500 theaters on that date for James Cameron's *True Lies*. But Cameron informed the studio in February he needed more time. So Fox put *Baby* on that date, forcing it to go up against *The Lion King*, which opened the week before. The Lion ate the Baby alive.

Its final box-office tally was $16,671,505, on a budget around $51 million.

Ebert once wrote that, when visiting the largest movie theater in Calcutta, he asked if *Star Wars* had been its most successful American film.

"No, I was told. It was a Hughes comedy, *Baby's Day Out*, about a baby wandering through a big city, which played for more than a year."

At least the film had found its audience.

John turned his attention to a remake of an old Fox property, *Miracle on 34th Street*. Meanwhile, he was losing employees.

After just over a year on the job, Alan Riche quit. Instead of the company expanding into TV, music, and books, as promised, John was instead focusing solely on filmmaking.

"I felt I couldn't accomplish things I wanted to do," said Riche. "I was not earning my money and wanted to move forward."

Richard Vane left during the following year. "I wasn't into *Miracle on 34th Street*," said Vane. "Why isn't he doing his great scripts? I joined the company because I liked the new ideas he had, not to do remakes."

Meanwhile, *The Bee* again moved studios, this time landing at Disney.

"This is where it probably should have been in the first place," John told me. "This is a combination of Disney cartoons and *The Living Desert*. Comedy and nature photography—what a combination!

"It's a thrill to do a Walt Disney Presents. I love how they have resurrected their animation and with *Honey, I Shrunk the Kids*, Disney live action is back. I'm really fascinated by (the studio), looking on from the outside. If I can get in and brush up against some of those ideas and talent, it would be fun."

John approached a third actor to play the developer, this the most intriguing of all—Jackie Chan. Think about it: Jackie Chan versus a bee, a developer wrecking his own home with martial arts as he seeks to eradicate a bee.

Above: Promotional poster for the John Hughes production of *Miracle on 34th Street* (1994).

10

POST-
HOLLYWOOD

In January 1993, the irreverent satirical magazine *Spy* ran an article on John Hughes entitled "Big Baby." The writer accused John of throwing childish tantrums that have caused all "Hollywood big boys" to despise him, and of getting at least $10 million a year for cranking out consistently mediocre money-losers. It even tried to give Chris Columbus "98 percent" of the credit for *Home Alone* without supporting that claim. The article put no names to any of its quotes, either.

Nevertheless, the revolving door and erratic management at Hughes Entertainment were making their way into the press. John would also play into this "Big Baby" perception by switching agencies twice within a month.

At the end of December 1994, he left CAA, his agency for a decade, to sign with rival ICM. Two week later, he went back to CAA and Rapke. It was just another day in the cornfield.

An episode of *The Twilight Zone* called "It's a Good Life," which aired November 3, 1961,

Opposite: John Hughes on the set for *Miracle on 34th Street* in 1994. Right: Referencing an episode of *The Twilight Zone* called "It's a Good Life," those who worked closely to John never knew if they were "in the cornfield" (a place from which there was no return).

concerned a mutant monster in the small town of Peaksville, Ohio. When displeased with people, the monster could wish them away with its mental powers into a "cornfield," from which there was no return.

Rapke and Bloom, who spoke almost daily about their shared client, would often jokingly wonder who was in John's cornfield today.

"You never knew who was going to be in the cornfield," remarked Rapke. Not too many years later, when John again put Rapke in the cornfield only to ask to come back to CAA for representation, the agent cut his ties with John.

"I really worked very hard for John Hughes," said Rapke. "I put a lot of myself into our relationship. When he chose to leave me the last time—as he had done a couple of times and come back quickly—I could no longer be involved in his representation.

"There are also sensitive people on other sides too. He doesn't have the monopoly on being the only one who has feelings."

At this point in John's career, his twenty-seven films had amassed more than $1.5 billion at the box office. If he was a baby, he was a powerful one.

Indeed, within days of John's return to CAA, Rapke and Bloom completed a multi-picture, multi-year deal at Walt Disney that reunited John with Joe Roth, the former Fox boss who had crossed town to head Disney. Just over a month later, the deal became a full-fledged partnership.

Ricardo Mestres, a former Disney executive, had an exclusive long-term production deal on the lot. John had met Mestres in 1981 at Paramount when they were both getting started. They became friends but had seen little of each other until John came to the Disney lot.

In February, the two formed a new company called Great Oaks Entertainment, which merged their two companies and projects. The idea was for John to admit finally that he was not a manager, or at least not a good one, and to partner with someone familiar with the Disney culture and with being an executive producer, packager, and manager. This, presumably, would allow John to focus on writing and producing in Chicago and leave management in his partner's hands in L.A. This proved a false assumption.

Hughes projects announced at the time included *The Bee*—tellingly, though, John was no longer listed as its director—and *Jack*, with Francis Ford Coppola set to direct Robin Williams. As usual with such Hughes announcements, the press release insisted Great Oaks would pursue projects in TV, publishing, and interactive media.

But John never strayed from movies. That's where he felt comfortable.

101 DALMATIONS

Before Roth landed at Disney, the studio had three labels—Touchstone Pictures, Hollywood Pictures, and Walt Disney Pictures, the latter producing family entertainment. The Disney label had made movies such as *Mighty Ducks*, *Cool Runnings*, and *Homeward Bound* for well under $30 million. Often its pictures cost as little as $10 million.

When Roth arrived, he retired the Hollywood label and repositioned Walt Disney to produce family films with larger budgets, on the scale of *Home Alone*. So Roth immediately put John to work on Disney "tent-pole" projects, the first being a live-action version of *101 Dalmatians*.

The original 1961 feature cartoon, made in the waning days of the first great wave of Disney animation—the film was among the last made under Walt Disney's personal supervision—is a lightly amusing affair. It contents itself with entertaining children, while adults may find themselves taking frequent popcorn-and-soda breaks.

For a live-action version, John tried to extricate the story from its cartoon world of anthropomorphic animals that talk to one another and relocate the tale in a more or less human realm. In this he was only partially successful, as the film never rises above being a live-action cartoon.

A first act gets the dogs' owners, played by Jeff Daniels and Joely Richardson, to meet cute in contemporary London. Their dalmatians, Pongo and Perdy, fall in love during an outing on Hampstead Heath. The dogs' amorous chase propels their owners, on bicycles with dog leashes, into all sorts of slapstick near-collisions and a subsequent dousing in the park's pond.

This results in a dual wedding—meaning humans and canines—of such swiftness that, even before they can properly date, Daniels asks Richardson, "Do you want a cup of marriage ... uh, tea?"

Disney Pictures president David Vogel was particularly taken with that particular scene's wry, romantic tone.

"I talked to John about that beautiful tea scene and hoped it might inspire him to write a romantic comedy," said Vogel. "He had a wonderful romantic comedy in him. But I don't recall one ever arriving on my desk."

When you do think about that scene and the

Above: Oscar-winning actress Glenn Close played the vampy villainess Cruella de Vil in *101 Dalmations*.

John speeds through plot developments as fast as possible—Cruella's evil desire to round up dalmatian puppies for the sake of a black-spotted fashion statement, their kidnapping by yet another pair of imbecilic thieves (Hugh Laurie and Mark Williams)—to get to the puppy rescue by Pongo, Perdy, and seemingly the entire animal population of London.

Thanks to the visual effects and animation wizardry of Industrial Light & Magic (ILM) and the animatronics by Jim Henson's Creature Shop, the non-human actors outsmart the villains at every turn.

Dogs, raccoons, pigs, crows, a cat, woodpecker, skunk, and sheep all contribute to foiling the insidious plot, and return not only the fifteen pups belonging to Pongo and Perdy home, but an additional eighty-four, which means the household must accommodate 101 Dalmatians.

Stephen Herek, who had previously directed *The Mighty Ducks*, makes no pretense of making a "date movie." All pranks, pratfalls, and villainy maintain a cartoony mode and, other than Close, humans are tolerated but mostly ignored, other than as victims of canine comedy.

Released Thanksgiving weekend in 1996 amid a wave of hype and merchandise, the film made back less than its estimated budget of $54 million in domestic box-office gross sales.

Vogel, for one, didn't see it that way. "With merchandising, ancillaries, something like six video sell-throughs, TV and cable, that film must have grossed near to $1 billion worldwide to the studio," he insisted.

John told friends he made more money on this film than any other, due to the deal engineered by Rapke and Bloom that gave him a cut of the merchandising.

even greater romantic practice-kissing scene in *Some Kind of Wonderful*, you realize how right Vogel was.

Glenn Close, among the many Oscar winners to join the Hughes Players, plunges into the vampy role of fashion designer Cruella de Vil with relish. Not to mention hair—black on one side, white on the other, and teased upward in every direction so she actually approximates her cartoon counterpart some thirty-five years earlier.

Rapke called them "designer deals," giving John part of merchandising and soundtracks on the theatrical deals the two made: "Nobody had deals like John Hughes. They were contemporary, cutting-edge deals."

FLUBBER

In 1997, Great Oaks remade Disney's 1961 family comedy *The Absent-Minded Professor* as *Flubber*. Reworking the original screenplay by the late Disney studio producer-writer Bill Walsh, John made only a few changes to the original story. The changes he did make, however, found him tinkering with ways to get *The Bee* up and running.

The story concerns an easily distracted science professor who inadvertently invents a flexible rubber substance that generates its own energy, a kind of flying rubber he dubs "flubber." John decided that Prof. Brainard (Robin Williams) should have his entire household run by robots who do all the menial household chores, including fixing meals.

His favorite robot, though, a flying cyber sidekick named Weebo, acts as a female companion, offering advice and admonitions to the perpetually absent-minded scientist on whom she clearly has a crush.

While much larger than a bee, Weebo nonetheless offered John an opportunity to see what a flying creature generated by puppeteers, animation, and ILM could do on screen. The results—child's play today with CGI—must have encouraged John. The flying gizmo, complete with pop-up computer screen that shows vintage movie and TV clips to fit the emotions of the moment, did hold out hope for future flying objects in a Hughes comedy.

John's screenplay also contained some DNA from *Weird Science* and *Home Alone*. In the former instance, Weebo creates a diaphanous female for Brainard by searching and downloading images of beautiful fashion models from magazines. In the latter, yet another pair of bumbling thugs (Clancy Brown and Ted Levine) break into Brainard's makeshift lab to steal the flubber.

Above: Promotional poster for *Flubber*, a re-make of the 1961 comedy *The Absent-Minded Professor*.

Above: Robin Williams as Professor Brainard in the family comedy *Flubber* (1997).

The movie, though, directed by Les Mayfield, is so routine and dull that even a surprisingly un-animated Williams can't inject any life into it.

As for *The Bee*, the Disney hierarchy never could figure out if the project belonged to the animation or live-action department. "It was a very big budget for a single-point-of-view movie at that time," noted Vogel. "Its expense was part of the issue."

Before going under, Great Oaks produced *101 Dalmatians* and *Flubber*, and co-produced *Jack* and *Just Visiting*. John and Mestres also shared credits on *Reach the Rock* and *Home Alone 3*. By the end of 1997, the two men gave up on what was described in *The Hollywood Reporter* as an "uneasy alliance."

"John didn't really have a commitment to build a company," said Vogel. "This was probably the later stages of his career. It was not so much that there were problems, but more John losing his fire to be sufficiently productive to warrant such an operation with staff and overhead.

"Also, John was in Chicago and not the easiest person to access. He lived in two houses and he liked to write late into the night. Ricardo would sit in an office, trying to run a business without having his creative partner on the other end of the phone. It was difficult."

John was clearly in the process of disengagement with all things Hollywood. He had given up on directing. He continued writing for the rest of his life but little of this was sent to Hollywood.

When Roth left Disney, he formed Revolution Studios, and would try luring John back into making movies, even announcing one film, *The Grisbys*, about a wealthy family that loses its money and is forced to spend Christmas in poverty, and *The Chambermaid*, about a hotel maid. The latter was to star Sandra Bullock and then Hilary Swank, but wound up with Jennifer Lopez starring and the title changed to *Maid in Manhattan*.

John collaborated on the screenplay for *Just Visiting*—a 2001 film based on *Les Visiteurs* (1993)—a goofy time-travel French comedy that became one of that country's biggest hits. Other than John, the French team behind the original performed their same roles in this English-language remake.

It's a broadly played comedy with fish-out-of-water gags involving men of the Dark Ages encountering twenty-first century kitchen appliances, indoor plumbing, and, most confounding of all, a social hierarchy at distinct odds with a feudal one.

Jokes don't go much beyond crude table manners and the sight of a knight in armor galloping a horse up stairs, across an "L" platform, and down Michigan Avenue.

It is curious that John Hughes, with his vast knowledge and love of music, never delved into that world, other than on soundtrack albums. For that matter, a man with his restless mind should have explored TV, publishing, and interactive media.

Jeffrey Jones recalled that, at the time he was offered the sitcom *The People Next Door* by CBS, which wound up on its 1989 schedule, John approached him about reprising his role as Principal Rooney and doing a TV series based on *Ferris Bueller*. This coincided with Columbia Pictures Television's development of *Parker Lewis Can't Lose*, whose clear antecedent was *Ferris*.

"John was pissed, I think, that someone was going to horn in on his successful film, and so he slapped together a plan to compete," said Jones. "John wanted me to move to Chicago, where it would be filmed. He said he wouldn't actually direct it, but would 'have a hand in it.'

Above: John collaborated on the screenplay for *Just Visiting* (2001), based on the popular French comedy *Les Visiteurs*.

"Basically my stuff is just John Hughes with four-letter words." —Kevin Smith

"I don't think at that point Matthew had been asked or was involved, and I doubt he would have done it anyway. I'm reasonably sure John was pissed that we—my agent and myself—did the higher-paying, sure-bet offer, and as a result 'turned him down.' "

Jacobson said Kevin Reilly, when he was NBC's entertainment president, flew to Chicago to discuss a TV series with John. Nothing came of this either.

John formed Hughes Music in 1987, a record company with the intent of putting out albums, with distribution and marketing by MCA Records.

Pop music certainly played a strong role in his films. And he was such a purist he never allowed a *Ferris Bueller's Day Off* album, since all the music in that film came not from new groups, but existing material. He knew it would be a hit—but not a great album.

Yet in music he lacked follow-through, even though he certainly could have tapped a person such as Tarquin Gotch to oversee A&R.

And, for all his enthusiasm about developing a film musical, he lost interest with the passing of time.

"When I did *How to Succeed in Business Without Really Trying* on stage, I thought it was perfect material for him," said Broderick. "He was friendly but not interested."

His old pals Vance and Deutch wanted to do *Pretty in Pink* as a stage musical.

"John hated the idea," said Vance. "I never heard him like that: 'No … NO! No one touches my work!'

"I couldn't believe he wouldn't want to do something like that. I thought he'd love it. He didn't want to even talk about it. He was absolutely adamant his material was not to be put in any other form."

When he announced the formation of Great Oaks, John told me he was serious about working in interactive media.

"I can't talk about my idea, but I'm very excited about the interactive area," he said. "I have to retool creatively to work in a different format. But I have found in messing around [with interactive] the past couple of years a way to translate my style and tone to another medium."

He never retooled creatively.

Instead, he retreated to his 11,233 square-foot Lake Forest English-style home with its red brick chimneys, dramatic beamed ceilings, stone fireplaces, large windows, French doors, six bedrooms and a media room, and, of course, Redwing Farm.

He always wanted to be an English gentleman-farmer, so as he acquired the barren land that became Redwing, he put in the hedgerows he saw on English farms. He set up a section of the property as a refuge and working farmstead, growing crops and raising Devon cattle. He put a pontoon boat on a lake that was only three times longer than the boat itself.

When he learned one hill on the property was the second-highest point in Illinois, he declared, "Well, that won't do!"

So he paid for enough cubic feet of dirt to be hauled in until it became the highest point in the state. As undoubtedly the richest screenwriter in Hollywood history, he could afford to do so.

John and Nancy flew to New York on August 5, 2009, to visit their son James, his wife, and their new grandson. The following morning John woke up early and left his Manhattan hotel to take a walk and shoot photographs. He collapsed on a sidewalk a few blocks away on West 55th Street. He was rushed to Roosevelt Hospital, where he was pronounced dead of a heart attack.

His sons told *Vanity Fair* that John had kicked his tobacco habit in 2001. But chain-smoking for decades must have taken its toll. He was fifty-nine.

The mystery of John Hughes's disappearance did not really turn him into "our generation's J.D. Salinger," as filmmaker Kevin Smith would have it. He simply didn't grant press interviews. Meanwhile, in his absence, his stock rose as many filmmakers who admit his influence—Smith (*Clerks*), Todd Phillips (*Old School*), Judd Apatow (*The 40-Year-Old Virgin*), David Dobkin (*Wedding Crashers*)—all created their own take on outsiders as leading characters.

"Basically, my stuff is just John Hughes with four-letter words," Smith told the *Los Angeles Times*.

In 2007, Simons & Schuster published *Don't You Forget About Me*, a series of Hughes-examining essays by a clutch of contemporary writers, ranging from novelist Lisa Borders and poet Rebecca Wolff to actress/author Moon Unit Zappa. Some loved him and saw themselves in his characters. Others saw nothing like themselves or anyone they ever knew.

Either way, as these essays showed, his characters are the benchmark of assessing who we are or aren't.

A Canadian documentary film, curiously with the same name as the book, featured decent-enough interviews with Hughes collaborators, surrounded by a poor road-trip doc wherein the director and his producers head for suburban Illinois in a van in search of the reclusive

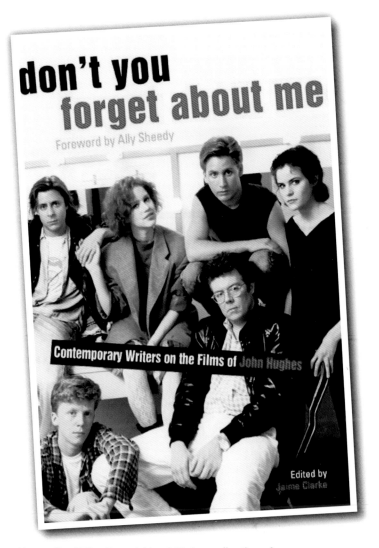

Above: *Don't You Forget About Me* is a collection of essays by modern writers on the films of John Hughes, published in 2007.

filmmaker. It was not released until after John's death.

Perhaps John felt his time had passed. Teen films such as *Heathers* (1988) and *Mean Girls* (2004), with their post-modern irony and cynicism, had supplanted *The Breakfast Club* and *Pretty in Pink*. Then again, as Rapke put it: "It's hard to be the Teen King when you're in your fifties."

Never tiring of writing, but unwilling to direct any longer, he searched for a successor to direct his screenplays. Patrick Read Johnson recalled having dinner with John one night before their *Dennis the Menace* meltdown.

"UTTERLY UNMISSABLE" "BRILLIANT BLACK SATIRE"

CITY LIMITS   YOU MAGAZINE

"OUTRAGEOUS"

FILM MONTHLY

"A teen movie to end all teen movies . . .
bites at all the conventions until real blood
flows along with the tears of laughter."

THE GUARDIAN

**WINONA RYDER
CHRISTIAN SLATER**

HEATHERS

Heathers enjoy
absolute authority
at
Westerburg High . . .
UNTIL THEY DIE!

NEW WORLD PICTURES IN ASSOCIATION WITH CINEMARQUE ENTERTAINMENT (USA) LTD. PRESENTS
'HEATHERS' STARRING WINONA RYDER · CHRISTIAN SLATER · SHANNEN DOHERTY
FRANCIS KENNY NORMAN HOLLYN DAVID NEWMAN
CHRISTOPHER WEBSTER DANIEL WATERS DENISE DI NOVI MICHAEL LEHMANN

Above: Cynical teen films like *Heathers* (starring
Winona Ryder and Christian Slater) were becoming the
new norm for teen comedies.

John told him, "Patrick, you do this movie and
you're me. You'll become me. You can go further."

Seeing the incredulous look on Johnson's face,
John insisted, "No, no, trust and work with me.
Come back here [to Chicago] to live with your
family and everything I'm doing you'll do. You'll
be me. Not like Chris Columbus, who's now in
the Chris Columbus business."

To Johnson this was a telling remark.

"Somehow, Chris had betrayed John by not
staying in Chicago, in the fold, after *Home Alone 2*,"
Johnson said. "Then when John Candy died that
shook him to the core. Not only had he lost his best

friend, but it shook him on the mortality level as
well—on his relationship to his family and Hollywood and how much he wanted to deal with bullshit.

"He wanted to make small films in his back-
yard. My theory is John wanted to create a world
with a bunch of friends, where he was making
movies in Chicago, like he would have as a teenager if he'd had the time and equipment. All he
wanted was a little gang in Chicago to make
movies with him.

"But it felt like John wanted people to get close
and as soon as they did he immediately started to
distrust them—'When are you going to fuck me
over?' There was this intense scrutiny for danger
to his happiness."

"When John Candy died that shook him to the core. Not only had he lost his best friend, but it shook on the mortality level as well…" —Patrick Read Johnson

Others take a less charitable view. "I think he burned himself out and lost interest," said Michael Chinich. "He was working on fumes, wasn't in touch with things after a while. I always pushed him to do something more adult but he never was really interested in that.

"He had no sense of what an adult's mind was like. All adults in his movies, except *Planes, Trains and Autombiles* were stick figures, like a cartoon figure there to service the youth.

"John couldn't write adults. He wasn't an adult himself. He didn't know how to be an adult. And he started drying up. Everything was getting more and more tired."

"He was a kid," Manning agreed. "He saw the world the way a kid sees the world. Which is why to me *The Breakfast Club* is so much about him in a weird way. It's the way a kid sees everything, as black-and-white—it's a jock, it's a brain—but by the end of the movie he realizes nothing is black and white. But he doesn't want to grow up and live in that world, necessarily. So he kind of lived in the black-and-white world where he could easily compartmentalize things."

Some friends did reach out from time to time.

"I would call every now and then," said Broderick, "when I read a script and say, 'Do you want to look at this or talk about other things?' But he was not interested in doing that again."

"When I returned to Paramount [as an executive], I told them, 'You guys are sitting on a goldmine of old John Hughes scripts,' " said Manning. "The story department pulled them out and later

Above: John Hughes and John Candy in 1991.

I got in touch with Jake Bloom, since John had become a recluse.

"So I called John up and offered to send them to him. 'I don't need to read them,' he said. 'I remember them. I wrote them. I don't want those movies getting made.' "

"I can't tell you the number of times Jake was approached by every studio to please talk him out of retirement," said Sean Daniel. "John never did."

Above: Matthew Broderick, Macaulay Culkin, Ally Sheedy, Molly Ringwald, Judd Nelson, Jon Cryer, and Anthony Michael Hall commemorate John Hughes at the 82nd Academy Awards.

A TRIBUTE FROM JUDD NELSON

Judd Nelson had sent **the writers of the 82nd Academy Awards** his own written tribute to John to incorporate to incorporate into the words he was to deliver, but little of it was used. He later sent it to John's family.

In the tribute, he noted that "I have long felt that part of the younger audience's strong affinity for the work of John Hughes is due to John's ability, both conscious and not, to view someone that is *young* without seeing that person as *less*... Young people face excruciatingly difficult decisions far more often than most of us are willing to examine and therein lies the entranceway John Hughes calmly walked straight through. No need to smash down walls. The opening was always there, but no one bothered to look or, for that matter, to remember high school has always been fraught with peril for more than a few."

Deutch is not entirely certain he would have remained retired. John's granddaughter told him one day that the kids at school thought she had "the coolest grandpa" because he had written *Ferris Bueller*.

"That got him to want to make a movie again, I think. Not in a full blown way, but he was considering doing something," said Deutch.

We'll never know.

He continued to write—memoirs, short fiction, and even screenplays, but never for publication or production. Even in his Hollywood years he would write stories and books, he said, but showed them to no one "because I don't think they are very good. My prose style is very weak."

"He always felt like an outsider in high school so he wrote these alienated, subversive stories and underdog characters," said Deutch. "He felt that way and captured that. Then he comes to Hollywood and becomes the biggest thing since sliced bread. He's in the club, not an outsider. He became the ultimate insider and understood he couldn't write that way. So he packed up and left. That's my analysis."

The 82nd Academy Awards included a film-clip tribute to John's work, following with cast members from his teen films gathered on stage to commemorate the man: Molly Ringwald, Anthony Michael Hall, Ally Sheedy, Judd Nelson, Jon Cryer, Matthew Broderick, and Macaulay Culkin. "Many beautiful writers, such as Truman Capote, had disturbed personal lives," noted P. J. O'Rourke. "Not John. John had a quiet and happy personal life. He was very private. You will not find a tortured soul but an extremely intelligent yet not complex character. People sometimes mix up intelligence with complexity. His was a clear and straightforward intelligence."

"He liked being at home, he liked being with his family," said Gotch. "He was a family guy. He loved his kids and hanging out at home. He and Nancy went everywhere together. He was the quintessential American suburban family guy. He didn't want to be standing on set talking to actors anymore. He wanted to be home with the kids. He realized how quickly the kids were growing."

During pre-production on *Baby's Day Out*, John drove Johnson back to his hotel. The director mentioned that he and his wife had not been getting along as she was moody while pregnant and he was working a lot.

John stopped the car.

"You take care of her," he admonished Johnson. "She is the best thing about you. Your wife and your children are best thing you have. If you don't fuck this up, they'll always be the best thing about you."

For John Hughes, that most certainly was true.

JOHN HUGHES FILMOGRAPHY

This list includes only produced screenplays where John Hughes received credit either under his own name or his writing pseudonym, Edmond Dantès.

Director

1984 *Sixteen Candles*
1985 *The Breakfast Club*
1985 *Weird Science*
1986 *Ferris Bueller's Day Off*
1987 *Planes, Trains and Automobiles*
1988 *She's Having a Baby*
1989 *Uncle Buck*
1991 *Curly Sue*

Writer

1982 *National Lampoon's Class Reunion*
1983 *Mr. Mom*
1983 *National Lampoon's Vacation*
1984 *Sixteen Candles*
1985 *The Breakfast Club*
1985 *Natiional Lampoon's European Vacation*
1985 *Weird Science*
1986 *Pretty in Pink*
1986 *Ferris Bueller's Day Off*
1987 *Some Kind of Wonderful*
1987 *Planes, Trains and Automobiles*

1988 *She's Having a Baby*
1988 *The Great Outdoors*
1989 *Uncle Buck*
1989 *National Lampoon's Christmas Vacation*
1990 *Home Alone*
1991 *Career Opportunities*
1991 *Dutch*
1991 *Curly Sue*
1992 *Beethoven*
1992 *Home Alone 2: Lost in New York*
1993 *Dennis the Menace*
1994 *Baby's Day Out*
1994 *Miracle on 34th Street*
1996 *101 Dalmatians*
1997 *Flubber*
1997 *Home Alone 3*
1998 *Reach the Rock*
2001 *Just Visiting*
2002 *Maid in Manhattan*
2008 *Drillbit Taylor*

Executive Producer/Producer

1985 *The Breakfast Club*
1986 *Pretty in Pink*
1986 *Ferris Bueller's Day Off*
1987 *Some Kind of Wonderful*
1987 *Planes, Trains and Automobiles*
1988 *She's Having a Baby*
1988 *The Great Outdoors*
1989 *Uncle Buck*
1989 *National Lampoon's Christmas Vacation*
1990 *Home Alone*
1991 *Career Opportunities*
1991 *Only the Lonely*
1991 *Curly Sue*
1992 *Home Alone 2: Lost in New York*
1993 *Dennis the Menace*
1994 *Baby's Day Out*
1994 *Miracle on 34th Street*
1996 *101 Dalmatians*
1997 *Home Alone 3*
1998 *Reach the Rock*
2001 *New Port South*

ACKNOWLEDGMENTS
NOTES/SOURCES

INTRODUCTION
Interviews
Michael Chinich, March 5, 2014
Martha Coolidge, Dec. 1, 2013
Howard Deutch, March 6, 2014
Jeffrey Jones, February 15, 2014
Michelle Manning, February 27, 2014
Fredell Pogodin, January 8, 2014
Jack Rapke, March 28, 2014

Publications
King, Andrea, John Hughes Special Issue, *Hollywood Reporter*, February 1991.
Zonkel, Phillip, *Village View*, November 23–29, 1990.

CHAPTER 1: WELCOME TO HUGHES WORLD
Interviews
Tarquin Gotch, January 31, 2014
Tom Jacobson, January 14, 2014
Steve Martin, April 2, 2014
P. J. O'Rourke, January 10, 2013
Mia Sara, January 24, 2014

Ally Sheedy, February 22, 2014
Marilyn Vance, January 17, 2014
Richard Vane, March 12, 2014

Publications
Spitz, Bob, *Mirabella*, December 1992.

Other sources
Press Notes, *Sixteen Candles*
Transcript of AFI Seminar, March 1, 1985

CHAPTER 2: THE BLIZZARD
Interviews
Jeffrey Jones, February 15, 2014
Judd Nelson, March 4, 2014
P. J. O'Rourke, January 10 and April 14, 2014
Matty Simmons, January 9, 2014

Publications
Christensen, Mark, *Ampersand*, Summer 1986.
Farr, Louise, *Women's Wear Daily*, July 14, 1986.

Honeycutt, Kirk, *Hollywood Reporter*, November 16, 1992.
Hughes, John, "20 Questions: Cheryl Tiegs," *Playboy*, October 1978.
Hughes, John, "Vacation '58," *National Lampoon*, September 1979.
Hughes, John, "Vacation '58/Foreword '08," *Zoetrope: All-Story*, Summer 2008.
King, Andrea, ShoWest 1991 Producer of the Year Special Issue, *Hollywood Reporter*, 1991.
Matousek, Mark, "John Hughes in Interview," *Interview*, August 1985.
O'Rourke, P. J., and John Hughes, "Sunday Newspaper Parody," *National Lampoon*, February 1978.
Spitz, Bob, *Mirabella*, December 1992.
Stein, Ellin, *That's Not Funny, That's Sick: The National Lampoon and the Comedy of Insurgents Who Captured the Mainstream*. New York: W. W. Norton & Company, 2013.
Zonkel, Phillip, *Village View*, November 23–29, 1990.

Other sources

John Hughes DVD commentary for *Some Kind of Wonderful*

Transcript of AFI Seminar, March 1, 1985

CHAPTER 3: THE LAMPOONER
Interviews

Beverly D'Angelo, February 28, 2014

Sean Daniel, June 18, 2014

P. J. O'Rourke, April 14, 2014

Lauren Shuler Donner, February 3, 2014

Matty Simmons, January 9, 2014; June 30, 2014

Publications

Hughes, John, "Vacation '58/Foreword '08," *Zoetrope: All-Story*, Summer 2008.

Stein, Ellin, *That's Not Funny, That's Sick: The National Lampoon and the Comedy of Insurgents Who Captured the Mainstream*. New York: W. W. Norton & Company, 2013.

Other sources

Harold Ramis on *Vacation* DVD Extras

Jaws 3—People 0 Script Review on awcgfilmlog.blogspot.com

CHAPTER 4: THE COMING OF BOOTH TARKINGTON JR.
Interviews

Jackie Burch, January 23, 2014

Sean Daniel, June 18, 2014

Michelle Manning, February 27, 2014

Fredell Pogodin, January 8, 2014

Ally Sheedy, February 22, 2014

Matty Simmons, January 9, 2014

Marilyn Vance, January 17, 2014

Gedde Watanabe, January 20, 2014

Publications

Hughes, John, "Vacation '58/Foreword '08," *Zoetrope: All-Story*, Summer 2008.

Kilday, Gregg, *US Magazine*, August 12, 1985.

Matousek, Mark. "John Hughes in Interview," *Interview*, August 1985.

Willman, Chris, *BAM*, March 29, 1985.

Other sources

Transcript of AFI Seminar, March 1, 1985

CHAPTER 5: HOLLYWOOD BOUND
Interviews

Matthew Broderick, March 21, 2014

Jackie Burch, January 23, 2014

Michael Chinich, March 5, 2014

Jon Cryer, February 26, 2014

Howie Deutch, March 6, 2014

Lauren Shuler Donner, February 3, 2014

Tom Jacobson, January 14, 2014

Jeffrey Jones, February 15, 2014

Michelle Manning, February 27, 2014

Fredell Pogodin, January 8, 2014

Jack Rapke, March 28, 2014

Mia Sara, January 24, 2014

Marilyn Vance, January 17, 2014

Publications

Cameron, Julia, "John Hughes' Rational Anthem: 'I Won't Grow Up,'" *Chicago Tribune*, June 8, 1986.

Farr, Louise, *Women's Wear Daily*, July 14, 1986.

Hughes, James, "John Hughes' Day Off," Grantland.com, May 1, 2013.

Kael, Pauline, "The Current Cinema: Coddled," *The New Yorker*, April 8, 1985.

Matousek, Mark. "John Hughes in Interview," *Interview*, August 1985.

Ringwald, Molly, "The Neverland Club" op-ed, *The New York Times*, August 12, 2009.

CHAPTER 6: MOVIE MOGUL
Interviews

Matthew Broderick, March 21, 2014

Michael Chinich, March 5, 2014

Martha Coolidge, Dec. 1, 2013

Jon Cryer, February 26, 2014

Beverly D'Angelo, February 28, 2014

Howard Deutch, March 7, 2014

Tarquin Gotch, January31, 2014

Fredell Pogodin, January 8, 2014

Matty Simmons, January 9, 2014

Marilyn Vance, January 17, 2014

Publications

King, Andrea, ShoWest 1991 Producer of the Year Special Issue, *Hollywood Reporter*, 1991.

Other sources

Transcript of AFI Seminar, March 1, 1985

CHAPTER 7: JOHN CANDY
Interviews

Chris Columbus, June 10, 2014

Bob Crane, January 29. 2014

Sean Daniel, June 18, 2014

Howard Deutch, March 6, 2014

Tarquin Gotch, January 31, 2014

Tom Jacobson, January 14, 2014

Jeffrey Jones, February 15, 2014

Steve Martin, April 2, 2014

Ally Sheedy, February 22, 2014

Publications

Goldstein, Patrick, "John Hughes, candle-lighter," *Los Angeles Times*, March 25, 2008.

Honeycutt, Kirk, *Hollywood Reporter*, March 7, 1994.

CHAPTER 8: ANTIC COMEDY
Interviews

Nick Castle, March 7, 2014

Chris Columbus, June 10, 2014

Patrick Read Johnson, March 13, 2104

Jack Rapke, March 28, 2014
Alan Riche, April 14, 2014
Richard Vane, March 12, 2014

Publications

Bart, Peter, *Daily Chapter*, April 8, 1991.
Eller, Claudia, *Daily Variety*, July 18, 1991.
Eller, Claudia, and Suzan Ayscough, *Daily Variety*, March 24, 1993.
Honeycutt, Kirk, *Hollywood Reporter*, June 24, 1994.

CHAPTER 9: ENFANT TERRIBLE
Interviews

Patrick Read Johnson, May 13, 2014
Alan Riche, April 14, 2014
Richard Vane, March 12, 2014

Publications

Honeycutt, Kirk, *Hollywood Reporter*, February 16, 1995.

CHAPTER 10: POST-HOLLYWOOD
Interviews

Michael Chinich, March 5, 2014
Sean Daniel, June 18, 2014
Tarquin Gotch, January 31, 2014
Patrick Read Johnson, May 13, 2014
Jeffrey Jones, June 11, 2014
Michelle Manning, March 25, 2014
P. J. O'Rourke, January 10, 2013
Jack Rapke, March 28, 2014
Marilyn Vance, January 17, 2014
David Vogel, April 19, 2014

Publications

Bart, Peter, *Variety*, April 8, 1991.
Busch, Anita, *Daily Variety*, January 9, 1995.
Goldstein, Patrick, "John Hughes, candle-lighter," *Los Angeles Times*, March 25, 2008.
Honeycutt, Kirk, *Hollywood Reporter*, December 29, 1994.
Honeycutt, Kirk, *Hollywood Reporter*, February 16, 1995.
Hughes, James, "John Hughes' Day Off," Grantland.com, May 1, 2013.
Kamp, David, "Sweet Bard of Youth," *Vanity Fair*, March 2010.
King, Andrea, ShoWest 1991 Producer of the Year Special Issue, *Hollywood Reporter*, 1991.
Lallch, Richard, "Big Baby," *Spy*, January 1993.

PHOTOGRAPHY CREDITS

pp.44–45: © MGM/courtesy Everett Collection.

pp.47–49: © Warner Bros./courtesy Everett Collection

p.51: Courtesy Everett Collection

p.52: © Warner Bros./courtesy Everett Collection

CHAPTER 4: THE COMING OF BOOTH TARKINGTON JR.

p.54: © Universal Pictures/courtesy Everett Collection.

p.55: © Jeff Slocomb/Corbis

p.56: © Michael Ochs Archives/Stringer

p.57: © Universal Pictures/courtesy Everett Collection

p.58: © top and bottom: © Columbia Pictures Corporation/courtesy Everett Collection

pp.59–67: © Universal Pictures/courtesy Everett Collection

p.68, top: Courtesy Everett Collection

p.68, bottom: © Universal Pictures/courtesy Everett Collection

pp.69–72: © Universal Pictures/courtesy Everett Collection

p.73: © Glasshouse Images/Alamy

p.75: © Universal Pictures/courtesy Everett Collection

p.76: © Chris Walter/WireImage/Getty Images

p.78: © Charley Gallay/Getty Images for CDG

p.79: © Marilyn Vance

p.80: © Universal Pictures/courtesy Everett Collection

p.81: © Virginia Turbett/Redferns/Getty Images

p.82: © Universal Pictures/courtesy Everett Collection

p.83: Courtesy Everett Collection

p.84: © Universal Pictures/courtesy Everett Collection

p.85: Courtesy Everett Collection

p.88: © Universal Pictures/courtesy Everett Collection

CHAPTER 5: HOLLYWOOD BOUND

p.90: Courtesy Everett Collection

p.91: © Universal Pictures/courtesy Everett Collection

p.92: © Universal Pictures/courtesy Everett Collection

p.93: Courtesy Everett Collection

p.94: © Universal Pictures/courtesy Everett Collection

p.95, top: Courtesy Everett Collection

p.95, bottom: © AF archive/Alamy

p.97: Courtesy Everett Collection

pp.99–104: © Paramount Pictures/courtesy Everett Collection

p.105: Courtesy Everett Collection

pp.106–107: © Paramount Pictures/courtesy Everett Collection

p.108: Courtesy Everett Collection

pp.110–111: © Paramount Pictures/Courtesy Everett Collection

p.112: Courtesy Everett Collection

p.115: © Paramount Pictures/courtesy Everett Collection

p.116: Courtesy Everett Collection

CHAPTER 6: MOVIE MOGUL

p.118: © Mary Evans Picture Library/Everett Collection

p.119: Courtesy Everett Collection

pp.121–128: © Paramount Pictures/courtesy Everett Collection.

p.129: © AF archive/Alamy

p.130: © Paramount Pictures/courtesy Everett Collection

pp.131–133: Courtesy Everett Collection

p.134: © Warner Bros./courtesy Everett Collection

p.135: Courtesy Everett Collection

CHAPTER 7: JOHN CANDY

p.136: © Patti Gower/*Toronto Star* via Getty Images

p.137: © Mary Evans Picture Library/Everett Collection

p.138: © Dick Darrell/*Toronto Star* via Getty Images

p.139: © Jeff Kravitz/FilmMagic/Getty Images

pp.140–144: © Paramount Pictures/courtesy Everett Collection

p.146: © Universal Pictures/RGA/Ronald Grant Archive/Alamy

p.147: © Universal Pictures/courtesy Everett Collection

p.148: © Ron Galella, Ltd./WireImage/Getty Images

p.149: ©Universal Pictures/courtesy Everett Collection

p.150: Courtesy Everett Collection

p.152: © Universal Pictures/courtesy Everett Collection

p.153: © Keith Beaty/*Toronto Star* via Getty Images

p.154: © 20th Century Fox Film Corp. All rights reserved. Courtesy Everett Collection

p.155: © Moviestore Collection Ltd/Alamy

p.157: © Michael Stuparyk/*Toronto Star* via Getty Images

CHAPTER 8: ANTIC COMEDY

p.158: © Ron Galella, Ltd./WireImage/Getty Images

pp.159–165: © 20th Century Fox Film Corp. All rights reserved. Courtesy Everett Collection

p.166: © Moviestore Collection Ltd/Alamy

p.167: © Ron Galella, Ltd./WireImage/Getty Images

p.168: © Universal Pictures/courtesy Everett Collection

p.169, top: © 20th Century Fox Film Corp. All rights reserved. Courtesy Everett Collection

p.169, bottom: © Warner Bros./courtesy Everett Collection

p.170: © Warner Bros./courtesy
Everett Collection

p.171, top: © AF archive/Alamy

p.171, bottom: © Warner Bros./
courtesy Everett Collection

p.173: Courtesy Everett Collection

p.175: © Warner Bros./courtesy
Everett Collection

p.177: © Mary Evans Picture Library/
Everett Collection

CHAPTER 9: ENFANT TERRIBLE

pp.178–179: © 20th Century Fox Film
Corp. All rights reserved. Courtesy
Everett Collection

p.180: © Moviestore Collection Ltd/
Alamy

p.181: Courtesy Everett Collection

pp.182–184: © 20th Century Fox Film
Corp. All rights reserved. Courtesy
Everett Collection

p.185: © AF archive/Alamy

CHAPTER 10: POST-HOLLYWOOD

p.186: © 20th Century Fox Film Corp.
All rights reserved. Courtesy Everett
Collection

pp.187–189: Courtesy Everett
Collection

p.190: © Buena Vista Pictures/
courtesy Everett Collection

p.191: © Walt Disney Pictures/
courtesy Everett Collection

pp.192–193: © Buena Vista Pictures/
courtesy Everett Collection

p.196: © New World Pictures/
courtesy Everett Collection

p.197: © Ron Galella, Ltd./
WireImage/Getty Images

p.198: © Jason Merritt/Getty Images

INDEX

ABOUT THE CONTRIBUTORS

KIRK HONEYCUTT

Kirk Honeycutt was chief film critic for *The Hollywood Reporter* for many years and subsequent to that senior film reporter for that publication. He has covered major industry developments and has regularly attended such film festivals as Cannes, Sundance, Berlin, Toronto, Pusan, and Montreal while serving on juries at other festivals.

Prior to that, he was chief film critic for the *Los Angeles Daily News*, a regular contributor to the *New York Times'* Arts & Leisure section, and a film columnist for the *Los Angeles Times*.

Mr. Honeycutt is a member of the prestigious Los Angeles Film Critics Association, and is the creator of *Honeycutt's Hollywood* (honeycuttshollywood.com), a popular film review website. He appears regularly on television, radio, and podcasts, and currently teaches at Chapman University's Dodge College of Film and Media Arts. He lives with this wife, Mira, in Los Angeles, California.

CHRIS COLUMBUS

For more than twenty-five years, Academy Award–nominated filmmaker Chris Columbus has written, directed, and produced some of the most successful box office hits, establishing him as a major force in contemporary Hollywood. He is also the *New York Times* best-selling author of *House of Secrets*, the first iteration of an epic new fantasy series which published in April 2013 to rave reviews and quickly rose to the top of the charts.

In Hollywood, Columbus first gained prominence by writing several original scripts produced by Steven Spielberg, including the back-to-back hits *Gremlins* (1984) and *The Goonies* (1985), which became decade-defining films. These screen-writing achievements led Columbus to direct his first feature, *Adventures in Babysitting* (1987) starring Elisabeth Shue.

Columbus directed and produced the first three *Harry Potter* films which triumphed at the box office and went on to collectively gross over $2.6 billion worldwide. He also produced the highly successful family/adventure comedy *Night at the Museum* (2006) and its sequel, *Night at the Museum: Battle of the Smithsonian* (2009). Other film credits include: the 2005 screen adaptation of the Pulitzer Prize–winning Broadway musical *RENT*; *Stepmom* (1998); *Nine Months* (1995); *Mrs. Doubtfire* (1993); *Only the Lonely* (1991), based on his original screenplay; and the hits *Home Alone* (1990) and *Home Alone 2: Lost in New York* (1992). In 2011, Columbus released the blockbuster hit *The Help* under his 1492 Pictures banner. The film garnered four Academy Award nominations, including one for Best Picture.